White Racism on the Western Urban Frontier

White Racism on the Western Urban Frontier

Dynamics of Race and Class in Dubuque, Iowa (1800-2000)

Mohammad A. Chaichian

Africa World Press, Inc.

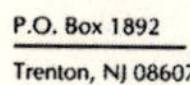
P.O. Box 1892
Trenton, NJ 08607

P.O. Box 48
Asmara, ERITREA

Africa World Press, Inc.

P.O. Box 1892
Trenton, NJ 08607

P.O. Box 48
Asmara, ERITREA

First Printing 2006

Book design: Saverance Publishing Services
Cover design: Dapo Ojo-Ade

Library of Congress Cataloging-in-Publication Data

Chaichian, Mohammad A.
White racism on the Western urban frontier : dynamics of race and class in Dubuque, Iowa (1800-2000) / Mohammad A. Chaichian.
p. cm.
Includes bibliographical references and index.
ISBN 1-59221-375-8 (hard cover) -- ISBN 1-59221-376-6 (pbk.)
1. Racism--Iowa--Dubuque--History--19th century. 2. Racism--Iowa--Dubuque--History--20th century. 3. Whites--Iowa--Dubuque--Attitudes--History--19th century. 4. Whites--Iowa--Dubuque--Attitudes--History--20th century. 5 Dubuque (Iowa)--Race relations--History--19th century. 6. Dubuque (Iowa)--Race relations--History--20th century. 7. Social classes--Iowa--Dubuque--History--19th century. 8. Social classes--Iowa--Dubuque--History--20th century. 9. Dubuque (Iowa)--Social conditions--19th century. 10. Dubuque (Iowa)--Social conditions--20th century. I. Title.

F629.D8C46 2006
305.896'073077739--dc22

2005033625

TABLE OF CONTENTS

ACKNOWLEDGEMENTS

I am indebted to many colleagues and friends who have loaned books and pamphlets, offered suggestions and leads and diligently read chapter drafts. Some wish to remain anonymous, and I am grateful for their help and support. I am particularly indebted to professors James B. McKee and Roger Waldinger, my colleagues and mentors, whose thoughtful, critical, and expert opinions and recommendations greatly helped me to reconceptualize the book's theoretical foundations and to restructure its organization. My gratitude and many thanks also go to my colleagues Vinay Bahl, Deb Brydon, Jo Dohoney, and Steven Colatrella, who carefully read various drafts and made valuable suggestions; Mary Bennett and Marvin Bergman at the State Historical Society of Iowa in Iowa City, who graciously helped me find historical documents; John Cloward from Zoning Department at the Dubuque City Hall, who helped me with maps and vital statistics; Michael Gibson, the archivist at the Center for Dubuque History, without whose help this project would not have been possible; Francis Giunta, President of the Dubuque Federation of Labor, with whom I had long conversations about race relations in Dubuque; Guy Hemenway at the Planning services Department, who generously shared some hard-to-find data on Dubuque; Richard Kemmer, director of university relations at the University of Dubuque, who painstakingly read and edited the earlier drafts and made many helpful and constructive suggestions; The late Ruth and Russell Nash, my good friends and longtime community activists who also read the earlier drafts and helped me locate hard-to-find data; Karen O'Rourke, Director of the Center for Public Ministry, who shared her critical views on racism in Dubuque; and Roger Osburn, Curator of history and Special Collections at the Dubuque Historical Society who diligently searched his files to find rare documents and shared his knowledge with me.

Several sources proved to be of utmost value for this research. First, the Center for Dubuque History at Loras College in Dubuque provided me with an invaluable collection of primary sources, such as books, manuscripts, monographs, maps, and statistics pertaining to local history. Second, I had access to an almost complete collection of local newspapers on microfilm at the above center as well as the Carnegie-Stout Public Library in Dubuque. Third, the archives of the Dubuque Historical Society, the Iowa Historical Society in Iowa City, and the University of Dubuque provided me with a wealth of material that often helped to fill the missing historical gaps. I also wish to acknowledge the support services provided by the Obermann Center for Advanced Studies at the University of Iowa, as well as Mount Mercy College, that facilitated the research and writing of this book. Last but not the least, my deepest debt is owed to my wife Dina and my son Yashaar, without whose unconditional love and support the completion of this book would have been unthinkable.

Needless to say, although the book is the product of a collective effort, I am solely responsible for its contents in terms of collection, presentation and interpretation of data.

INTRODUCTION
WHITE-ON-BLACK RACISM WHERE THERE ARE NO BLACKS

This book is about race and ethnicity in an old industrial town in the American heartland. It is a historical and sociological voyage with European immigrants and their progeny, mainly of German and Irish origin, who have established and maintained a beautiful frontier town west of the Mississippi River. Despite the pleasant landscape, the journey is an unsettling one, as the traveler witnesses how the Eurocentric ethnic pride of the city residents has been reinforced and maintained by excluding other ethnic groups from the community. The residents' exclusionist attitude is applied most harshly toward African Americans despite African Americans having always been an insignificant ethnic minority in the town. The residents' fear or dislike of African Americans is in most part a product of their *perceptions* of cultural and racial differences between blacks and whites, rather than from a genuine cultural and social interaction.

A typical mid-size industrial city and the oldest in the state of Iowa, Dubuque has experienced more than 160 years of urban development. Established as a center for fur trading and lead mining in the early nineteenth century, Dubuque evolved as a booming industrial town in the post-Civil War period, with major industries such as lumbering, milling, meat packing, and wagon making. With a population of 20,000, Dubuque in 1870 was among the top 25 major urban centers in the country. Although the city maintained its industrial base, in the early decades of the 20th century it experienced a period of no growth. In the post-WWII years Dubuque was on the move again and the city had a period of industrial growth and economic prosperity. However, as the American corporate capitalist economy became increasingly global in the last decades of the 20th century the city did not grow at the same pace, and once again there was a gradual decline in industrial production. Similar to many other American cities, in order to revive the city's ailing economy Dubuque planners resorted to tourism and related service industries, an economic policy that has continued to the present time.

Little known beyond its regional boundaries, this picturesque town with its Victorian style houses and mansions made the national headlines when there was a sudden eruption of hate crimes during the 1989-1991 period. Articles on Dubuque's race problem appeared in the *New York Times* and other national papers, and television talk show hosts like *Oprah* and *Phil Donahue* aired special programs on Dubuque. While racial and ethnic prejudice has always been a part of Dubuque's social and cultural reality, the intensity of events took many by surprise. The media attributed this revived racism to a cross burning incident in 1989, which in turn prompted a group of concerned citizens to devise a plan to attract one hundred "families of color" to the city in the next five years. Known as the *Constructive Integration Plan,* the news of its approval by the city hall officials ignited a backlash of fear, intolerance, and hatred among some residents in a city that has historically been inhospitable to African Americans. Following a rash of cross burnings, demonstrations by the members of the Ku Klux Klan, a strong opposition by many Dubuque residents, and behind-the-scene efforts by certain elements within the business community, the plan was eventually abandoned. Under the auspices of the Chamber of Commerce and major powerbrokers in town, the original plan for enforcing affirmative action policies and racial diversity was then replaced by a call for cultural diversity and a plan to educate the citizenry on the issue of racial tolerance.

When I started my tenure at the University of Dubuque in 1986, I found this city of about 65,000 a charming and fascinating old midwestern community. However, I also found Dubuque to be caught in the midst of persistent economic crisis, struggling to survive and at the same time planning for its future growth and development. My fascination and interest in the city's history of urbanization culminated in the design and execution of a course titled "Sociology of Dubuque," which dealt with the city's urban political economy within a comparative historical framework.[1] A recurrent and highly controversial topic of discussion in this class involved questions concerning civil rights issues, particularly related to racial and ethnic inequalities and conflicts in the city. As I closely watched the intense racial strife unfold on a day-to-day basis, and monitored incidents of hate crimes, I became interested in the politics of citizen participation and debates on the prospects of bringing about racial and ethnic equality and harmony in the city. I could discern a link between an emerging racism in the 1980s and certain economic and political decisions made by the "movers and shakers" which were negatively affecting Dubuque residents, particularly the working class and the poor. Not wanting to base my understanding of race relations on only a speculative theory, I became determined to examine the issue in a systematic way. The only logical and appropriate method was historical documentation and analysis, and that is how this book is organized.

But readers may legitimately ask, why bother with studying race relations in a rather obscure and relatively small metropolitan area in the Midwest that only has less than one-percent minority population? In her report on the aftermath of racial tensions in Dubuque in the early 1990s, Ann Treneman of the *London Observer* (1992) made an insightful and interesting observation:

> While technically a city of 57,500 doesn't qualify as a small town, in many ways *Dubuque is the epitome of Main Street USA.* You certainly couldn't get any farther from the ghettos of Los Angeles. It is suburban to the point of sit-com: *the hilly streets are wide and pleasant, lined with the neat lawns, roomy houses*

> *and large cars of comfortable middle class America.* The many churches make God particularly next-door neighbor, and a nun was once the mayor. But loving thy neighbor is not so easy for some people when their neighbor may be black.(italics mine)

An examination of the census data for the racial and ethnic composition of the American metropolitan areas(SMSAs) also indicates that Dubuque is neither unique nor an exception to the rule. For instance, the census data indicate that in 1996 out of 273 metropolitan areas 105 had less than 5 percent black population, with a total combined population of more than 36 million for the 105 SMSAs. This represented about 14 percent of the nation's population.[2] A closer look at the census data also reveals three general trends. First, almost all metropolitan areas with less than 5 percent black population are in states north of the old Mason-Dixon Line, and west of the Mississippi, and scattered throughout the country. Second, race relations in the midwest may merit more careful and closer attention, as blacks in most major metropolitan areas in the three midwestern states of Iowa, Minnesota and Wisconsin are conspicuously underrepresented. Finally, blacks are also underrepresented in five metropolitan areas with populations exceeding one million.[3] This may suggest that many urban areas in comparable socio-economic situations either have encountered problems similar to Dubuque in the past, or may do so in the future in the area of race relations.

Analysis of race relations in Dubuque can serve as a case study with much wider applications at the national level. But two distinct and clearly interrelated issues must be studied. First, the historical evolution of ideas of "race" and "racism" in the American social and cultural context must be appreciated. In particular, the nature and dynamics of white-on-black prejudice and discrimination that some scholars of race relations identify as *white racism* merits a close attention. Second, the economic and political dimensions of the presence of blacks, as well as the nature of interaction and racial tensions between whites and blacks in urban America during different historical periods must be examined.

AMERICAN RACE RELATIONS AND "WHITE-ON-BLACK" RACISM

It is not an overstatement to say that most of us use the concepts of "race" and "racism" in our daily conversations, social criticism, and even academic discussions without providing a clear definition, or even without being conscious of their intrinsic meanings and subsequent implications. In a race culture that is visual and emphasizes people's "appearance" for their racial identity, we in a sense know race when we see it. But as a concept, race must be defined within the context of "social situations" that in turn are historically created. American race relations also have to be understood as an evolving historical process within the context of colonization of the "New World." In *Race, The History of an Idea,* Thomas Gossett(1997: Chapter 1) succinctly documents the existence of "race consciousness," particularly based on physical differences in pre-modern and ancient history. However, he concludes that modern race-based theories are the product of European colonization of the New World, Africa and Asia. In addition, Gossett recognizes American cultural consciousness of race in general, and recognition of new racial categories in particular, as an evolving historical process. "When the English colonists first landed in this country, they immediately encountered one race 'problem' in the Indians," according to Gossett, but then he adds that "in a few years they imported another when, in 1619, the first boat load of Negro slaves arrived."[4] As the new colonies evolved and the new nation was created, this immigrant-based country had to continuously deal with new racial definitions and to revise the old ones. Earlier perceptions of race used a combination of geographical location and skin color as a basis for racial classification. As is illustrated in Table 1, 18th century classifications of race by Linnaeus and Blumenbach clearly represent this theoretical tendency.[5]

Table 1: 18th Century Racial Classifications Based on Geographic Location and Skin Color

	Racial Categories				
Classified By:	1	2	3	4	5
Linnaeus (1738)	African (Afer)	American (americanus)	Asian (asiaticus)	European (europeaus)	--
Blumenbach (1775)	Black (Ethiopian)	Red (American)	Yellow (Mongolian)	White (Caucasian)	Brown (Malayan)

Source: Gossett (1997: 35-39).

Not all the originators of these models believed in the inherent inferiority or superiority of different races. For instance, Blumenbach considered "Negroes, Indians, and Mongolians as potentially valuable members of society," and was convinced that "they bear no hereditary taint"(cf. Gossett, 1997:39).[6] Later in the 19th century Charles Darwin's *theory of evolution* challenged the prevalent belief that supported the existence of different races. But Darwin "did not change the argument that some races are superior to others" (op. cit.: 67). Anthropological studies and sociological arguments in the 20th century gradually challenged the biological definitions of race. For example, in a study of sociology textbooks during the 1930s, Brewton Berry (1940:415) concluded that while sociological definitions of race still had strong residues of biological arguments, they nonetheless inclined to agree that "the innate intellectual and temperamental differences between the races are small, insignificant, and doubtful." Later, as the Civil Rights movement challenged the American conscience on the question of race and racism, American mainstream culture continued to link one's race to innate biological differences. Representing the intellectual mindset of the time, in his book *Race and Racism,* van den Berghe (1967:9) defined race as "A human group that defines itself and/or is defined by other groups as different from other groups by virtue of innate and immutable physical characteristics." He further argued that physical characteristics are "believed to be intrinsically related to moral, intellectual, and other non-physical attitudes and abilities."

At the social-psychological level, white racism manifests itself in a set of racist rituals that, as Feagin and Vera (1995:9) describe, are used by whites as "physical, psychological, or symbolic force" in order to "deprive their victims of fundamental human rights and destroy talents, energy and lives." Racist rituals range from white supremacist groups' initiation ceremonies and utilization of ceremonial regalia, to cross burning and lynching. Pertaining to Iowa and Dubuque, as I will show in the following chapters, support for white racist rituals is also provided at different levels of social participation. In a study of ideological roots of white supremacist groups, Harper (1993, cf. Feagin and Vera, 1995:10) found that participation in racist rituals includes active male members of white supremacist groups who take part in "aggressive racist actions;" male and female supporters or "acolytes;" and "passive white sympathizers" who do not take part in racist rituals, but believe in the racist myths that "portray African Americans as less competent and less human than whites."

As a concept subjected to peculiarities of social situations and historical developments, race only becomes socially meaningful "as long as people believe that differences in selected physical traits are meaningful" (Marger, 2000:23). Relating the ways social definitions of race relations acquire lives of their own, there is the sociologist W.I. Thompson's oft-quoted statement that "If men define situations as real, they are real in their consequences" (Thomas and Znaniecki, 1918:79). Furthermore, as anthropologist Robert Redfield(1958:67) explains it, "it is on the level of habit, custom, sentiment, and attitudes that race, as a matter of practical significance, is to be understood." He then concludes, "Race is, so to speak, a human invention."

In its fluid form, this "human invention" in turn provides the context in which colonizing groups and settler-based societies such as the United States find justification for racism, or race-based discrimination. Marger (2000:26-27) provides a clear definition of racism both as a belief system and ideology that by-and-large represents the sociological consensus. First, it is a belief that "humans are divided naturally into different physical types." Second, these physical types in turn are "intrinsically related to their culture, personality, and intelligence." Finally, racist ideology concludes that "on the basis of their genetic inheritance, some groups are innately superior to others." The modern ideology of racism therefore becomes a pretext for situational exclusion and discrimination of targeted groups, depending on historical circumstances and political and economic interests of dominant groups.

The concept of race also has to be understood within the context of the American cultural experience which sets it apart from the way other societies may define it. For instance, white Europeans' racial oppression of Native Americans, blacks, and other non-European immigrants in the New World has been present for nearly 400 years. But depending on the social situation of targeted groups and their historical, political, and economic status, this racism has taken different forms and been enforced with varying degrees of intensity. Schaefer (2001:13) calls this socio-historical process "racial formation" by which "racial categories are related, inhabited, transformed, and destroyed." For example, as a conquered people Native Americans were dealt with much more harshly than other oppressed groups, and primarily for two reasons. First, early Anglo-Saxon and other European settlers were not interested in Native Americans' assimilation into their settler communities, but rather in taking over their lands. Second, faced with Native Americans' resistance to European subjugation and economic and cultural domination, creation of a racist ideology based on dehumanization of the indigenous population by settlers was a historical necessity. Thus, dissemination of a racist ideology by the ruling elite paved the way for settlers' brutal treatment of natives that in most cases ended in outright genocide. In comparison, although as a subjugated and enslaved group blacks have also been present since the early days of American colonization, for practical purposes and economic reasons they were nonetheless incorporated into the social fabric of the white settler society.

blacks in urban America during different historical periods must be examined.

AMERICAN RACE RELATIONS AND "WHITE-ON-BLACK" RACISM

It is not an overstatement to say that most of us use the concepts of "race" and "racism" in our daily conversations, social criticism, and even academic discussions without providing a clear definition, or even without being conscious of their intrinsic meanings and subsequent implications. In a race culture that is visual and emphasizes people's "appearance" for their racial identity, we in a sense know race when we see it. But as a concept, race must be defined within the context of "social situations" that in turn are historically created. American race relations also have to be understood as an evolving historical process within the context of colonization of the "New World." In *Race, The History of an Idea,* Thomas Gossett(1997: Chapter 1) succinctly documents the existence of "race consciousness," particularly based on physical differences in pre-modern and ancient history. However, he concludes that modern race-based theories are the product of European colonization of the New World, Africa and Asia. In addition, Gossett recognizes American cultural consciousness of race in general, and recognition of new racial categories in particular, as an evolving historical process. "When the English colonists first landed in this country, they immediately encountered one race 'problem' in the Indians," according to Gossett, but then he adds that "in a few years they imported another when, in 1619, the first boat load of Negro slaves arrived."[4] As the new colonies evolved and the new nation was created, this immigrant-based country had to continuously deal with new racial definitions and to revise the old ones. Earlier perceptions of race used a combination of geographical location and skin color as a basis for racial classification. As is illustrated in Table 1, 18th century classifications of race by Linnaeus and Blumenbach clearly represent this theoretical tendency.[5]

Table 1: 18th Century Racial Classifications Based on Geographic Location and Skin Color

	Racial Categories				
Classified By:	1	2	3	4	5
Linnaeus (1738)	African (Afer)	American (americanus)	Asian (asiaticus)	European (europeaus)	--
Blumenbach (1775)	Black (Ethiopian)	Red (American)	Yellow (Mongolian)	White (Caucasian)	Brown (Malayan)

Source: Gossett (1997: 35-39).

Not all the originators of these models believed in the inherent inferiority or superiority of different races. For instance, Blumenbach considered "Negroes, Indians, and Mongolians as potentially valuable members of society," and was convinced that "they bear no hereditary taint"(cf. Gossett, 1997:39).[6] Later in the 19th century Charles Darwin's *theory of evolution* challenged the prevalent belief that supported the existence of different races. But Darwin "did not change the argument that some races are superior to others" (op. cit.: 67). Anthropological studies and sociological arguments in the 20th century gradually challenged the biological definitions of race. For example, in a study of sociology textbooks during the 1930s, Brewton Berry (1940:415) concluded that while sociological definitions of race still had strong residues of biological arguments, they nonetheless inclined to agree that "the innate intellectual and temperamental differences between the races are small, insignificant, and doubtful." Later, as the Civil Rights movement challenged the American conscience on the question of race and racism, American mainstream culture continued to link one's race to innate biological differences. Representing the intellectual mindset of the time, in his book *Race and Racism,* van den Berghe (1967:9) defined race as "A human group that defines itself and/or is defined by other groups as different from other groups by virtue of innate and immutable physical characteristics." He further argued that physical characteristics are "believed to be intrinsically related to moral, intellectual, and other non-physical attitudes and abilities."

Recent scientific attempts in sequencing the human genetic code have raised hopes that new genetic discoveries, including the recently published research findings by the Human Genome Project (HGP) will do away with the long-standing myth that race is a biological reality.[7] Published in 2001, the project's findings indicate that humans are identical in 99.9 percent of their DNA. The remaining 0.1 percent is considered to be the "human genome diversity" that is "distributed across populations in an overwhelmingly statistical pattern" (Gannett, 2001: 487). As an offshoot of the HGP, in 1993 a collaborative effort by anthropologists, geneticists, linguists and others also launched the Human Genome Diversity Project (HGDP) to study these statistically insignificant but apparently important genetic differences among various racial and ethnic groups. The project aimed at collecting tissue samples from 7,000 indigenous groups worldwide that were identified by their distinct languages (Connor, 2001). Supporters of the HGDP claimed that they believed in the non-existence of biological races, but recognized genetic differences in certain "human populations." They also emphasized "health disparities between whites and other ethnic and racial groups," and thus medical significance of HGDP findings (Duster, 2001).

But from its inception, the HGDP has been surrounded by controversy. As early as 1996, the United Nations' Economic, Scientific, and Cultural Organization (UNESCO) published a report by its International Bioethics Committee and cited the following reasons that lent support to a skeptical public's fear that the findings of the HGDP could be misappropriated and misused by racists:

> The history of objectification of colonized (especially indigenous) peoples by Western scientists; the political vulnerability of many ethnic minorities; the ties between religious and ethnic discrimination; and the likelihood that racists will continue to look to science for whatever support they might find there. (cf. Gannett, 2001:480)

The fiercest attack came from a coalition of 30 groups representing indigenous peoples in North, Central, and South America who, in 1997, produced the *Ukupseni Declaration*. They opposed the HGDP on the grounds that it "intends to collect and make available our genetic materials which may be used for commercial, scientific and military purposes." They also demanded that the HGDP and other similar scientific projects "cease any attempts to seduce or coerce participation in their project through promises of benefits and financial gain in order to obtain consent and participation of indigenous peoples" (*Ukupseni Declaration*, 1997). In his book *The Emperor's New Clothes: Biological Theories of Race in the Millennium,* Joseph Graves (2001) also rejects the HGDP's use of "human populations" to trace genetic differences as a new form of scientific racism in disguise, and argues that "race is simply a social and political construct the world would be better without" (cf. Villarosa, 2002). Finally, in a compelling article, Lisa Gannett (2001:490-91) also rejects the claims that "population thinking" is rejection of "biological racism," and is instead reconceptualization of "races" as "populations."[8]

In academic circles, studies that emphasize innate biological differences between whites and blacks also provide scientific support for white racism. A most recent seminal work is *the Bell Curve* by Richard Hernstein and Charles Murray (1994), who characterize "blacks" and "whites" as two distinct racial categories and then provide quantitative evidence to prove that the two group's genetic differences result in different I.Q. scores. "White racism" has been defined and analyzed from a variety of perspectives in the social sciences and humanities. For instance, Joel Kovel (1984: xli-xlvii) defines it as a psychological reaction to "blackness" by whites, as they have been socialized to associate blackness with darkness, ignorance or the unknown. Feagin and Vera (1995:7) view white racism as the "socially organized set of attitudes, ideas, and practices that deny African Americans and other people of color the dignity, opportunities, freedoms, and rewards that this nation offers white Americans."

At the social-psychological level, white racism manifests itself in a set of racist rituals that, as Feagin and Vera (1995:9) describe, are used by whites as "physical, psychological, or symbolic force" in order to "deprive their victims of fundamental human rights and destroy talents, energy and lives." Racist rituals range from white supremacist groups' initiation ceremonies and utilization of ceremonial regalia, to cross burning and lynching. Pertaining to Iowa and Dubuque, as I will show in the following chapters, support for white racist rituals is also provided at different levels of social participation. In a study of ideological roots of white supremacist groups, Harper (1993, cf. Feagin and Vera, 1995:10) found that participation in racist rituals includes active male members of white supremacist groups who take part in "aggressive racist actions;" male and female supporters or "acolytes;" and "passive white sympathizers" who do not take part in racist rituals, but believe in the racist myths that "portray African Americans as less competent and less human than whites."

As a concept subjected to peculiarities of social situations and historical developments, race only becomes socially meaningful "as long as people believe that differences in selected physical traits are meaningful" (Marger, 2000:23). Relating the ways social definitions of race relations acquire lives of their own, there is the sociologist W.I. Thompson's oft-quoted statement that "If men define situations as real, they are real in their consequences" (Thomas and Znaniecki, 1918:79). Furthermore, as anthropologist Robert Redfield(1958:67) explains it, "it is on the level of habit, custom, sentiment, and attitudes that race, as a matter of practical significance, is to be understood." He then concludes, "Race is, so to speak, a human invention."

In its fluid form, this "human invention" in turn provides the context in which colonizing groups and settler-based societies such as the United States find justification for racism, or race-based discrimination. Marger (2000:26-27) provides a clear definition of racism both as a belief system and ideology that by-and-large represents the sociological consensus. First, it is a belief that "humans are divided naturally into different physical types." Second, these physical types in turn are "intrinsically related to their culture, personality, and intelligence." Finally, racist ideology concludes that "on the basis of their genetic inheritance, some groups are innately superior to others." The modern ideology of racism therefore becomes a pretext for situational exclusion and discrimination of targeted groups, depending on historical circumstances and political and economic interests of dominant groups.

The concept of race also has to be understood within the context of the American cultural experience which sets it apart from the way other societies may define it. For instance, white Europeans' racial oppression of Native Americans, blacks, and other non-European immigrants in the New World has been present for nearly 400 years. But depending on the social situation of targeted groups and their historical, political, and economic status, this racism has taken different forms and been enforced with varying degrees of intensity. Schaefer (2001:13) calls this socio-historical process "racial formation" by which "racial categories are related, inhabited, transformed, and destroyed." For example, as a conquered people Native Americans were dealt with much more harshly than other oppressed groups, and primarily for two reasons. First, early Anglo-Saxon and other European settlers were not interested in Native Americans' assimilation into their settler communities, but rather in taking over their lands. Second, faced with Native Americans' resistance to European subjugation and economic and cultural domination, creation of a racist ideology based on dehumanization of the indigenous population by settlers was a historical necessity. Thus, dissemination of a racist ideology by the ruling elite paved the way for settlers' brutal treatment of natives that in most cases ended in outright genocide. In comparison, although as a subjugated and enslaved group blacks have also been present since the early days of American colonization, for practical purposes and economic reasons they were nonetheless incorporated into the social fabric of the white settler society.

In their book *White Racism,* Feagin and Vera (1995: xi-xii) argue that both before and after emancipation blacks have always served as a "point of reference" for racial differentiation and discrimination related to the white European socio-economic, cultural and religious values, and even white self-perceptions. Feagin and Vera also argue that white racism toward blacks should be considered as "an archetype for other subsequent patterns of white treatment of people of color," as immigrants of non-European origin often find themselves being treated "more like African Americans than like Euro-American whites." Using blacks as a "point of reference" in the process of racial formation is interesting, particularly pertaining to some European immigrants such as the Irish, who were seen by white settlers as undesirable white ethnics. Being victims of the British racist oppression in Ireland, and entering at the lowest rungs of the American class system, often in close proximity to African Americans, the majority of Irish immigrants realized that the only route to citizenship and becoming "white" was to differentiate themselves from blacks (see Ignatiev, 1995). As I shall discuss Dubuque's case later, in their assimilation into "white America" the Irish immigrants in most cases became vigorously anti-black both in thoughts and actions.

White-on-black racism as an attitude and social behavior has persevered and at the same time evolved with social changes in American society. Putting it in a historical context, Louis Kushnick (1996) argues that white racism first emerged as the foundations of the American settler society and slavery were laid, and was later institutionalized through Jim Crow legislation as American capitalism evolved after the Civil War. However, he also argues that the increasing involvement of the United States in the world economy and a claim for global moral leadership in the 20th century required suppression of overt racial discrimination. Thus, according to Kushnick, a suppressed white racism led to the emergence of more subtle and indirect forms of discrimination that manifested itself in social processes such as white flight to the suburbs, which gradually left urban black residents behind in inner cities and urban ghettos. As I shall discuss in the following section, post-WWII race relations in urban America culminated in the eruption of race riots that have continued to plague the nation's major cities. For example, in an investigation of the causes of urban race riots during the 1964-67 period, the Kerner Commission's report concluded that white racism was the major cause of social strife in urban America, with "racial attitude and behavior of white Americans toward black Americans" being the most fundamental factor (*Report of the Advisory Committee on Civil Disorders*, 1968:9).

In this book I shall examine white racism in Iowa and Dubuque by considering it not so much as a product of direct, day-to-day interaction of blacks and whites, but as a complex socio-historical product that is affected by a myriad of economic, political, cultural and social-psychological factors. Our historical journey into Dubuque's past and examination of its residents' experience of race relations will also shed light on an interesting aspect of white-on-black racism: there appears to be a strong link between economic welfare and degrees of anti-black prejudice among white ethnics. Finally, as I will document in the following chapters, white racism in regions with little or no black populations is also a social phenomenon that is extremely resilient and resistant to social change.

PRESENCE OF BLACKS IN URBAN AMERICA

Without a doubt, the history of race relations in urban America since the early 20th century has been the history of its largest cities, such as New York, Chicago, Philadelphia, Los Angeles and Detroit. This is in sharp contrast to the 19th century social conditions, particularly in the North, as few cities had sizable black populations. In fact, as late as 1910 about 90 percent of the nation's black population still resided in the rural areas of the South (Grant, 1972:27). Concentration of blacks in the rural south was a direct product of its plantation system and utilization of slaves as field workers. For one thing, as an agricultural-based institution, the southern plantation economy necessitated attachment of slave-laborers to

the land and severely restricted their spatial movement. However, slaves also comprised a considerable portion of the urban population in the South, engaging either in commercial occupations or domestic work. Based on some estimates, as early as 1820 about 20 percent of southern black slaves resided in major urban centers (Wade, 1964, cf. Palen, 1992:223).

The more flexible working conditions in urban areas required a different kind of master-slave relations in southern cities. According to Sowell (1975:12), urban slaves were "engaged in a wide variety of occupations, skilled as well as unskilled, in addition to those who worked as domestic servants for their owners." In his book *Industrial Slavery in the Old South,* Robert Starobin states that in the 1850s between 160,000 and 200,000 slaves, or about 5 percent of slave population worked in Southern industries. But since most of the industries in the South were located in rural areas, only about 25,000 industrial slaves worked in urban factories (Starobin, 1970:11-12). Many urban slaves were also hired out to work for other white employers. Some argue that the relaxed and less restrictive social environment in the cities forced urban slaveholders to deviate from strict rules of controlling the slaves as practiced in plantations, and to instead "rule with a lighter hand" (Palen, 1992:224). In addition, based on some estimates, in the early 1860s about one out of eight southern blacks was a "free Negro," mostly living in urban areas (Ibid.).[9]

In the aftermath of the Civil War and during the Reconstruction era, freed blacks moved to towns and urban areas of the South in greater numbers. But this proved to be a short lived phenomenon, as many emancipated blacks had to return to rural areas and work as new sharecroppers for their former masters in order to "find a basis for subsistence"(Grant, 1972:27). In the meantime, as the North became increasingly industrialized in the post-Civil War period, Europe provided a steady flow of migrant workers for American industries. In the first decade of the 20th century alone a total of 8.8 million European immigrants came to America. But the outbreak of WWI disrupted the European immigration tide, and the American wartime economic machine was desperate to find a substitute labor pool. This was found in the South, and labor recruiting agents of northern industries were dispatched to the South to recruit blacks and encourage them to migrate to the "Promised Land" of the North. These recruiting efforts were one of the reasons for the massive emigration of blacks from the southern states, as between 1910 and 1930 about 1 million blacks moved to major northeastern and midwestern cities. By 1930, black populations in major cities in the north ranged from 5 percent in New York City to more than 11 percent in Philadelphia and St. Louis.[10]

Several factors contributed to the massive migration of southern blacks to northern industrial cities. First, labor-recruiting agents for northern factories lured blacks as cheap laborers to the north, often bribing them with free train tickets. Second, blacks that had migrated earlier also wrote letters to friends and relatives about the advantages of living in the north. Third, the "Promised Land" seemed to offer prospects of living freely in the North without the fear of Jim Crow laws. All things considered, southern blacks had every reason to head north, as in relative terms the social environment in the North was more hospitable for blacks than the one they wished to emigrate from. Several newspapers in the North also encouraged black migration. For example, the black-run *Chicago Defender* had a circulation of 100,000 in 1917, and was widely circulated and read south of the Mason-Dixon Line. The *Defender's* editorials advised blacks to "come north to the land of opportunity, where they could find employment and, if not equality, at least an escape from harassment and violence"(Judd, 1988:231).

Migration of Southern blacks to the North "Promised Land" proved to be less than ideal for blacks and more problematic for the northern white population. On the one hand, newly arrived black immigrants were confronted with persistent discrimination in housing and jobs and soon realized that "equal opportunity" promises by employers and the government did not include black workers. On the other hand, white Americans did not perceive blacks as "just another ethnic group" who would in time acculturate and assimilate into mainstream American culture, but rather as a lower caste that had to "be separated residentially from whites"(Abu-Lughod, 1991:187). To prevent black families from moving into white neighborhoods, white residents in many northern cities introduced restrictive covenants attached to property deeds and many were officially recorded with the county Clerks of Court. For example, in 1944 more than 11 square miles of Chicago were covered by restrictive deeds (Grant, 1972:71). Many newly incorporated small towns and neighborhood associations also enforced restrictive covenants, either *de facto* (by social persuasion of residents) or *de jure*.

White-on-black racism in the North manifested itself in discrimination in jobs, housing, and provision of services for blacks, which in turn resulted in much higher rates of unemployment and poverty among blacks and creation of dilapidated residential neighborhoods and ghettos. Adding to the problem was the difficulty of adjusting to urban life for black immigrants who previously lived in the rural South. Escaping from the overt violence of the southern system of racial apartheid, blacks sought refuge in the North only to find out that the social conditions were also ripe with violence, though in a more subtle fashion. Persistent racism, poverty and unemployment in northern cities with a sizable black population led to the eruption of urban riots in the late 1910s and early 1920s. In the "Red Summer" of 1919 alone more than 20 cities, including Chicago, "experienced race riots, all of them initiated by whites attacking blacks" (Judd, 1988:232-33).

The Great Depression temporarily put a damper on South-North migration of blacks, but the post-WWII economic boom once again accelerated the migration process. Between 1940 and 1970 more than 4 million blacks migrated from the South and settled in northern metropolitan areas, while white urban residents moved to the newly developed suburbs in great numbers (235). In addition to several other factors that promoted suburbanization, such as the construction of the national highway system and flight of industrial and commercial activities to the suburbs, the high concentration of newly arrived blacks in the cities also contributed to the "white flight" to suburban residential neighborhoods. As a consequence, central cities in many large metropolitan areas were left with high concentrations of blacks and other "non-white" low-income, working class ethnic groups, while the newly developed suburbs absorbed almost exclusively white urbanites. Blacks and other non-white groups also managed to move to the suburbs. But as is illustrated in Table 2, they remained an insignificant minority in most suburban rings of major metropolitan areas. Thus, the white flight to the suburbs contributed to *de facto* segregation and increasing spatial isolation of blacks in central cities.

Table 2: Changes in Percentage of Blacks in Central Cities and Suburban Rings in 12 Selected SMSAs, 1940-1980

	Central City		Suburban Ring	
SMSA	1940	1980	1940	1980
East:				
New York	6.4	25.2	4.6	7.6
Philadelphia	13.1	37.8	6.6	8.1
Boston	3.3	22.4	0.9	1.6
Baltimore	19.4	54.8	11.9	9.1
Washington, DC	28.5	76.6	13.7	16.7
Pittsburgh	9.3	24.0	3.6	4.0
Midwest:				
Chicago	8.3	39.8	2.2	5.6
Detroit	9.3	63.1	2.9	4.2
St. Louis	13.4	45.6	6.7	10.6
Cleveland	9.7	43.8	0.9	7.1
West:				
Los Angeles-Long Beach	6.0	16.4	2.3	9.6
San Francisco-Oakland	4.9	24.1	3.6	9.4

Source: Table constructed based on information in Judd (1988:237, Table 8-2).

Similar to the 1910-1930 period, the post-WWII economic development also contributed to intensification of conflict between whites and blacks, culminating in a series of urban riots in major metropolitan areas with sizable black populations, especially during the 1960s. However, the nature of conflict and the patterns of violence were distinctly different. In most cases, white-on-black violence in the former period resulted from direct interaction of the two groups who were forced to live and work together in the northern cities. For example, the Chicago riot in the summer of 1919 was ignited when a black youth tried to swim across a "no-man's land" that separated a "colored" beach and a white beach. The black boy was stoned to death by a white mob. The riots left 38 people dead (see Judd, 1988:233; Kleniewski, 2002:339). This happened at a time, and in a social and cultural environment that neither acknowledged nor supported civil rights of black residents. In contrast, in the aftermath of the Civil Rights movement and legal gains for blacks, almost all riots since the 1960s have been ignited by the actions of law enforcement agencies against black residents. The most significant and most violent urban riot in the 1960s erupted in the Watts area of Los Angeles. The police ignited the riot when a crowd of angry black residents protested the arrest of a black youth. The riots lasted three years, and left 220 people dead (Feagin and Hahn, 1967:102).

The unprecedented frequency of urban riots during the 1964-67 period prompted President Johnson to establish the National Advisory Commission on Civil Disorders to investigate the causes of urban riots and to recommend policy measures to prevent them in the future. Known as the "Kerner Commission Report," the investigation concluded that several factors have contributed to the eruption of urban riots:

> A history of racial oppression that blacks were beginning to challenge, mass migration of black people from the rural South to the urban North, an economic structure of blocked or limited opportunities

> for urban blacks, and less than positive conditions in urban ghetto neighborhoods, including tense police-community relations.(cf. Kleniewski, 2002:340)

Unlike the pre-1960s period when white residents took the law in their own hands to confront blacks, in the post-1960s era the task of "putting blacks back in their place" has been delegated to the police and law enforcement agents while white residents have taken refuge in the suburbs. Thus, in the hundreds of urban disturbances that have occurred since the 1960s most participants are members of the African American minority. However, the changing ethnic composition of major American cities has created urban ethnic landscapes that are more represented by a coalition of working class and poor nonwhite population. The Los Angeles riots of 1992 is a good example: although the riots were ignited when news broke out that a jury had acquitted the four police officers accused of the brutal beating of Rodney King, the majority of those arrested in the riot's aftermath were Hispanic.[11]

The preceding brief historical review of race relations in urban America suggests that in most cases the real presence and interaction of both whites and blacks in major metropolitan areas have fueled racial conflicts and white antagonism toward blacks. But this race-based antagonism took different shapes as the two groups competed for scarce resources such as jobs, housing, and political power in different historical periods. A prerequisite for the ignition of white-on-black violence and race-based urban riots has always been the active presence of blacks in the city in significant numbers. But if this explanation is plausible, as was indicated in the Kerner Commission Report, then how can one make sense of a long history of white-on-black racism and eruption of anti-black sentiments in mid-size cities like Dubuque, Iowa, where throughout its history it has been home to an insignificant black population? If anything, Iowa cities like Waterloo-Cedar Falls and Des Moines with average black populations of 8.3 and 7.0 percent in 1990, respectively, would have been better candidates for race-related disturbances.[12]

An historical investigation of race relations in Dubuque indicates that white-on-black racism does not require the physical and historical presence of blacks in large numbers. Rather, it is an ideological tool that is historically used by white ethnics to resolve their intra-group conflicts and to reassert and establish their own ethnic identities. This makes the Dubuque story neither a unique nor an isolated case.

THE SCOPE OF THE STUDY

Writing about this issue, I did not want to limit my research and analysis to what happened only in the 1980s and early 1990s. Rather, I was inclined to go beyond the obvious, and explore the historical root causes of periodic violent outbursts of racial hatred and ethnic conflict in a city that has never had a sizable "non-white" racial or ethnic population. I have used both local and national documents to accomplish this task. In addition to secondary sources, I have used census data from 1840 to the present time, both federal and state, in order to document the socio-economic status of various ethnic groups in Dubuque. The census data is problematic, however, due to its inconsistencies in terms of enumeration techniques and usage of concepts and terminologies to define racial and ethnic groups. Local newspapers also proved to be invaluable primary sources of information, and in the course of my research I exhausted most local archives. Finally, I have used personal interviews and correspondence; oral history accounts and personal letters, many at the State Historical Society in Iowa City; and essays written by college students, some in my own classes, who have had first-hand social experience in the community. These sources helped me to find answers for social situations and changes unexplainable by census data alone, or to fill the historical gaps left by missing newspaper reports or other documents for certain time periods.

As a first step, in chapter one I examine historical roots of the formation of Dubuque as a frontier town. Established and developed mostly during the 19th century, the founders of

American western frontier towns capitalized on the experience of almost two centuries of settlement on the eastern seaboard, particularly pertaining to race relations. Similar to many other frontier communities, the early European settlers in Dubuque were able to reassert their ethnic identity by winning a political and economic battle against the indigenous Native American population. However, this was at the expense of the latter group's virtual exclusion from social processes, expulsion from the area, and at times total annihilation.

In the first chapter I also review the process of community formation for various European ethnic groups during more than 160 years of Dubuque's history. The findings indicate that after the initial stage of colonial domination and reaffirmation of the community's European ethnic identity, ethnic conflicts and rivalries were shifted to a new level, mainly between the Germans and the Irish as the two most important and numerically significant ethnic groups in the Dubuque area. This chapter also chronicles the presence and contribution of Jews as the city's only "white" minority ethnic group. Although mostly accepted by Dubuque citizens during the city's two centuries of urban development, Jewish residents have also been subjected to prejudicial attitudes and periodic discriminatory acts. But for the most part they appear to have succeeded in establishing themselves as a viable minority group, both through partial assimilation to local culture, and their engagement in the community's economic and political affairs.

Chapters two, three, and four examine the historical presence and contributions of African Americans as the most important (or discernible?) "nonwhite" ethnic minority group in Dubuque. In chapter two I briefly review almost two centuries of changes in blacks' socio-economic and occupational status, their residential location and the extent of spatial segregation for this minority population.

Chapter three chronicles race and ethnic relations during the 19th century, Dubuque's first century of urban development as a frontier town. Of note are the expressed attitudes and political positions of pro-Union and pro-Confederacy contingents and the changing nature of white-on-black racism among Dubuque residents during several periods of economic prosperity and decline and political crises, including the Civil War period and the Reconstruction Era.

In chapter four I chronicle race relations throughout the 20th century in this regional metropolis. In particular, I focus on the nature and extent of white-on-black racism during the Jim Crow era, the Great Depression, the 1960s, and finally the turbulent decades of the 1980s and 1990s. With its 19th century status as a western frontier town and as an industrial and predominantly working class community, the city had to cope with the challenges of corporate capitalism that by the 1960s was pulling its workers into the nuances of a globalized economy. Similar to the previous century, race relations are greatly affected by economic fluctuations and dynamics of intra-class conflict among workers. The findings indicate that while African Americans have never been a sizeable ethnic group in Dubuque, racial prejudice and discrimination have always been based on white-on-black racism. Thus as residents of European origin historically competed with each other to secure their share of Dubuque's economic resources, their "perceived" prejudice toward an almost non-existent African American population created an easy to defeat external enemy and scapegoat at the local level, especially during hard economic times.

Related to white-on-black prejudice and discrimination, the role and presence of white supremacist groups in urban America also merits close attention, since they are the product of post-Civil War American capitalism and have been active participants in most ethnic and racial conflicts. Chapter five sketches the presence of the Ku Klux Klan in Dubuque and Iowa, particularly during the 1920s and late 1980s to early 1990s. A historical review of race relations indicates that both the targets and social support bases of this white supremacist group were different during each of the two above-mentioned periods. As the United States allied itself with the British against Germans during WWI, the Klan found Dubuque residents of German descent, mostly Catholic, an easy target to attack in order to promote their ideals of white supremacy based on "one hundred percent American" values. For them, being "German" was unpatriotic at the national level, and at the local level the Klan perceived Catholics as promoters of parochial education and accomplices to German-Americans who were out to undermine Americanism and Protestant values. Of note is the Klan's new focus on local social issues in the 1920s that mostly spared blacks from its rhetorical attacks. In contrast, while during the 1980s and early 1990s the Klan again capitalized on a weak economy and high unemployment rates, this time it targeted blacks after local liberals devised a plan to enhance Dubuque's ethnic diversity by attracting one hundred "families of color."

The comparative historical data help us to identify one important characteristic of Klan supporters during these two periods: their broad social class base and their shifting class alliances. For instance, while Klan supporters and sympathizers during the 1920s mostly came from upper and middle class backgrounds, members of the working class provided the most support for the Klan in the late 1980s to early 1990s period.

My findings indicate that Dubuque residents have experienced several periods of intense racial conflict: the 1840s, the 1870s, the 1920s, and finally the 1980s-1990s. But only the latter period stands out as one in which a significant number of Dubuque residents firmly and resolutely stood up for racial equality and social justice. Although to assume that the community's struggle to fight racism and prejudice was supported by the majority of its residents is erroneous, the strong conviction of participants and the intensity of their involvement to bring about racial justice during the last period merit close examination.

Therefore, in chapter six I begin with a narrative of recent events in the 1990s that led to the formation of the Constructive Integration Task Force. Using mostly primary sources, I examine the proposed plan that aimed to bring about racial harmony in Dubuque; the community's reaction to its controversial provisions; and the original plan's derailment and eventual defeat.

Since Dubuque has historically been a working class town with a strong cultural and political presence of labor unions, in chapter seven I review organized labor's position on black workers both in Iowa and Dubuque. A historical survey of local and state labor documents indicates that, except for a few unions and in brief periods, organized labor has been slow to promote human rights and fight racial discrimination among its rank and file. A combination of factors, including black workers' historical role as a cheap source of labor and strike breakers as well as a culture of white-on-black prejudice have contributed to this less than ideal reality.

Chapter eight is the culmination of my journey into the past in search of historical clues and reasons for the resurgence of an otherwise dormant racism in the community. Using Dubuque as a case study, I analyze racist ideology as a multifaceted and complex social and cultural phenomenon deeply rooted in the local, national and international political economy. The chapter's focus is on the dynamics of race and class and the periodic resurgence of racial and ethnic intolerance in Dubuque, particularly during the 1920s and 1980s, when city residents suffered immensely from long periods of economic downturn. Finally, in an epilogue I revisit Dubuque a decade after racial tensions in the early 1990s polarized its residents on the issues of racial diversity and human rights. While there have been some efforts to raise citizens' awareness about racial and ethnic diversity, prejudice and discrimination continue to affect blacks and other nonwhite ethnic groups in town, although in more subtle forms. Dubuque's persistent economic crisis and subsequent loss of jobs in the last decade have certainly been a contributing factor to this problem. The links between economic crisis and prejudice can also be discerned at the state level. Faced with the loss of younger and more educated Iowans who leave the state for better jobs and higher pay, state planners have scrambled to attract workers to Iowa in order to compensate for the loss. Since existing and newly created jobs are mostly geared to lower paid and less skilled workers, employers have sought migrant workers, in particular Hispanics, to fill those positions. This has stirred anti-immigrant and anti-Hispanic sentiments among Iowans, culminating in the passage of the "English Only" legislation in 2002. Thus while African Americans continue to be subjected to prejudicial attitudes, Hispanic migrant laborers have become the new problematic "race" in Iowa and Dubuque.

Dubuque serves as an interesting case study to gain insight on race relations in not just an obscure midwestern metropolis, but in "any town USA" with similar historical experiences. Using historical documentation and analysis, I will demonstrate that white racism should not be considered as an individual mental malaise, a social-psychological moral impasse that can be confronted or outright eliminated by educating the public, or a personal attitude problem. Rather, racism, and in particular white-on-black racism should be examined and understood as a socially created ideology that is intertwined with periodic turns and twists of the American political economy, evolves historically, and is modified and revised in response to political and economic developments, group and ethnic interaction dynamics and class conflicts.

Notes

1. See Chaichian (1989).
2. U.S. Bureau of the Census, State and Metropolitan Area Data Book 1997-98, Table B-2. Accessed 12-10-01: http://www.census.gov/press-releasee/ metro11.prn. According to census data, in 1999 blacks numbered 35.1 million, or 13 percent of the total population (U.S. Census Bureau, 2000:1). The adopted 5 percent cut-off point here is assumed to be well below the desired *proportiona*l black population distribution, whereby the average black population in a given SMSA should be around 13 percent.
3. The five metropolitan areas are Seattle-Tacoma, WA; Minneapolis-St. Paul, MN; Phoenix-Mesa, AZ; Portland-Salem, OR-WA; and

Salt Lake City-Ogden, UT with a total combined population of more than 12 million residents. See the U.S. Bureau of the Census, State and Metropolitan Data Book 1997-98, Table B-2.

4. Ibid., p. 3.
5. See Dunn and Dobzhansky, 1964; Gossett, 1997.
6. Even more than two centuries later, one can find the earlier classifications based on skin color and geographical location, especially the one formulated by Blumenbach, to still have considerable acceptance, and widely used by Americans on a daily basis.
7. Conceived in the mid-1980s, the Human Genome Project (HGP) began as an international collaborative effort to map the genes on human chromosomes, and sequence DNA base pairs that match up the genes. In the United States, the project was financed by the Department of Energy (DOE) and the National Institute of Health (NIH). In 1998, a private company also started the use of new DNA sequencing machines to achieve the above objectives.
8. For contrasting arguments on HGDP also see King and Motulsky (2002); Couzin (2002), Cooper, Kaufman and Ward (2003); Burchard et. al. (2003); and Juengst (1988). The *Human Genome Diversity Project* at Stanford University (<http:www.stanford.edu/group/Morrison/hqdp/faq.html>) and the government-sponsored *International HapMap Project* (http://www.genome.gov/11511175)also provide vital information.
9. Starobin (1970:4) puts the number of free blacks around "one-quarter million.' Considering that black population is estimated at around 4 million by 1860, Starobin's figure is much lower than the one estimated by Palen.
10. During the same decade blacks comprised 7 percent of population in Chicago and 8 percent in Cleveland (Judd, 1988:229-30).
11. It is also interesting to note that about 7 percent of those arrested were white (see Madhubuti, 1993).
12. For comparative data of various racial and ethnic population for Iowa cities see Iowa State University, Department of Economics: http://ia.profiles.iastate.edu/data/census/city/race.htm.letterw. Accessed 3-6-02.

CHAPTER 1

THE MAKING OF ETHNIC IDENTITIES IN THE FRONTIER TOWN

As the oldest city and the site of the first white settlement in the state of Iowa, Dubuque is well qualified to be studied as an important frontier town that along with many other European settlements in the Midwest facilitated American westward expansion. Two factors were instrumental in the Midwest's early years of urban development. First, the Louisiana Purchase of 1803 doubled the national domain from the Mississippi River to the Rocky Mountains, and from the Gulf of Mexico to British North America. Second, completion of the Erie Canal linked New York and the East to the Great Lakes. However, in the last decades of the 18th century several French settlements were already established along the Mississippi and Missouri Rivers. These included Dubuque in the soon-to-be Iowa Territories; Kaskaskia in Illinois, which in the early 19th century served as the state capital; and St. Louis and St. Genevieve in Missouri.

In the process of getting settled in the area, white settlers in Dubuque had to deal with the "Native American question" in terms of their legitimate claims and presence in the Iowa territories. Similar to many other frontier towns in the Midwest, the federal government's active role and participation to secure new lands helped the new immigrants get settled in Dubuque. The early white settlers in Iowa had their share of firsthand racial and ethnic conflict with the indigenous population that in most part was generated and fueled by the former group's interest in gaining ownership rights and control of land and natural resources. Among many Indian tribes that inhabited the northeastern parts of North America were the Mesquakie Indians or the "Red Earth" people. Also known by settlers as the "Fox," the Mesquakie came to the Dubuque area in the mid-1700s (Wilkie, 1987:48-49). With 1,600 to 2,000 members out of approximately 50,000 Native Americans, the Mesquakie were one of the smaller tribes who resided in Wisconsin, Illinois, and eastern Iowa in the 1600s (Callender, 1978:645).

The city of Dubuque borrowed its name from a French-Canadian fur trader and settler, Julien Dubuque, who, along with others in 1788 established a settlement north of the mouth of a stream known as Catfish Creek on the rugged bluffs west of the Upper Mississippi River. Located south of present-day Dubuque, the Catfish Creek Village was the second largest Mesquakie settlement in Iowa. As late as 1820 it had a population of about 250 people (Hoffmann, 1930: 43).[1] Some local historians and popular narrators of Dubuque's history have portrayed the encounters between Julien Dubuque, the French "founding father" of the city, and the Mesquakie as one based on friendship, mutual respect, trust and cooperation (Hermann, 1922). Local legend glorifies Julien Dubuque as a noble white settler who mingled with Indians, treated them as friends and even married an Indian woman. That Dubuque married Potosa, the young daughter of Peosta, the chief of the Mesquakie tribe is widely believed. Potosa may have been Dubuque's first wife, as at his death "his widow was identified as a Mesquakie Métisse from prairie du Chien named Josette Peltier *dit* Antaya" (Murphy, 2000:85). Marrying Indian women was a common practice among French Canadian residents in Dubuque and the nearby Prairie du Chien settlement. Apparently this was reluctantly condoned by the Native American communities "because it created the assurance of mutuality and reciprocal obligations between the spouses' families"(Ibid.). Other historians argue that Dubuque's intentions to marry Potosa were based more on economic interests and less out of his genuine love and affection for the chief's daughter (Herman, 1922:44).

Revisionist local historians also portray Dubuque as a "full-blooded white man" and "one of the shrewd, ingenious men" who managed to carry on a prosperous trade with local natives in pursuit of his own personal interests (*The History of Dubuque County*, 1880:495). But Julien Dubuque was also known to be a charismatic individual and an "outgoing man of great charm and generosity with a notable sense of humor" (Murphy, 2000:86). Gaining the Native's trust, Dubuque reportedly received lifetime permission from the Mesquakie to work the lead mines in the area. However, there were no indications of land ownership rights for him in the pact, which he tried to secure by calling the lead mines the "Mines of Spain" and getting the approval of the Spanish Governor in New Orleans in 1796 (Somner, 1975:5).[2] Until his death in 1810, for 22 years Julien Dubuque mined hundreds of thousands of pounds of lead with the help of about a dozen white and mulatto workers, as well as the labor of Native American elderly and women (Petersen, 1966:108). The extracted lead was transported down the Mississippi River to St. Louis, where he made a hefty profit.

Some chroniclers of Dubuque's early history contend that despite his pursuit of personal and material interests, Julien Dubuque represented a century-old tradition of amicable coexistence between the French fur traders and Indian inhabitants of the upper Mississippi Valley. According to Auge (1980:33), during the eighteenth and early nineteenth centuries this relationship "produced a 'bi-racial' frontier culture in which the two peoples managed to live in close proximity without losing their individuality." An inevitable outcome of this social and cultural interaction was the birth of many children of "mixed ancestry," or what is referred to as "half-breeds." Unlike other French settlements in the area such as Prairie du Chien located north of Dubuque, where the Indian-French cohabitation is well documented, the evidence concerning the Mesquakie village near Dubuque's Mines of Spain is more limited.[3] However, according to Auge (op. cit.:44), "it would appear that this settlement contained a high proportion of persons of mixed ancestry." In fact, Julien Dubuque had about ten Creole associates, that according to "scattered records" many of them were "Métis or Native and long-time residents of the Fox-Wisconsin region" (Murphy, 2000:88).

After Dubuque's death in 1810, the Mesquakie guarded the Dubuque territory and successfully operated some of the lead mines.[4] Based on some estimates one year after Dubuque's death "Sauk and Mesquakies sold 400,000 pounds of lead to traders," which by all standards was "a sizeable amount in a year that the United States imported 1,837,702 pounds of lead from overseas" (Ibid, 98). But distrusting American government officials and citizens, the natives prevented white settlers and miners from entering the region. The white settlers' interest in the area led to a series of confrontations with the indigenous population in the early decades of the 19th century. The events culminated in the last encounter known as the Battle of the Bad Axe, and ended in the Sauk tribe's defeat and a forced settlement that permanently removed Native American tribes from the Iowa Territory. The seeds of the war were planted in 1804 in St. Louis, when several members of the Sauk tribes were tricked into signing a treaty with the United States government, represented by William Henry Harrison, who later became the president of the United States. According to this treaty, the Sauk and Mesquakie relinquished 6 million acres of land from Missouri to Minnesota east of the Mississippi River. In return, the tribes were granted $1,000 a year in goods and commodities, and were allowed to stay in the area as long as the land was not sold to white settlers (Kappler, 1904:74-77; Waldman, 1988:212). The Sauk and Mesquakie tribal leaders immediately denounced the treaty and questioned its legality, as

> the warriors were not authorized to speak for the entire Sauk tribe; the Mesquakie tribe was not represented at all; and the Euro-American negotiators entertained the Sauk with quantities of liquor before, during, and after the treaty negotiations.(Dockstader, 1977:35)

The St. Louis treaty was a historical turning point for the Mesquakie and the Sauk, as this first land cession completely undermined their pastoral-nomadic lifestyle and economic system and led to their eventual defeat and demise in the region (Kapller, 1904:74). Forced out of Illinois into Iowa, in 1832 about 1,000 Sauk Indians tried to return to their lands east of the Mississippi River. But when the Illinois settlers killed an Indian peace emissary dispatched by their leader Black Hawk, a series of battles were fought. The Battle of Bad Axe was the last confrontation that ended in the massacre of Native Americans by the American Militia. The battle was fought on extremely unequal terms: more than 12,000 American soldiers and militia against 1,000 men, women and children of the Sauk Tribe. While the white military and civilian casualties totaled 72, only 40 people, mostly women and children survived from the Black Hawk's tribe (*The Telegraph Herald Special*, 1977:37-38). The Mesquakie did not participate in the Black Hawk War, and while maintaining their neutrality in the conflict at times they indirectly sided with the American government. However, the war's outcome was detrimental to their presence and territorial claims in the Dubuque area, as in 1832 the United States government forced them to cede land as reparations and denied the Mesquakie any claims to Dubuque's lead mines (Callender, 1978:644).

After the Black Hawk Treaty Native Americans completely disappear from the Dubuque scene in most of the region's historical accounts.[5] From then on, they were neither considered as a serious threat nor a viable ethnic group in Dubuque's historical memory.

WITHERING AWAY THE NATIVES: EMERGENCE OF DUBUQUE AS A WHITE FRONTIER TOWN

The establishment and operation of the Mines of Spain was an example of a "small Creole community" in the tradition of other French Canadian settlements such as Prairie du Chien and Green Bay, whereby "European-descended men and Native-descended women lived and worked together" (Murphy, 2000:99). But once the Dubuque region was thrown open to white settlers in 1833, between 2 and 3 hundred settlers crossed the Mississippi River, established the Dubuque village and engaged in lead mining and other enterprises characteristic of frontier towns. The benign nature of the relationship between Julien Dubuque and the Mesquakie of the Catfish Creek village did not have any bearing on the treatment of indigenous people by those settlers who later on laid the foundations of the city of Dubuque. For one thing, there were significant differences between the colonial policies of the French and those of the American government and settlers on the Western frontier.

First, the former took possession of the Native American lands in the name of the French king but returned them to the natives under the protection of the French crown. The American government on the other hand assumed a "legal fiction" that Native Americans constituted sovereign nations from whom it could buy lands through negotiations (Wilkie, 1987:58-59). When on many occasions the negotiations failed, the American government followed the British colonial policy which assumed the territories were uninhabited lands, which in turn justified the dispossession, resettlement, and in most cases outright annihilation of the Native Americans.

Second, the French and American colonization of the new world was also different in terms of their relationship with the natives. While the former allowed social interaction between the French settlers and the natives, the latter followed the British colonial policy which disapproved of any social contact and miscegenation between colonizers and colonized. This apparently was the dominant attitude among the Dubuque elite during the early decades of the city's development. For example, in a lecture delivered before the Dubuque Literary Association in 1854 a pioneer settler and a prominent member of the upper class in Dubuque characterized Julien Dubuque as an individual "greatly addicted to the vices incident upon the commingling of Spanish and Indian races in America..."(Lucius Langworthy, quoted in Dubuque City Directory, 1856-57:18).

In his accounts of the reality of social interaction between whites and indigenous populations in frontier towns, Hamer (1990: Chapter 9) also makes several interesting points that are certainly applicable to Dubuque. First, he argues that Native Americans were often presented as "the antithesis to civilization." This was often the theme of early drawings and paintings of frontier towns, whereby the artist depicted "the figure of the Indian or the aborigine standing to the side and in the foreground and pointing at the newly risen town which is the focus of the scene"(Hamer, 1990:214-15). In a similar fashion, when in certain occasions "a ragged Sac or Dacotah" entered Dubuque's scene, "the savage dignity of the red man" was still reported as a symbol of "barbarity" confronting the city's "top-heavy civilization" *(Herald*, April 17, 1859, cf. Oldt,1910:49).

Second, indigenous people in frontier towns were "either scorned as 'miserable vagabonds' or else tolerated for a time and even welcomed as freaks, sources of entertainment"(Hamer, 1990:222). The "savagery" of Native Americans and their unruly behavior outside the "civilized" etiquette of a frontier town was also reported in early Dubuque papers and chronicles as amusing and entertaining.[6] Third, he contends that indigenous people perceived the use of lands and territories to be "intermittent" rather than the "permanent possession" to which European settlers were accustomed. Thus was the element of surprise and astonishment by white settlers, says Hamer, when the indigenous people who used to live in the area "would suddenly turn up and commence some sort of activity on land within the town's boundaries" (216). In his childhood memoirs, a local historian describes how in 1867 after giving a war dance in downtown Dubuque, a group of 30 Indians "roamed about all over the city from house to house and into the stores"(Hoffmann, 1936:58).

The expulsion of Native Americans from the region and consolidation of the newly established communities such as

Dubuque was the beginning of a new era in the history of race relations on the Western frontier. New historical necessities and the peculiarities of frontier-town political economy replaced one form of ethnic conflict with another, as newly settled immigrants struggled to survive in their harsh environment and to gain a credible local and national identity. After the Civil War there was a tendency to refute the city's multi-racial social reality in the early 1800s, and some began to question the authenticity of reports pertaining to Dubuque's intimate relations with local indigenous population. For example, as late as 1866 the Dubuque *Herald* which was known for its strong pro-slavery position and represented the Democratic Party in the city questioned the myth that Dubuque married an Indian woman (*Herald,* January 8, 1866, cf. Oldt, 1910:42). Two decades later, a prominent Dubuque judge whose position on the ideological and political legitimacy of the North and the South oscillated and eventually tilted toward the latter during the Civil War period, also doubted that Dubuque ever had an Indian connection by marriage (Judge T.S. Wilson in the *Herald,* February 6, 1887, cf. Oldt, 1910:42).

The real reasons behind these public denunciations of the city's early inter-racial history are not clear. One probable interpretation is that they were reactions to a mounting social pressure to incorporate blacks and other "colored" population during and after the Reconstruction Era. Another possible explanation is that by denouncing inter-racial socialization between white settlers and the Native Americans in early Dubuque, opponents of racial integration hoped to make a historical case to legitimate Dubuque's growth as an all-white city.

THE MAKING OF DUBUQUE'S WHITE EUROPEAN ETHNIC FABRIC

When the Dubuque territory was opened for settlement after the Black Hawk Treaty in 1833, about 300 people crossed the Mississippi to take advantage of what was left behind by the Native Americans and the few white settlers who had worked

Dubuque's lead mines. Based on some estimates by 1838 there were 600 or more inhabitants in Dubuque, mostly engaged in mining activities. Dubuque's appeal for settlers was "not the site's agricultural prospects," writes a local historian, but rather "the rich deposits of top-grade lead ore on the encircling bluffs that beckoned irresistibility to frontier entrepreneurs"(Dykstra, 1993:7). The "lead rush" in Dubuque also brought in a group of settlers who were "mostly male, largely illiterate, and given to drinking, gambling and quarrelling" (Wilkie, 1987:152). Others evaluate Dubuque's new inhabitants in more favorable terms, as being a mixture of "renegades and ruffians among men of education and sophistication, some graduates of the best Eastern colleges" (Mercer, 1982:55).

Frontier towns from the Ohio River to the western banks of the Mississippi River were distinctly different from settlements established earlier on the Eastern Seaboard. Not all new European immigrants and American citizens were eager to rush to the western frontier. Rather, for various ethnic, religious and economic reasons the most destitute, the most adventurous, and the least wanted or accepted individuals on the East coast were forced to move into the heartland and settle in the new frontier towns. In Dubuque's case, even more than two decades after its establishment as a mining town, the city's population was mostly illiterate. According to Oldt (1910:915), based on the 1856 census out of 2,808 school age children only 264 were in school. The city's population "almost without exception was of the roughest sort," reported the *Herald,* who apparently had a low standard of morality and considered "the taking of life or any other species of crime" as social pastime." (*Herald*, April 17, 1859, cf. Oldt, 1910:49)

A seemingly "striking" feature of the ethnic mix of early Dubuque was its heterogeneity. In a letter to the Dubuque *Iowa News* in 1839, a reader writes about a regiment of soldiers in Dubuque which consisted of the Irish, Germans, Dutch, French and other immigrants of European origin. He further writes that "such a heterogeneous mixed multitude of nations, tongues, languages, and people is to be found nowhere on this earth except in the Dubuque lead mines" (cf. Calkin, 1964:48-49). Impressed with Dubuque's ethnic diversity, another observer of the time stated that he was "struck with the mixed mass of Germans, French, English, Irish, etc., intermingling with each other in that cheerful manner, which is the true indication of happy hearts and smiling prospects." (ibid.)

For several decades, Dubuque's population consisted mainly of first generation European immigrants and their American born offspring. According to some estimates, by 1860 more than three quarters of the households in Dubuque County had at least one foreign born parent (Auge, n.d.:1), and 42 percent of residents were foreign born (Wilkie, 1987:185). Reporting on Dubuque's diverse population of European origin, in 1860 a newspaper editor described the crowd on a "busy market day" in the town as being comprised of "the sturdy American yeoman, the pale faced occupant of the city store, the honest German but recently from the Faderland, the rollicking Irishman, the quick and polite Frenchman, the staid but solid Englishman, and the canny Scotsman"(cf. Gjerde, 1997:236). With the passage of time, the children of foreign born immigrants started to change the scene, and by 1915 the foreign born Dubuquers comprised only one out of eight residents compared to one out of two in the 1860s (ibid.: 335).

The intricate links among race, ethnicity, and social class require an analysis of both the powerless "ethnic minorities" and dominant ethnic groups with considerable economic and political power. Among Dubuque's European immigrants, certainly the Germans and to some extent the Irish fall in the latter category, whose presence and role in weaving Dubuque's social and ethnic fabric has been instrumental. This is the focus of the following section.

SETTLING ETHNIC DIFFERENCES: THE GERMANS AND IRISH

From its early days as a village, Dubuque's cultural environment has always been dominated by a combination of German and Irish cultures, flavored with the strong religious ethos of the Catholic Church. Mathias Loras, bishop of the newly established Dubuque Diocese in 1854, wrote letters to dozens of newspapers on the East coast and called on Catholics to "come in haste to the west of Iowa," as they will "soon make whole Catholic settlements — some Irish, some German, some French"(Jerde, 1995:72). And come they did to Dubuque and Iowa by the thousands. According to a local historian, "It was these parents and grandparents (all once foreign born), Irish but especially the German ones, who gave Dubuque its strongest cultural accents. It was a German-language culture, heavily Catholic but also Lutheran and Reformed, that favored beer, song and male dominance." (Wilkie, 1987:335)

German immigration to the United States and to Iowa in particular during the 19th century was fueled by two factors: an escape from extensive military service and compulsory conscription in Germany; and the promise of a better quality of life and prosperous future for their offspring in the New World (Calkin, 1962:153). The latter factor attracted many German citizens who voluntarily left the homeland for a better future in America. But some also fled Germany because of regional conflicts. For example, thousands of Germans from the Schelswig-Holstein region, a duchy torn between Denmark and Germany, came to Davenport, many of whom eventually moved north and settled in Dubuque (McGarvey, 2000).

While after their initial immigration to America the Irish tended to stay on the East coast for a longer period of time, newly arrived German immigrants sought to move inland as quickly as possible in order to join German immigrant communities in the Midwest. The main reason for Germans' uneasiness on the

East coast was cultural, mainly linguistic, since Eastern seaboard culture did not appreciate and accommodate newcomers who could not speak English (Auge, n.d.:8).

German immigrants settled in nearly all 16 counties in the tri-state area, with the heaviest concentration in Dubuque County.[7] Having reached a critical mass the Germans had a distinct advantage over other European ethnic groups in Iowa, as they did not suffer from being an ethnic minority and an "outsider" which would have forced them to close ranks in order to preserve their ethnic identity (Stevens, 1960). The voluntary nature of German immigration facilitated their assimilation into American culture and language, and their sheer numbers in Iowa also reinforced their sense of ethnic pride and identity.

Furthermore, Germans in Dubuque became active in business and politics and soon provided leadership in the community. Yet despite their embrace of American culture and engagement in business and politics, Germans in 19th-century Dubuque maintained their "old world" traditional values, language, and culture (Mercer, 1982:57). For instance, a report on the high school curriculum in Dubuque in 1859 indicates that students were required to take German language for two years (Oldt, 1910:917-18). There were also two German newspapers in town, *Der National Demokrat* and *Die Iowa*; and as late as 1906 about 15 to 20 German organizations such as "*Turnerverein*"(a social-athletic club) and "*Germania Halle*" were still serving nearly 18,000 German-Americans in Dubuque (Stevens, 1960). The "*Saengerbund*," a German social and musical organization was in operation until 1945. As late as 1979, a German club was holding "dances with traditional German costumes, bands and beers," and German lessons were given after each social meeting (Guilfoyle, 1979). One of the oldest German clubs in town was the German Shooting Society. As an exclusively male club, it was incorporated in 1865 to cater to the upper class Germans in Dubuque. Although it later ceased to operate as an exclusive German club, it nonetheless remained as an upper class club and as late as 1985 its members included several bank and corporate executives, doctors, lawyers and other professionals (Kirchen, 1985).

Notwithstanding this strong social, economic, and political presence in the community, German Americans suffered from continued anti-German sentiments. One common problem reported by the two German language newspapers was "prejudice against Germans" during the 19th century (Kritzman, 1982:52). Irish residents played a crucial part in this, but this ethnic prejudice was caused by social class differences, competition in the city's job market and inequalities in wealth among the two groups. For instance, as a fast growing frontier town public works projects created significant number of jobs in Dubuque. In order to secure jobs for their own people, the two ethnic groups fiercely competed with each other to control city politics. In the 1850s a German-language weekly in Dubuque voiced concerns about the city government being controlled by the Irish. But "twenty years later, Germans who found themselves in position of power let their benevolence shine on a German rather than an Irishman"(Gjerde, 1997:244-245). Furthermore, separated along economic class lines, Irish and German residents fiercely protected their ethnic identity through spatial and territorial segregation, while reinforcing ethnocentrist beliefs in each ethnic group's social and cultural superiority among their cohorts. A local historian of German descent recalls that "when any of the Irish came up town, or any of the Germans ventured down to Dublin, there generally was a fight," and as a young boy he "had to run" while going through Dublin "in order to escape a crowd of boys down there for fear of getting a licking." (Hoffmann, 1936)[8]

The first serious and well-documented case of overt prejudice and discrimination against German Americans in Dubuque was in the aftermath of the WWI. With the outbreak of the war, the American government launched a nationwide pro-British and anti-German propaganda campaign that also made life miserable for many Dubuquers of German descent. The use of German language was considered anti-American and unpatriotic; and, in the words of a local historian, "Dubuque's already patriotic Germans were expected to bear abuse and still work twice as hard as others to prove their patriotism" (Wilkie, 1987:393). Businesses bearing German names were forced to adopt American names. For example, as a patriotic gesture during WWI the German-American Savings Bank changed its name to "American Trust and Savings Bank" (Guilfoyle, 1979). A worker and longtime North End resident remembered his boyhood experience during the war years when "they changed all the German titles — like sauerkraut, they changed that to liberty cabbage. And war bonds and stuff like that. They used to teach German. The prayers were in German. Then the war came on and they hated Germans."[9]

Most German newspapers were also forced to close down, and by 1925 it was hard to find one in Dubuque (Rapp, 1991). The outcomes of the two world wars seem to have affected the immigration of Germans into Dubuque County, as the number of foreign born Germans dropped sharply between 1920 and 1950. However, the foreign born German residents continuously ranked first among all European immigrants (see Calkin, 1962:176-77).

On the other ethnic front, the Irish had also been present in Dubuque's politics and economy since it was incorporated in 1837. Even before the Black Hawk purchase opened the Dubuque territory to white settlers, a group of 51 miners came to the area, of whom at least two-thirds were Irish (Calkin, 1964:48). The Irish came to Dubuque for its rolling hills and beautiful landscape, says a local Irish genealogist, because "this part of the country looked so much like Ireland that it felt like home to them" (Harold McCarville, cf. McGarvey, 2000). As early as 1840, the first ward, comprising the southern part of the city was an Irish enclave called "Dublin." A local historian characterizes the early Irish immigrants as "tough and hard bitten veterans of the southern Missouri diggings," at times well armed, and "often drunk on corn liquor or cheap brandy" and who made Dubuque look like "a kind of legendary mining camps of the American West"(Dykstra, 1993:7). In the early years of Dubuque's growth the flow of Irish immigrants continued to the point that, by 1840, about a quarter of the heads of households in Dubuque County were Irish. A decade later, the Irish still remained the largest ethnic group (24.6 percent) followed by Germans (17.8 percent) and the British (10.3 percent). The numerical superiority of Irish Dubuquers started to erode by 1860, and for the first time German households surpassed the Irish (32.4 and 29.8 percent, respectively) followed by British as a distant third (5.4 percent)(Auge, n.d.:2).[10] From then on, Germans maintained their numerical dominance among the ethnic groups of European origin in Dubuque, followed closely by the Irish.

Compared to Germans, the Irish in Dubuque were of a lower socio-economic status and many lived in poverty. Based on data on property ownership from the 1860 census, Auge (n.d.:7) reports that the Irish immigrants were "the poorest" in Dubuque: whereas 41.9 percent of the German and 28 percent of the British households had $300 or less in real estate value, the figure for the Irish was 50 percent. When the Irish famine displaced millions of its countrymen and women, many of them migrated to America during the 1845-55 period. Dubuque also had its share of Irish immigrants who in most part were destitute. By 1860, the majority of Irish in the work force held manual jobs and/or owned small businesses, and there were only 15 Irish residents who held professional jobs such as lawyers, doctors, or teachers (*The Dubuque Telegraph Herald*, 1964).[11] For the poor Irish immigrants the Western frontier in general and Dubuque in particular had a lot to offer, from "cheap land-wooded areas" to "plenty of jobs to be had in the lead mines."(Jerde, 1995:72)

Both in terms of social activities and the town's spatial organization there appeared to be *de facto* segregation between the Germans and the Irish in place. For instance, like their German neighbors, the Irish had their own social clubs, businesses and religious institutions. German and Irish Catholic churches were built a few blocks away and sometimes across from each other to cater to a segregated community along ethnic lines.

While Germans went to their "*Turnerverein*" to socialize, the Irish patronized their "*Royal Order of Hibernians*" in the 19th century. The Irish residents patronized Irish-owned neighborhood businesses only, which further separated the two groups along economic lines. German and Irish immigrants in Dubuque therefore created a two-tiered community along social class and cultural lines, each bringing their cultural traditions, ethnocentric values, and speech patterns to their own neighborhoods. They also became increasingly clannish, settling on opposite ends of the town: the Germans lived mostly in the north end while most of the latter group resided in the south of town, dubbed "Dublin" (Mercer, 1982:55). Outsiders' observation of life and people in Dublin was reflected in reports that often remarked on the neighborhood's negative features, including its lower class residents who "were guilty of the crime of being poor" (the *Herald,* cf. Oldt, 1910; 132-33). But Dublin was not a homogeneous ethnic neighborhood, and in the words of one Irish worker and Dublin resident in the 1920s, "It was fairly mixed where we lived"; nor did its residents perceive it in negative terms.[12]

For the major part of the 19th century the Irish continued to be targets of prejudice, ridicule and ethnic stereotyping by the more affluent population in town that was predominantly German. While the powerless Irish often had to settle their ethnic-based disputes in street fights, the privileged class, a good number of them Germans, used the local papers to put down the residents of Irish descent. During a murder trial in 1860, for example, a local paper reported a court session in which an Irish witness, "one Mickey McDonald" answered the lawyers' questions in broken English and heavy Irish accent for which the court room was reportedly "convulsed with laughter."(cf. Oldt, 1910:457)

Regardless of the above-mentioned examples of ethnic-based hostilities, some residents have minimized the extent of German-Irish animosity in town. As one old-time Dubuquer commented, he "never put too much stock in the German-versus-Irish talk. Back then, everybody was fighting just to make a buck and put food on the table." Eventually ethnic hostilities between the two nationalities faded. Peter Hoffmann, a German grocer who chronicled Dubuque life from the 1860s to the 1930s mentions in his memoirs how by the 1930s "the sons and daughters of the old antagonists" began to socialize and even marry each other (Guilfoyle, 1979). Thus, if not the deep rooted cultural loyalties and class differences, at least the open ethnic conflicts between the Irish and the "Dutch"(German) seem to have come to an end. As Hoffmann put it, by the 1930s they were "all Americans." (ibid)

With the passage of time, many Irish residents shed their ethnic clothes and neighborhoods with strong Irish ethnic culture could no longer be found. But as the economic hardships of the late 1970s and early 1980s began to take their toll, for the first time in recent history the Irish became more vocal in their resentment of the local establishment that they historically affiliated with German Dubuquers. Exploiting an age-old ethnic rivalry between the Irish and the Germans in town, a local newsletter, *The Little Dublin News,* published by a few Irish residents in the 1980s, had a homegrown target to attack. Associating Germans with power and money, yet presenting the Irish Dubuquers as a hard working, down-to-earth, poverty stricken but proud people, the newsletter indirectly attacked Dubuque's ruling elite by degrading residents with German background.[13] While most of the Irish social and cultural organizations have long been disbanded, a renewed emphasis on Irish ethnic pride in the 1970s signaled their eroding social status. For instance, after almost a century's interruption in 1979 the Irish held their St. Patrick's day parade in Dubuque, with "six hundred members" and "one dog dyed green" (Guilfoyle, 1979). As I will discuss in more detail in chapter 8, *The Little Dublin News* became the voice of the working class residents, many of Irish descent, who during the 1980s rightfully felt they were not getting their fair share of the local economy.

ETHNIC MINORITIES IN DUBUQUE: JEWS AND AFRICAN AMERICANS

Among the "white" and "nonwhite" minorities, two groups, namely Jews and African Americans have had considerable visibility and presence in Dubuque's social, economic and political reality. In general, Dubuque residents were more tolerant of religious minorities like Jews, and nationalities such as the Chinese, Japanese, and people of Central and Latin American origin. Of the above mentioned nationalities and ethnic groups, only Jewish immigrants were present in significant numbers, and in most cases they were classified as "white," or at times as "Hebrew" people. African Americans also had a significant presence in Dubuque's early years of development (1833-1845). But by 1850 their numbers dwindled to a level, which has remained more or less the same to this day. The following is a historical sketch of the socio-economic and political status of Jewish residents in Dubuque. Since the presence of African Americans has always played a special role in shaping the mentality of Dubuque citizens on the issue of race and ethnicity, their story will be discussed in more detail in the following chapters.

JEWS IN DUBUQUE

The early Jewish immigrants to Iowa and Dubuque have been mostly self-employed and involved in certain areas of trade and business. Many of Iowa's Jewish merchants in the 19th century began their careers as rural peddlers "with packs on their backs," traveling long distances on foot to supply the scattered rural population with needed merchandise (Conzett, 1941:22). Based on some estimates, "there were at least 100 Jewish peddlers in Iowa" during the first year of Iowa's recognition as a state in 1846 (Glazer, 1904:175).

One of the first permanent settlers who landed in Dubuque in 1833 was Alexander Levi, a French-born Jew who is also known as "the founder of Jewry" in Iowa (Conzett, 1941:16; Fleishaker,

1957:53-54)). He opened a grocery store in the newly established village of Dubuque and later accumulated wealth by engaging in "mining on a large and extensive scale" (Fleishaker, 1957:44). After years of hard work and perseverance, Levi became "one of Dubuque's wealthiest and most influential figures" (Conzett, 1941): 239). Early Jewish immigrants, mostly of Russian, Polish, and Lithuanian origins, appear to have settled in one specific geographical locality. According to one study, Jews resided "near the vicinity of Maple and Elm on the 1500 through 1700 blocks," which was then north of the downtown area (Van Speybroeck, ca 1986:11-13). In another study Fleishaker (1957:58) calls the Jewish neighborhood "Jerusalem," a five-block stretch on Maple Street as "Dubuque's [Jewish] ghetto." The only synagogue in Dubuque was also located in "Jerusalem."

Information about Jewish residents in Dubuque during various periods is inconsistent and at best sketchy. The census data for 19th-century Dubuque consider Jews as "white," and there are no indications of their religious orientation. Prior to the Civil War there were reportedly seven Jewish families. Four heads of households were engaged in the clothing business, one was a lead miner, one owned a grocery store, and another was involved in a dry goods business (Conzett, 1941:32). During and after the Civil War in the 1860s, however, there appears to have been a constant exodus of Jews from Dubuque (Belskey, n.d.:3). This changed after the Reconstruction period, and reportedly between 1884 and 1889 about 150 Jewish families lived in Dubuque (Wolf, 1941:294). Assuming an average of four persons per household, there could have been about 600 Jews living in Dubuque during the 1880s. This figure seems to be consistent with the number of Jews in the next decade, as a report in the *Dubuque Daily Herald* (1895) estimated that in 1895 there were as many as 700 Jews in the city.

The last decade of the 19th century seems to have been the peak period in terms of Dubuque's Jewish population, and thereafter in the early decades of the 20th century their numbers drastically declined (van Speybroeck, ca 1986:13-14). The 1910 U.S. census identifies 14 "Yiddish speaking" Jews in Dubuque, mostly of Russian origin. Of the 6 recorded Jewish households, 2 heads of households were peddlers, one was a tailor, and 3 were unemployed.[14] Post-war economic conditions and a "temporary kosher meat industry" apparently gave a boost to Dubuque's Jewish community (Fleishaker, 1957:59). The 1920 population census for Dubuque County is the first to provide some reliable information about Jews' socio-economic status. Reportedly, there were a total of 252 Jews residing in Dubuque.[15] At less than 1 percent, the unemployment rate was extremely low for male Jews. Two-thirds of the male Jewish residents either owned their businesses or were self-employed artisans. Finally, junk peddling and dealership was the dominant occupation for Jews, followed by retail businesses in clothing. By 1950, there remained only 50 Jewish families in Dubuque, and their numbers continued to decline to the present time (Conzett, 1941:244; fleishaker, 1957:58).

Unlike in many other urban communities, rather than establishing their own ethnic enclaves Dubuque Jews eventually blended in and became accepted by the community (Van Speybroeck, ca 1986:13). 1920 census data provides information about spatial location of Jews in Dubuque. It appears that Jewish residents were scattered throughout the city, but with heavier concentration in wards 3 and 4, the latter being mostly a well-to-do area in town.[16] For instance, the residence of Alexander Levi, the first Jewish resident, was reportedly "one of the finest and commodious homes in the city."(Fleishaker, 1957:44)

Despite their religious differences in a predominantly Catholic town, Jews have rarely been targets of overt racist, anti-Semitic, or discriminatory acts. This may be attributed to their relatively high social and occupational status, their extensive community involvement, as well as their reputation of being "hard working" and "self-reliant" people. Jews have certainly been regarded as part of the city's establishment, as in many occasions they have served on the city's board of education; have been active members and board representatives of the Chamber of Commerce, the YMCA, the Rotary Club, the Kiwanis and many other social and charitable organizations (Belskey, n.d.:5). One prominent Jewish Dubuquer of the early 20th century was Abraham Slimmer, a cattle businessman, banker, and philanthropist, who donated more than $3,000,000 to charitable institutions and was considered "the friend of the poor and downtrodden."(Fleishaker, 1957:43-52; Belskey, n.d.:5)

As Iowa's Jewish population grew smaller, there was a considerable increase in inter-marriages and "many Jewish men married non-Jewish women." This was reportedly due to "both the general friendliness towards Jews and the limited opportunities of meeting other young Jewish men and women" in Dubuque (Fleishaker, 1957:45, 58). As a result of their structural assimilation and active involvement in civic and charitable organizations, there are very few recorded incidents of anti-Semitism by local newspapers and historians. But despite Dubuque residents' acceptance of Jews in their midst, "misbehaving Jews" occasionally stirred anti-Semitic sentiments. One local chronicler tells a tale of a "certain Jewish merchant" who settled in Dubuque in the late 1830s, married a Gentile lady, and converted to Christianity (Conzett, 1941:50). Being involved in trade activities, he apparently started having financial problems and allegedly smuggled some merchandise belonging to his creditors out of Dubuque. According to this story, "he was found guilty and lost credit and many friends and *brought a reputation for Jews as being tricky"* (ibid., italics mine). But by and large, Jews appear to have blended into Dubuque's social fabric and have been well received by the Gentiles. For example, Alexander Levi, the first Jewish settler in Dubuque became an active member of the Masonic order once he rose to prominence.

One indicator of the extent of Jewish presence in the community is the membership figures for Dubuque's only synagogue. Up until 1884 Dubuque Jews did not have an organized congregation. Between 1884 and 1905 various congregations provided a sense of community for Dubuque Jews. The first synagogue was built in 1905, followed by the construction of the second place of worship in 1939. These congregations remained traditional, but the Jewish community continuously grew smaller as "families left to raise their children in communities with better religious education and cultural advantages of larger Jewish communities"(Fleishaker, 1957:53-61). The *Dubuque Telegraph Herald* (1990) reported that by 1990 the synagogue had 25 to 30 members, who came from as far away as Platteville, Maquoketa, and Galena— small towns within a 30-mile radius. Based on the report, "the congregation was so small that it did not have a permanent Rabbi assigned to the Dubuque synagogue."

Documenting historical reasons for Dubuque's Jewish flight in the 1860s, a dramatic increase in their numbers in the last decades of the 19th century and again a continuous decline in their numbers since the 1920s is not an easy task. There is simply no recorded account of Jewish immigration patterns for the Dubuque area, and one can only resort to speculation. Apparently, during the 19th century the "newly arrived Jewish immigrants were sent to Dubuque by a New York Committee." But finding little support and lacking a sense of community, "most of them stayed but a short while and left for a bigger city" (Fleishaker, 1957:58). Although hard to document, the Ku Klux Klan's activities and their anti-Semitic propaganda in the 1920s might have been a significant factor for the sharp decline of the Jewish population during this period. Despite the turbulent years of the mid-1920s and the presence of the Ku Klux Klan in Dubuque, those Jewish families who did not leave the community seemingly maintained amicable relations with people of other ethnic groups. For example, in the 1930s a long-time Jewish resident commented that "relations between the Christians and Jews in Dubuque have always been most friendly, and we received generous donations from them to build our synagogue" (*The Dubuque Telegraph Herald*, 1938:218).

In the post-WWII period, as professionals and owners of small businesses Jews did not pose a threat to workers in a predominantly working class, industrial town. But with increasing deterioration of Dubuque's economy many jobs disappeared and small businesses failed, and anti-Semitic sentiments resurfaced again in the 1980s. This was particularly strong among the self-employed, some of whom came from Dublin, the old Irish stronghold. As was the case for residents of German origin, the *Little Dublin News* also attacked Jews for their alleged notoriety in running successful small businesses.[17] A more recent case of anti-Semitism was reported in 1989, when a city-wide distribution of anti-Semitic letters and posters blamed Jews for a variety of political and economic problems in the country and the world (Rodgers, 1989:3A). This was at a time when Jews' representation in town was at its lowest level. Based on one report, in 1989 there were about fifteen Jewish families still in Dubuque, and the numbers dwindled to less than a handful by 1993 (Rodgers, 1989).

In his book, *Postville: A Clash of Cultures in Heartland America,* Stephen Bloom (2000) also provides an interesting historical account of the increasing tensions between the locals and the new Jewish contingent and the emergence of anti-Semitic sentiments in nearby Postville, a tiny town northwest of Dubuque with less than 1,500 residents. The arrival of a group of ultra-Orthodox Hasidic Jews from New York in 1987 gave rise to anti-Semitic sentiments, as the newcomers revived the town's depressed economy by taking over an idle plant and converting it into a successful kosher slaughterhouse. The Hassidic Jews not only came with "large sums of money," says Bloom, but they also resisted assimilating to local culture and the valued traditions of a rural community. In fact, they "refused to acknowledge even the *presence* of anyone not Jewish"(Bloom, 2000:50-51). He argues that local residents' dislike and disapproval of Jews and their lifestyle was based on a combination of pent-up frustration of the locals' failure to move the town's economy forward, and their resentment of Hassidic Jews' higher socio-economic status and snobbery as the city's new "ruling class"(Bloom, 2000:xii). In his interviews with long-time Jewish residents in the area Bloom observed that in order to be accepted by locals, Jews in Postville had to keep their religion and traditions to themselves and assimilate to local culture. For Iowa Jews, "blending in with their neighbors was the only way to survive," argues Bloom (305). This was the case for "Doc Wolf," a Jewish physician who served Postville and its surrounding rural communities for six decades but kept his Jewish identity to himself, blended in with the locals and became involved with local politics and volunteer activities.[18] Bloom gives examples of hostile anti-Semitic sentiments expressed by locals that in most part were under the surface. He also gives credit to Postville residents for their non-prejudicial attitudes toward Doc Wolf, as "for six decades, no one in either Alamakee or Fayette County commanded anything near the respect" that he had (295).

In most cases, Dubuque Jews chose an approach similar to that of Doc Wolf in order to interact with the city's Christian majority population. In his study of the Jewish presence in Iowa, Michael Bell (1994:124) contends that most Jewish Iowans adopted the above strategy in order to survive in a state that has never had a sizable Jewish population. Thus "they surrendered their language, transformed their faith, and adapted their customs to the rhythms of the daily life that surrounded them." Again and again, when offered the choice to keep the public identity they brought with them from Europe, Iowa's Jews "chose to change themselves to be more like their neighbors and to adopt the values of American life." By and large, as a successful minority group Jews managed to survive in a predominantly Catholic working class community, and anti-Semitic sentiments were more related to their social status as a group with money and political power than their "Jewishness." Those who left the community did so not much because of anti-Jewish sentiments in town, but to join larger Jewish communities in other metropolitan areas.

Notes

1. According to Hoffman (1930:42), the principal village of the Mesquakie was near the site of the present day city of Davenport, about 65 miles south of Dubuque on the Mississippi River.
2. According to the original agreement between Julien Dubuque and the Mesquakie made at Prairie du Chien in 1788, the Mesquakie granted permission to Dubuque "to work at the mine as long as he shall please, and to withdraw from it, without specifying any term to him" (cf. Auge, 1976:3). Thus, conscious about his lack of ownership rights over the mines, Dubuque gained the recognition of the Spanish Governor over his property claims. But he repeatedly failed to get the same recognition from the American government, which was the emerging supreme power in the region at the time. Some historians have also mistakenly concluded that Dubuque was granted possession of the mines by the Mesquakie. See, for example, Petersen (1966:107).
3. "Mines of Spain" refers to lead mines near the Catfish Creek Village that were initially explored by Julien Dubuque.
4. For an interesting historical account of Julien Dubuque's life, the Mines of Spain, and early Dubuque community see Murphy (2000:84-99).
5. According to census data, by 1870, there were only 457 Native Americans left in Iowa (Stuart, 1987: Table 3.7, p.57), of which the Mesquakie numbered only 264. Gradually, their numbers increased to 403 in 1932 and 653 in 1955. Of the 653 Mesquakie, about 500 lived in and around Tama, a Mesquakie reservation in eastern Iowa (Callender, 1978:645).
6. See for example *Miners' Express,* June 6, 1849, cf. Oldt, 1910:45.
7. Dubuque borders the states of Wisconsin and Illinois, hence known as the "tri-state city."
8. The south side of Dubuque was dubbed "Dublin," where most residents of Irish ancestry resided.
9. Charles Dempsey, interviewed by Paul Kelso, 1977. *Iowa Labor History Oral Project*, Iowa Federation of Labor, AFL-CIO. State Historical Society of Iowa, Iowa City.
10. In his article "The Irish in Iowa," Calkin (1964:63) provides a much lower estimate for the Irish, and reports that "of the 13,045 inhab-

itants of Dubuque in 1860, 13.9 percent or 1,800 were born in Ireland.

11. See Calkin (1964:63-64) for a more detailed ranking of the Irish Dubuquers' occupational status.
12. On the quality of life in Dublin, he further remarked "It was a good working man's neighborhood, and there were a lot of kids there. We had a lot of fun in that area." See Hugh Clark, interviewed by Greg Zieren, 1980. *Iowa Labor History Oral Project*, Iowa Federation of Labor, AFL-CIO. State Historical Society of Iowa, Iowa City.
13. See for example the anecdote in the *Little Dublin News* (April 1983:7) in which the German Dubuquers are depicted as "house-broken" and speak English, who will "make wonderful pets." Also see the April 1988 issue (p. 4).
14. The figure is not accurate for two reasons. First, a few pages of the microfilmed document for Dubuque County are not legible. Second, the more established first generation as well as the second generation Jewish residents were most likely fluent in English and could have passed as "white."
15. Under a column headed "Nativity and Mother Tongue," each person's place of birth and mother tongue as well as parents' birthplace and mother tongue are identified. Under this heading, Jews are recognized either as "Jewish" or "Hebrew."
16. See the 14th Federal Census of population for Dubuque City-1920.
17. See *The Little Dublin News (n.d.: 8)* for the news letter editor's fictitious recollection of Jewish residents' past success as owners of small businesses. Of note is his disdain for Jews as "stinking" yet successful and "enterprising" small business owners.
18. Living in the nearby town of Elgin, Bloom writes, "to almost anyone within a fifty-mile radius, Henry Wolf was known simply as Doc Wolf." He died in 1996 (Bloom, 2000:295).

CHAPTER 2

TWO CENTURIES OF AFRICAN AMERICANS' PRESENCE IN IOWA AND DUBUQUE

Blacks have been present in Iowa since its early days as a new Territory. When the territories were opened to settlers after the Black Hawk purchase in 1833, many settler families from nearby southern states brought "a slave or two" with them into Iowa (Bergmann, 1969:6). By late 1830s the legislators of the new Iowa Territory, the majority of whom were southerners by birth, passed several laws to limit immigration of free blacks from other states into Iowa. The first of such laws, was the 1838 Act that required blacks and mulattoes to present a "fair certificate of actual freedom" and give a bond of $500 in order to be permitted to settle in Iowa (8-9).[1] Nonetheless the presence of free blacks is documented in the early 19th century census data, and by 1850 there were 324 free "colored" residents in Iowa (Goudy, 2001:23).[2] According to a local historian, in most cases blacks "worked in the mines of Dubuque, or as laborers in the river towns of Burlington, Davenport, and Keokuk and lived in shacks close to the water front"(Bergmann, 1969:14).

After the Emancipation Proclamation by President Lincoln in 1863, southern blacks started to migrate north in greater numbers. Bordering the slave state of Missouri, Iowa too had its share of black immigrants, and for several decades most southern blacks settled in the counties bordering the Mississippi River. In an era with no reliable roads, a settlement pattern that was purely due to the logistics of regional migration started to emerge in eastern Iowa: the southernmost counties neighboring navigable rivers began to receive the highest numbers of black immigrants.

Thus with the exception of Dubuque County, they came to four river counties of Lee, Des Moines, Scott, and Clinton, and got settled mostly in the counties' major river towns of Keokuk, Burlington, Davenport, and Clinton, respectively. For the most part, Dubuque County and the city of Dubuque remained one of the least receptive eastern Iowa urban frontier towns. Although in smaller numbers, after the Civil War blacks also settled in two western Iowa river towns of Council Bluffs and Sioux City, both located on the shores of the Missouri River(see figure 1).

At the peak of the river traffic on the Mississippi during the 1870s and 1880s, river towns of Burlington, Davenport, Clinton, and even Dubuque provided employment opportunities for black workers (Bergmann, 1969: 37-38). With the declining significance of rivers for transportation and the dawn of railroad industry many river towns experienced economic stagnation and a decline in their population, including black residents. Industrialization and an increase in manufacturing activities in the late 19th and early 20th centuries created a new pattern of black presence in Iowa's major urban centers. From then on, employment in industries, coal mines and related services such as the railroads became a determining factor in attracting black immigrants and workers to Iowa. Overall, the main characteristic of black immigrants since the early decades of 19th century has been their preference for settling in urban areas. African Americans continued to settle in Iowa's urban centers in the 20th century. Census data indicate that about 64 percent of black Iowans in 1900 were living in cities, and by 1990 only 3 percent of them resided in rural areas (Goudy, 2001:30).

In the post-WWII period three urban counties of Black Hawk, Polk, and Scott and their major metropolitan centers of Waterloo-Cedar Falls, Des Moines, and Davenport respectively have become home to more than 60 percent of Iowa's black population. Except in Dubuque and Council Bluffs, census data for 1990 and 2000 indicate that blacks are also present in signifi-

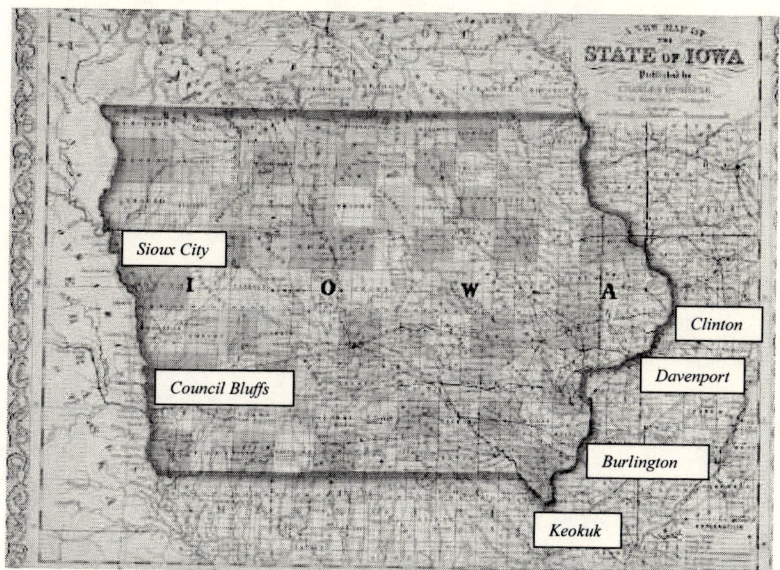

Figure 1: Iowa Towns with High Concentration of African Americans in the 1860s

Map Source: Charles Desilver, "A New Map of the State of Iowa, 1856." Accessed 11-3-05 <http://www.philaprintshop.com/iowa.html>

cant numbers in other metropolitan areas with 50,000 or more population (see Table 3).

In a historical context, Iowans have demonstrated both extreme levels of tolerance and accommodation of people of diverse ethnic backgrounds, and anti-black sentiments and racism. For example, at the same time that some Iowa politicians were diligently working on legislative acts to deny free blacks their basic civil rights; other Iowans were quietly but actively involved in the resistence movement known as the "Underground Railroad," helping hundreds of fugitive southern slaves to gain their freedom in the northern states and Canada.[3] Settled in the southern Iowa counties, the Quakers were "particularly vigilant" in helping fugutive blacks (Bergmann, 1969:22).

Table 3: Changes in Black Population for Major Metropolitan Areas in Iowa, 1990-2000

City	1990	2000	County	Total Population 1990	Total Population 2000
Des Moines	13,667	16,025	Polk	193,187	198,682
Cedar Falls/ Waterloo	8,477	10,097	Black Hawk	100,765	104,892
Davenport/ Bettendorf	7,761	9,587	Scott	115,419	129,634
Cedar Rapids/ Marion/ Hiawatha	3,224	4,778	Linn	124,190	153,532
Sioux City	1,993	2,047	Woodbury	80,505	85,013
Iowa City/ Coralville	1,883	2,973	Johnson	70,085	77,343
Burlington	1,212	1,354	Des Moines	27,208	26,839
Council Bluffs	409	614	Pottawattamie	54,315	58,268
Dubuque	295	700	Dubuque	57,546	57,686

Source: Iowa State University, Department of Economics. *Iowa Population By Race and Ethnic Origin City List.* Accessed 3/16/2002: <http://ia.profiles.iastate.edu/data/census/city/race.htm#LetterW>

Some historians have tried to give an impression that as a "covert operation of transporting fugitive slaves" the Underground Railroad in Iowa "moved with the dispatch, efficiency, and regularity of a time-table that would have been the envy of the Rock Island and Burlington Railroads"(Wall, 1978:89). But in his assessment of the movement, Berrier (2001:46) concludes that "there was in fact no large-scale, well-developed organization, but rather a few individuals who were loosely organized, and mostly at the local level."[4] Nonetheless, many Iowans with abolitionist and pro-black sympathies created an extensive informal network to assist fugitive blacks across the soutern counties, stretching from the western shores of the Mississippi River to the Missouri River on the Iowa-Nebraska border (Harnack, cf. Berrier, 2001:50).

Another example of Iowans' positive track record of racial tolerance, is the growth and development of Buxton, a coal mining company town located in Monroe County in southern Iowa where "blacks and whites lived and worked side by side with little racial strife"(Schwieder et. al., 1987:3). From its inception in 1900 until its demise in the mid-1920s Buxton was the only racially integrated community in Iowa with the majority of its population being black. In a city of 5,000-6,000 people at its peak, Buxton blacks socialized and intermarried with whites and held professional jobs and commercial positions, a phenomenon unherad of in other Iowa towns. When in the 1920s white supremacist groups held large rallies in other Iowa urban communities, Buxton was by-passed by groups such as the Ku Klux Klan (Gradwohl and Johnsen, 2001:4). But by all accounts Buxton's case was a highly unusual social experience both at state and national levels (Schwieder et. al., 1987:3).

In contrast to Buxton, Dubuque's track record of having the lowest number of African American residents makes it a significant case study of race relations in Iowa. As already discussed, since the Reconstruction era the main prerequisite for the outbreak of race riots and white-on-black racial violence in American cities has always been the presence of blacks in significant numbers. All things considered, then, racial unrests of the 1980s and 1990s in Iowa should have taken place in cities with considerable number of African-Americans, such as Des Moines, Davenport, and Waterloo-Cedar Falls and not Dubuque. This suggests that we have to go beyond a simplistic notion that somehow certain people, or states for that matter, are more prone to racial prejudice. But before examining Dubuque's historical record of race relations we need to review demographic changes in black population, changes in their socio-economic and occupational status and the extent of their presence and integration in Dubuque's stratified residential neighborhoods.

PRESENCE OF AFRICAN AMERICANS IN DUBUQUE'S URBAN ECONOMY

Like Jewish residents, blacks also have been present in Dubuque since its inception as a frontier town. But African Americans' presence and status, as well as others' perception of and relation to them, has been partially affected by certain social, economic, and political developments in the nation and the region. The pre-Civil War period (1833-1860) marked an era of immense growth in terms of Dubuque's spatial and commercial development as a pioneer frontier town in Iowa. During these formative years the foundations of future industrial and trade developments were laid down, and blacks undoubtedly contributed to the city's growth. Almost a century before Buxton could claim having the highest numbers of black residents, as a new frontier town Dubuque was home to considerable number of blacks, both free and slaves. In a study of Iowa's blacks prior to the Civil War, Dykstra (1982:70) considers Dubuque as the only place in Iowa's early years to have had a sizeable black community. According to the 1840 census, 72 blacks lived in Dubuque. This included 16 slaves and 56 "free colored" blacks, who comprised 8.6 percent of the city's population (see Table 4).[5]

In 1840 Dubuque's black population also constituted 42 percent of all blacks residing in the Iowa territory (Stanley, 1985:4). But as is shown in Table 4, while by 1850 the "white" population had a ten-fold growth, the number of Dubuque's black residents dropped sharply down to 29. The "new capital of African Americans in Iowa" was Muscatine, another Mississippi River settlement located 80 miles south of Dubuque (Dykstra, 1993:13). This sharp decline can be attributed to two factors: 1) a general decline in the lead mining business and related activities which reduced the need for manual and day laborers; and 2) a lynching incident in 1840 (Dykstra, 1982:75).[6] Reportedly, of the 10 free "colored" heads of household in the 1840 census, only 2 can be identified as "still there in 1850"(Ibid.).[7]

Table 4: "White" and "Nonwhite" Population in the City of Dubuque, 1840-1860.

Racial Classification	1840[1]	1850	1860
Free Inhabitants			
White	760	9,156	12,935
Colored	56	23	65
Mulatto	--	N.A.	N.A.
Slaves	16	N.A.	N.A.
Total "Colored" Population (slaves and Mulattoes)	72	29	65
Total Population	832[2]	9,185	13,000
Percent "Colored" to Total Population	8.6	0.3	0.5

Notes: 1. The 1850 data are for Dubuque County.
2. The figure is for 1838.

Sources: Table constructed based on data from Dykstra (1982:71); *the 1850 U.S. Census for Dubuque County*; and *the 1860 U.S. Census-Iowa, Dubuque County*, the National Archives of the United States (1934).

The city's population increased immensely between 1840 and 1860, but the number of black residents remained low, and its representation dropped to a meager 0.5 percent in 1860 compared to 8.6 percent in 1840. During this period blacks lacked any recognized social status, even as they tried to pay their share in laying the foundations of the newly established community. For instance, Dykstra (1993:7) reports that in the aftermath of sentencing and hanging an Irish man for the murder of his friend in 1834, Dubuque's Methodists "sought to elevate the spiritual tone of the place, undertaking the erection of the territory's first church." According to him, "at least six local blacks, some of them said to have been slaves, pledged modest sums to a Methodist building fund to build the territory's first church."[8] Blacks' contributions should be seen in light of possible coercive measures taken by white settlers, and as a matter of survival in an environment inhospitable to them. But Dykstra (1993:12) sees the possibility of some recognition of stratification among free blacks in town, and comments that "a case might be made that the relative value of contributions to the Methodist building fund indicates some gradation of status and seniority among black Dubuquers in 1834."

Related to economic status, few blacks were reported to own "real property." According to Dykstra (Ibid.), "Thomas C. Brown, the black barber, claimed eleven hundred dollars worth of land; a laborer, Anthony Arthur, claimed one thousand dollars worth; and Aaron Baptiste reported six hundred dollars worth." But in terms of occupational status blacks in general remained a powerless ethnic group in the pre-Civil War period, often working the least desired jobs. Out of 29 "colored" residents in 1850, only two were self-employed as barbers. The rest were identified as day laborers and house servants. While in many frontier towns black women mostly performed household chores, they appear to have fared better in Dubuque, as some were "self-employed operators of home-based enterprises." One such example, Agnes Arthur, ran a boarding house in the late 1850s in Dubuque (Scharnau, 2001:218).

A decade later, there were no significant changes in blacks' status, and a few "colored" farm workers identified as "stableman" were added to the rank of manual laborers in the 1860 census. From 1860 onward, blacks became an insignificant racial and ethnic minority. This was partly due to a declining river traffic and partly the result of a decline in lead mining activities (Bergmann, 1969:39). Yet despite their insignificant numerical presence, they nonetheless continued to be the targets of prejudicial attitudes, discrimination and sometimes vicious violence.

The census data for the 1870-1920 period provide a wealth of information on Dubuque's population in general and the "nonwhite" residents in particular. With an increase in population from 13,000 in 1860 to 18,434 in 1870, there was also an increase in the number of nonwhite residents from 65 to 157. More nonwhites seem to have moved to Dubuque, but proportionately they still remained an insignificant ethnic group comprising only 0.8 percent of total population. There is no documentation of possible reasons for this small increase, but the emancipation of southern blacks and population displacements caused by the Civil War might have had an effect on this matter.

Dubuque experienced a period of economic stagnation during the late 1850s and 1860s, but after the war it continued to grow and flourish as an important industrial city and center of trade in the Midwest. Compared to the pre-Civil War era, the socio-economic and occupational status of blacks for the 1870-1920 period does not appear to have improved, and in light of available data their overall status deteriorated. In 1870, for example, there were only three self-employed blacks in Dubuque— two barbers and one blacksmith. The remaining blacks were day laborers, porters, whitewashers, janitors, cooks and stablemen. By 1880, there remained only one "colored" blacksmith who was self-employed, and the rest were engaged in menial jobs similar to the previous decade. The 1900 census identifies a black engineer, the 42-year-old James Wood from Mississippi, who was aboard the U.S. Steamboat operating at the Ice Harbor.[9] Other black workers with a slightly improved occupational status were two painters and one bricklayer. The remaining black residents in the labor force were again listed as day laborers, janitors, waiters and porters. By 1910, semi-skilled black workers disappear altogether from Dubuque scene, with only the unskilled and poor blacks remaining in town. The only prominent black resident in 1920 was a minister of Dubuque's black congregation.[10] In fifty years, from 1870 to 1920, the city's population more than doubled, but in the same period the "nonwhite" population dwindled to 76 (or one-tenth of one percent of the population; see Table 5).

During the 1920s organized labor was dealt a severe blow, and many people lost their jobs or had to settle for less pay. Despite the hardships, the tiny African American population in Dubuque persevered and their numbers remained relatively steady.[11] Although African Americans were not the main target of the white supremacist groups, the 1920s were particularly difficult years for Dubuque's black residents due to a resurgence of

Table 5: "White" and "Nonwhite" Population in the City Of Dubuque, 1870-1920*

	1870	1880	1900	1910	1920
Nonwhite Population for Wards					
First	5	0	16	14	1
Second	32	25	32	17	44
Third	40	22	5	0	0
Fourth	72	32	42	32	28
Fifth	5	4	0	0	3
Nonwhite Racial Classification					
Black	35	33	94	51	54
Mulatto	118	48	N.A.	12	18
Chinese	0	2	1	0	4
Indian	1	0	0	0	0
Japanese	0	0	0	0	4
Total Nonwhite	154	83	95	63	76
Total population	18,434	22,254	36,297	38,444	39,141
% Nonwhite to Total Population	0.8	0.4	0.3	0.2	0.2
% Black to Total Population	0.2	0.1	0.3	0.1	0.1

* The 1890 census data are not available, as most of the population schedules for the state of Iowa were badly damaged in the Commerce Building fire in January 1921 (Bowerman, 1991:17).

Sources: *Population Schedules of the 9th, 10th, 12th, 13th and 14th Censuses of the United States* (1870, 1880, 1900, 1910 and 1920, respectively) for the Dubuque County. Washington, D.C.: The National Archives of the United States. All data are available on microfilm at the Center for Dubuque History, Loras College, Dubuque, Iowa.

the Ku Klux Klan both at local and national levels.[12] In general, nonwhite residents continued to be underrepresented, and between 1930 and 1970 the average nonwhite contingent in Dubuque remained as low as 0.2 percent of total population (see Table 6).[13]

There is little documentation of African-Americans' occupational status for the 1920-1960 period in Dubuque. Census data for this period provide only crude figures for the employed and unemployed. The employment figures for 1950 and 1970 indicate that all African Americans 16 years and older in Dubuque's labor force were employed. Probably as an outcome of the nation-wide civil rights victories for African Americans and other minority groups, blacks made considerable gains in Dubuque after the 1960s. Unlike the pre-WWII period, a typical African American worker in Dubuque was no longer a janitor, porter or whitewasher. In fact, in 1970 none of the employed blacks in town were classified as private household workers, and only four, or 7.5 percent, were classified as "laborers." African-Americans were, however, absent at the upper ranks — there were no black managers, executives or administrators in Dubuque. But a major shift in the occupational status of blacks was their conspicuous presence in the mid-level occupations and semi-skilled jobs, with 32 percent being employed in clerical positions, 21 percent in service-related professions, and another 13 percent in professional and technical areas.[20]

Table 6: "White" and "Nonwhite" Population in the City of Dubuque 1930-1990

Ethnic Groups	1930[14]	1950[15]	1960[16]	1970[17]	1980[18]	1990[19]
Whites	38,691	49,596	56,463	62,092	61,742	56,626
"Negroes"/"Blacks"	88	58	143	100	219	331
Asian and Pacific Islanders	N.A.	15	N.A.	N.A.	194	368
Native Americans	N.A.	N.A.	N.A.	N.A.	52	69
Other Races	N.A.	2	N.A.	17	167	152
Persons of Spanish Origin	N.A.	18	N.A.	142	359	370
Total Population	41,679	49,671	56,606	62,209	62,374	57,546
Percent "Nonwhite" to "White"	0.2	0.15	0.25	0.3	1.0	1.6

Thus for the first time in the 1970s blacks moved out of the past stereotypical occupations — they were not the unemployed, manual laborers or welfare recipients, but the gainfully employed in the average paid and mid-level occupations. Furthermore, a comparison of employment figures and occupational status of Dubuque black residents in 1970 and 1980 indicates two significant changes. On the one hand, about 40 percent of blacks in 1980 were employed as managers, administrators and mid-level executives. On the other hand, for the first time the black unemployment rate also rose to 25 percent, a phenomenon unprecedented in the history of black employment in Dubuque. This was happening at a time when blacks were losing their strength in the service sector, clerical professions and professional and technical areas of employment. In terms of income, some studies have documented that in the 1970s Dubuque blacks had a competitive edge over whites. In Dubuque County, for example, 65 percent of African-Americans earned $20,000 or more per year, compared to 41 percent of their white counterparts (Hendricks, 1983).

Black recruitment by Dubuque's major industries and employers did not materialize until the mid-1970s. Both management and labor seem to have been opposed to employing blacks in Dubuque's industrial facilities. A longtime resident and three-time mayor of Dubuque remembered that in 1960 "the local UAW and the management did not have any blacks and, by God, they weren't going to have any" (James Brady, quoted in Hendricks, 1983). Among major employers in town, only one corporate entity, namely John Deere, had a positive reputation in hiring African Americans. As the first major industry to come from outside the community, in 1946 John Deere was perceived by local businesses somewhat negatively for its alleged efforts to recruit blacks, and resented for raising wages in the community.[21] In reality until the 1980s black employees at John Deere never exceeded 0.25 percent of its workforce. For example, of the 4,300 employees at the John Deere Dubuque Works in 1969 only 2 were African Americans (Anderson, 1969). Change came very slowly in the 1970s, and by 1980 John Deere employed about 20 blacks, mostly in skilled and professional level jobs (Hendricks, 1983; Herndons, 1981).

Despite significant gains in the 1970s black Dubuquers suffered a serious blow to their social status and economic well-being in the 1980s. Many African-Americans were laid off or forced out of the community as the economic crisis worsened during the 1970-1983 period. According to one estimate, by 1983 out of 20 blacks employed at John Deere only 5 were still there. Two factors were responsible for their plight. First, in many cases African-Americans who were recruited through Affirmative Action policies in the 1970s were laid off first in the 1980s since they lacked seniority. Second, many African Americans hired by Dubuque firms soon left town, and some asked to be transferred to other cities since there were not many blacks nor any community support to keep them in town (Hendricks, op. cit.). In fact, in 1980 Dubuque had one of the lowest rates of minority population at the state and national levels. Dubuque also had the lowest percentage of African Americans among the 7 metropolitan areas in Iowa. At the national level, in 1980 out of 323 metropolitan areas, Dubuque had the eighth-lowest percentage of African Americans, or less than 0.3 percent of its total population (Kraske, 1983a)(see Table 7).[22]

Table 7: Metropolitan Areas With the Smallest African-American Population, 1980

City	Rank*	Total Metro	# of Blacks	% Blacks to Whites
Wausau, WI	1	111,270	38	0.03
Bismark, ND	2	79,988	53	0.07
Laredo, TX	3	99,258	98	0.09
Eau Claire, WI	4	130,507	168	0.13
Medford, OR	5	132,456	173	0.13
Fargo, ND-Moorehead, MN	6	137,574	290	0.20
Sioux Falls, SD	7	109,435	276	0.25
Dubuque, IA	**8**	**93,745**	**237**	**0.25**
Bangor, ME	9	83,919	244	0.29
Bellingham, WA	10	106,701	328	0.30

* Cities are ranked according to lowest percentage of African Americans for total metropolitan population.

Source: Table constructed based on information from Kraske (1983b).

BLACKS' URBAN RESIDENTIAL PATTERNS IN DUBUQUE

One method to evaluate the comparative status of African Americans during different periods is to study their residential patterns in terms of **spatial concentration** (segregated quarters) or **spatial dispersion** (desegregated and heterogeneous neighborhoods). Up until 1920, the Dubuque municipality was organized and governed based on a ward system. The census material for the 1870-1920 period thus provides information for each of the five wards in Dubuque, including the data for nonwhite population.[23]

During this fifty-year period black residents were conspicuously absent from certain neighborhoods. For instance, the fifth ward, also known as the "North End," was a German enclave and never had a sizeable African American contingent.[24] Another area that had very few black residents was the first ward, which included substantial segments of the Irish neighborhood known as "Dublin," as well as the southern outskirts of the city which later attracted upper-class residents to the area. Clearly, blacks' absence in the southern outskirts was due to their lower socioeconomic status. But they were also effectively excluded from both German and Irish working class neighborhoods.

In contrast, there was a heavy concentration of mulattos in the second and fourth wards. The second ward included the commercial district, factories, and warehouses in the "flats" area, which in local lexicon refers to an area between the Mississippi river to the east and the high bluffs to the west. The "Flats" area is the site of the old industrial core of Dubuque along the Mississippi river that was developed during the 19th century. The second ward also served as a buffer zone between the German neighborhoods in the north and the Irish residences in the south. Apparently, this may have been the only affordable area for the African American population of the time who were mostly manual laborers with limited income.

With further polarization of Dubuque along class lines, the better off and upper class distanced themselves from the stench of factories and crowded the downtown area by moving west and up on the bluffs, also known as the "Hill," which made the fourth ward. An affluent area dotted with upper-class residences and mansions, the fourth ward was the 19th century version of contemporary up-scale suburbs. Census data indicate that considerable number of blacks resided in the "Hills" area. But considering the socio-economic status of blacks in Dubuque at the turn of this century, the only explanation for their conspicuous presence in this ward is their employment as house servants, whitewashers and laborers.

A major change in Dubuque's form of city government in 1920 replaced the ward system of electing council members with an at-large electoral process. The census data, therefore, were no longer available at the ward level, as was the case prior to the 1920 enumeration. Thus in the absence of reliable data, a study of residential patterns for African Americans between 1920 and 1980 remains at best sketchy. One such example is a study conducted by students at the University of Dubuque. The project's findings indicate that in 1971 most black families were concentrated in one locality in the "Flats" area, residing mostly in substandard dwellings (Roberts, 1974:265-66). The Flats includes the downtown business district, which, similar to many other American cities, was devastated by the urban renewal projects of the late 1960s. This dilapidating urban area housed the working class, the poor and unemployed in Dubuque. As the city expanded in the 1970s and 1980s, in addition to the "Hill" area and western suburbs the more affluent gradually moved out of the Flats and settled in the southern expanses of town.

In 1980 the Dubuque city government returned to the ward system, and the 1980 and 1990 censuses once again provide data at the ward level. Since the tract and ward boundaries were redrawn in the 1980s a comparative study of the residential patterns for African Americans becomes a risky task. Overall, in comparing the 1980 and 1990 population data we can make two general conclusions. First, in terms of residential patterns, except for few high income bracket areas, in 1980 blacks were present in all other Dubuque residential neighborhoods. In particular, they were conspicuously present in tracts 1, 5, 7 and 9.[25] One plausible explanation for this selective spatial representation is that these three tracts were the sites of Dubuque's three liberal arts colleges and a few Bible schools with sizeable minority student populations.[26] Tracts 1 and 5 were also parts of the old Dubuque that included dilapidated neighborhoods with high concentration of rental properties. Again, despite their relative spatial dispersion, similar to the 1870-1920 period blacks were underrepresented in the most affluent sections of town due to their poverty (U.S. Bureau of the Census, 1983: Table P-7).[27]

Second, African Americans' residential pattern did not change drastically by 1990, as in several tracts their residences were clustered together, forming enclaves with a certain degree of visibility. This ghetto-like residential pattern is partly due to the limited availability of rental units to African Americans, often caused by a subtle and hard-to-document process of discrimination by some real estate agencies. Also, similar to many other working class and poor ethnic groups, for purely practical purposes of social networking and provision of intra-group support, African Americans in Dubuque have been forced to form their own residential enclaves. Finally, an increase in the number of African American students in Dubuque colleges contributed to a sharp increase in the number of blacks in tract 6 (U.S. Bureau of the Census, 1990; and Charvat, Burke and Goody, 1990).

CONCLUSION

Our historical examination of available data indicates that except during the first decade of its inception as a frontier river town in the 1830s Dubuque's African American population has remained conspicuously low. Throughout the 19th century blacks' socio-economic status also remained low and, though mostly employed, they were hired to do menial jobs as house servants, dock workers, porters, whitewashers and the like. Very little is known about their residential patterns prior to the Civil War. But except for those who lived in white households as maids, or in the city's boarding houses, in all likelihood the rest of black residents lived in shacks in the remote fringes of town. A reading of the census data after the Civil War indicates that similar to other urban communities blacks lived in segregated quarters, and in Dubuque's case separated from other working class and poor neighborhoods that housed the residents of Irish and German origin.

A historical survey of occupational status and residential patterns for Dubuque blacks during the 20th century testifies to their occupational advancements and increasing presence in residential neighborhoods across social class and income boundaries. Changes are particularly significant for the 1970-1990 period, as significant numbers of blacks are represented in mid-level occupational levels. A few blacks are even employed in higher-levels such as managerial and professional positions. Yet despite their gains, a review of race relations in Dubuque during the 20th century suggests that blacks' relative success has had no bearing on reducing white-on black prejudice in town. In fact, their improved socio-economic and occupational status in the 1980s appears to have backfired and worked to their disadvantage.

Notes

1. I will discuss the politics of race in chapter 3 in more detail.
2. Bergmann (1969:14) puts the number of blacks by the end of the 1840s at 333.
3. According to Berrier (2001:45) the origins of the term "Underground Railroad" are traced to a frustrated southern planter, who, after losing his slave allegedly stated that "the Negro escapes to Canada as easily as if they traveled on a railway which was beneath the ground!"
4. See also Dykstra (1993:91).

5. In another study of Iowa's black population, Haefner (1938:190) does not record the presence of black slaves in her examination of *the Second Census of Enumeration of the Inhabitants of the Territory of Wisconsin in 1838*, and states that "there were 112 'free negroes' in the 15 counties of the Iowa Territory, of which 72 lived in Dubuque County."
6. This will be discussed in detail in the following chapter.
7. The census data for 1850 are both sketchy and unreliable, since many pages in the microfilmed document are not legible, and the figures are for Dubuque County and not the city of Dubuque. While the 1840 census distinguishes between "whites," "free colored," and "slaves," the 1850 census excludes slaves and only enumerates whites and free colored residents. However, this is the only census that distinguishes between "blacks" and "mulattos," the latter including the "half-breeds" or offspring of mixed marriages. The mulatto category disappears from the 1860 census, and the only racial distinction made under the "free Inhabitants" heading, is between "whites" and "coloreds." The mulatto category resurfaces again in the post-Civil War era and remains until the 1920s.
8. Dykstra (1993:7) identifies black contributors and the amount of their contribution as 'Uncle Tom'(50¢), Caroline Brady (12½¢), Walton Baker (25¢), Sam Welsh (25¢), Nathaniel Morgan (50¢), and Tilda (25¢). Nathaniel Morgan was later lynched by a Dubuque mob.
9. The Ice Harbor is Dubuque's main port of entry on the Mississippi River and also served as a shipbuilding site during the 19th century and the early decades of the past century.
10. Data for this part are collected by the author from the *Population Schedules of the 9th, 10th, 12th, and 13th Censuses of the United States for the Dubuque County*, Washington, D.C.: The National Archives of the United States.
11. Layoffs of organized industrial workers in Dubuque did not affect black workers, as they were mostly employedas manual laborers.
12. During the 1920s blacks were not the main targets of the Klan propaganda and activities. In chapter 6 I will discuss the presence of the Klan in more detail.

13. The Census Bureau's ambiguous and tentative approach to racial designations prior to the 1960s Civil Rights Movement manifested itself in constant revision of racial categories for enumeration purposes. This conceptual inconsistency makes it difficult to have an accurate reading of the figures in Table 6, as well as to make a comparative and historical analysis of the African-American population in Dubuque.

    Similar to previous decades the 1930 census enumerators adopted an inconclusive method to tabulate the population by color and race. For example, the 1930 census clusters people into three racial categories of "Negro," "white," and "other races." The third group is also broken down into several racial subcategories including Mexican, Indian, Chinese, and Japanese. Two decades later, the 1950 census uses the term "color" to divide the population into two categories of "whites" and "nonwhites." The "mulatto" category once again disappears from census classification, and the terms "Negro" or "black" are interchangeably used to identify nonwhite population.

14. *Abstract of the 15th Census of the United States* (1953), Vol.II, Tables 48, P.109. U.S. Department of Commerce, Bureau of the Census, Washington, D.C.: Government Printing Office.
15. *A report of the 17th Decennial Census of the United States, the 1950 Census of Population* (1953), Vol.II, Part 15, Iowa. U.S. Department of Commerce, Bureau of the Census, Washington, D.C.: Government Printing Office.
16. U.S. Department of Commerce, Bureau of the Census (1966), *Special Census of Dubuque, Iowa*, October 7, 1966, Series P-28, No 1438.
17. U.S. Department of Commerce, The 1970 Census of Population and Housing, Census Tracts for Dubuque SMSA, Iowa, Tables P-1 and P-2, pp. 1-4.
18. U.S. Department of Coomerce, Bureau of the Census (1983). *The 1980 Census of Population and Housing, Census Tracts for Dubuque SMSA, Iowa*, Table P-7. Washington, D.C.: Government printing Office.
19. *Census of Population and Housing in Incorporated Places in Iowa* (1990). Des Moines, Iowa: The State Library of Iowa.

20. The data presented in preceding discussion are compiled from the following sources:

    a) For 1950: U.S. Bureau of the Census (1952), Vol.II, Part 15, Table 36, P.69 (itemized data not available).

    b) For 1970: U.S. Bureau of the Census (1973), Tables P5-P8, pp. 9-12.

    c) For 1980: U.S. Bureau of the Census (1983), Vol. I, Chapter C, part 17, Tables 134 and 135, pp. 209-216.
21. As a production branch of a major multinational corporate entity, in 1979 the John Deere Dubuque Works employed more than 8,000 workers, manufacturing heavy construction equipment. The corporation's status and role in the city's economy will be discussed in detail in chapter 7.
22. As discussed earlier, the situation did not get any better in the late 1990s.
23. The Census Bureau's conceptual inconsistency makes any assessment of the actual number of different ethnic groups in Dubuque and elsewhere extremely difficult (See endnote 12 above).
24. According to the 1920 census the fifth ward contained predominantly German population and/or people from Scandinavian Countries, as well as a sizeable representation by Polish Americans.
25. For instance, blacks were highly concentrated in tracts 1, 5, 7, and 9, with a total of 137 residents (or 62 percent of Dubuque's black population).
26. Tract 7 was also predominantly renter-occupied with a median household income of $15,677 in 1980.
27. This area is demarcated by census tract 8.02.

CHAPTER 3

WHITE-ON-BLACK RACISM IN DUBUQUE: THE FRONTIER TOWN'S FIRST CENTURY

To argue that racial prejudice and discrimination in Dubuque for the past 160 years or so has been predominantly a "white vs. black" issue would not be an overstatement. Once European settlers arrived in Dubuque after the Black Hawk Purchase in 1833, Native Americans disappeared altogether from the scene — and once the initial stage of Euro-ethnic conflict was over, the German-Irish rivalry diminished to a cultural war for ethnic affirmation and pride.[1] A study of race relations in Dubuque is, therefore, limited in scope, as it is dominated by white racism aimed only at African Americans. However, as one historian of race relations in Iowa points out, the peculiar nature of white racism in Iowa in general, and in Dubuque in particular, is that Iowans "reacted not to the *fact* of a black presence but to the *prospect* of it" (Dykstra, 1993:VIII). Unlike overt racial conflicts which emerge out of the political and economic reality of multiethnic urban communities where blacks and whites are represented in significant numbers, this kind of "anticipatory prejudice" is hard to detect and still harder to analyze. In this chapter I focus on the attitudes of white residents toward African Americans, and the nature and extent of white-on-black racism during the 19th century.

RACE RELATIONS PRIOR TO THE CIVIL WAR (1830-1860)

Both as free residents and slaves blacks have been present in Dubuque since the 1830s. Iowans never sanctioned slavery, and many were actively involved in helping fugitive slaves on their way to freedom. But according to the 1840 census, in addition to free blacks, 16 slaves were either owned or supervised by eleven Dubuque residents.[2] A few slave owners and prominent community members are worthy of note. George Wallace Jones, a delegate to the U.S. Congress for the Iowa Territory owned three slaves; Thomas McKnight, a receiver of the local U.S. land office owned two slaves; and Jack Thompson, a wealthy merchant owned one slave (Dykstra, 1982:74).

Slavery was never officially sanctioned or institutionalized in Iowa for two reasons. First, as part of the Louisiana Purchase the Northwest Ordinance outlawed slavery in the Northwest Territory that included Iowa. Second, after Congress adopted the Missouri Compromise in 1820, the area north of latitude 36° 30' was designated as "free of slavery" (Schwieder et. al, 1987:18).[3] But following the Black Hawk Purchase in 1833 many families who moved from neighboring southern states to Iowa brought their slaves into the Iowa Territory (Bergmann, 1948:5-6).[4] Owning slaves was not apparently considered a reprehensible practice in Dubuque and Iowa, and as was the case in southern states, slave owners in Dubuque area could place ads in papers and ask the public's assistance to capture their runaway slaves. For instance, in a public notice published in a Dubuque paper a slave owner cautioned the public of "harboring or trusting" a runaway "servant girl eleven years of age" with "short black hair and black eyes" (*Du Buque*, January 25, 1840, cf. Oldt, 1910:67). Referring to the prevalence of slave owning in Dubuque's early history, Dykstra (1993:11-12) comments that in the 1840s "Only in and around Dubuque lived Iowans callous enough to identify to the census marshals the servile status of their household blacks," and when elsewhere in Iowa "slave-holding Iowans at least had the grace to lie Dubuquers nonchalantly called a slave a slave."

For the majority of Iowans, opposing slavery and seeing blacks as equals in political and economic matters were two different issues. The relations between whites and free blacks in Iowa prior to the Civil War has to be understood within the context of the state's politics and existing laws. Later known as "Iowa's Black Code," the Iowa legislature passed two laws that slowed down the movement of free blacks into the Iowa territories. The first law that was passed in 1839 prevented "blacks and mulattoes" from settling in Iowa if they did not possess "a certificate of freedom and the ability to post a bond of $500," indicating that they "would not become a public charge." Passed in 1840, the second law effectively prohibited interracial marriages (Schwieder et. al., 1987:18). Finally, the passage of the state constitution in 1844 excluded free black males from voting and serving in the state legislature and the state militia (Dykstra, 1993:19). Thus Iowans had a clear position on free blacks' presence in their state: maintain their subordinate status, and if possible keep them out of Iowa altogether.

Iowans' dislike of blacks was in spite of their strong anti-slavery sentiments and active participation in the Underground Railroad movement.[5] Although Dubuque's track record of helping fugitive slaves in their passage to freedom is at best marginal, there are a few shining moments in the city's history of race relations. The first significant documented incident, and certainly the most positive case during the antebellum period, was that of "Ralph." In 1834, Ralph, a slave from Missouri entered into an agreement with his master to pay him $550 plus interest by 1838 in return for his freedom. He then came to Dubuque and worked in the lead mines. But working hard and gaining little, by 1839 he was unable to pay the overdue note for his freedom. Two Virginian mine workers who learned about Ralph's situation allegedly offered his owner to return Ralph for a $100 fee. By order of a local justice of the peace, the two men captured Ralph and headed south. But a Dubuque resident witnessed his capture and rushed to his rescue. T.S. Wilson, the District Judge, referred Ralph's case to the newly organized Iowa Supreme Court. The Supreme Court ruled that "Ralph was neither fugitive nor slave," and "once permitted by his owner to establish a residence on Iowa soil, he had become free" (Dykstra, 1982:71-72). From then on Ralph became a free man.[6]

Unfortunately, not all the incidents involving blacks in Dubuque had pleasant and happy endings. A year after Ralph's case, Nathaniel Morgan, a young and free African American, was lynched by a group of Dubuque residents. Led by the commander of the local militia, a group of white local men accused Morgan, a cook and waiter in a local hotel, of stealing a trunk full of clothes. He denied any wrongdoing but was severely beaten up and repeatedly whipped by the mob. Overwhelmed by pain and torture, Morgan admitted to the crime he had not committed and named a location up on the bluffs where he had hidden the stolen trunk. Obviously the mob could not find the trunk and, according to an eyewitness, Morgan's dead body was returned to the city with "his back broken and his ribs and sides all stove in" (*The History of Dubuque County*, 1880:395). The militia leader and several other men involved in the lynching were charged with murder, but the local judge acquitted all of them "on the grounds that their intent to commit so gross a crime had not been proved." (Dykstra, 1982:74)

Nowhere is there evidence that Dubuquers ever acknowledged Nathaniel Morgan's innocence in public, nor did the local media condemn his lynching. The only testimony to his good character and innocence is a letter written to a friend by William Allen (1865). In the letter he indicates that in 1833 he "hired this Negro Nat and his wife from Galena" and that he "always thought him honest." Morgan's death deprived Dubuque blacks of a potential leader and contributed to a sharp decline in Dubuque's black population, as after the lynching incident many African-American residents reportedly moved to Muscatine, another frontier river town south of Dubuque (Hawthorne, 1992:13). Those who stayed behind lost a sense of community or collective leadership, which made them more susceptible to racial prejudice (Dykstra, 1993:13).

A historical survey of white-on-black prejudice and overt acts of racism in this period suggests that Dubuque residents' national origin and social class affected the nature and extent of their prejudice toward blacks. For instance, residents of British origin came from a country with a long history of colonization and slavery that could have made them more lenient toward slavery. But slavery was abolished within the British empire in 1833, the same year as the Iowa territories were opened for settlement. Thus most settlers of British origin "tended to locate among New England settlers in the Middle West and to adapt themselves to the prevailing sentiments of their communities, which meant a dislike of slavery"(Bergmann, 1969:8). On the other hand, early settlers of German and Irish origin tended to sympathize with the Jacksonian tradition in the Midwest, and to join the Democratic Party that represented the South and proslavery sentiments. While "German elements" gradually shifted their position and aligned themselves with the Republican Party, the Irish "maintained their allegiance to the Democratic Party, even condoning slavery, since party, to them, came before principle"(Ibid.).

Social class membership also played a significant role in shaping individuals' attitudes toward blacks. The upper class and owners of capital for instance held prejudicial attitudes toward African Americans and condoned slavery at the time. For example Josiah Conzett, a prominent member of the community, wrote about his recollections of people and events in the 1870s, describing residents on Clay Street during the pre-Civil War period. Conzett (1905:212) talks about the house next door where "lived a Negro familie by name of Aaron. The man was very large almost *a giant with the strength of an ox. He was a dray man his wife was a coal black Negress*" (italics mine). Since the elite felt no direct threat by poor black residents, some even lent their support to blacks in public, and at times even implicitly recognized their basic civil rights. Lucius Langworthy, another prominent member of Dubuque's ruling elite and a pioneer lead miner, commented in somewhat positive terms supporting Ralph's freedom while condemning Morgan's lynching in a public speech. He praised those who came to Ralph's rescue as "liberty loving citizens," but he also portrayed the lynch mob as a "misguided group of people" whose brutality was "a mistaken zeal, and with entire ignorance, perhaps of the injury they were inflicting, or with reason blinded by prejudice" (Dykstra, 1982:74-76). In general, the white elite's racism was often channeled through political action and legislation. As influential local and regional power brokers, many prominent members of the upper class also supported legislation to limit the extent of black participation in local and state politics. For instance, when Dubuque was incorporated in 1838, white settlers made extra efforts to exclude blacks from the political process. In Dykstra's words, while "the customary clause setting the rules for a town's first election did not specify voter eligibility," the act asserted that "only 'free white' males would vote"(Dykstra, 1982:74-76). Also, at about the same time that Lucius Langworthy was praising Ralph's rescuers, Edward, another prominent Langworthy brother, was active in passing anti-black resolutions in the Constitutional Convention of 1844 in Iowa.[7]

In most cases, members of the white working class and the poor were the ones who, threatened by the presence of free blacks in Dubuque's job market, openly expressed their prejudicial attitudes and often acted on them. In fact, incidents of mob violence in pre-Civil War Dubuque were always related to free blacks and not black slaves. Divergence of attitudes on blacks based on social class is evident in one local historian's account of a racially motivated melee. In his discussion of blacks' status in Dubuque, Dykstra (1982:76) tells the tale of a "respectable businessman" who, on an election day in 1856, dared to declare publicly that he considered a "black person to be as good as himself." The angry crowd attacked and severely injured the man, and he was lucky to be rescued by the police before getting killed.

During the 1850s two major Dubuque newspapers, the *Times* and the *Dubuque Herald,* also reflected the sentiments of white property owners and workers, respectively. The Dubuque *Times* represented the views of upper class business community, mostly of German background, and was predominantly pro-Union. In contrast, the *Dubuque Herald*, the city's more influential paper, represented the prevalent and overt anti-black sentiments of the time, mostly expressed by workers and the poor. One such case was the paper's response to a progressive bill passed by the state senate's Republicans in 1856 to give the "Negroes, Indians and mulattos the right to testify in cases when white men were parties." A *Herald* editorial commented "the next proposition will be to allow Negroes, Indians and mulattos to acquire citizenship with all the rights of the whites and the next to court white daughters and have white wives." (*Dubuque Herald*, December 23, 1856, cf. Oldt, 1910:340)

Dubuquers cannot be singled out for their pro-slavery and anti-black attitudes. As involuntary migrants, many of the early Iowa settlers were southern small-scale farmers who could not compete with the large-scale plantation system and its political machine in the South. Naturally, pro-slavery sentiments were widespread among Iowa's new settlers who were afraid of emancipated blacks as potential competitors in the local labor market (Bergmann, 1948:6-7). For instance, when in 1854 news of the passage of the Kansas-Nebraska Bill by the U.S. Senate reached Dubuque, the city's Democrats reportedly "fired 100 rounds from the cannon and held a jubilee meeting"(Oldt, 1910:336).[8] But other Dubuque residents were incensed about Democrats' reaction, and mocked their pro-slavery sentiments by publishing the following ad in the *Tribune:*

Nebraska Slave Market

Constantly on Hand Negroes of All Ages; Boys and Girls, Men and Women, for Sale at Low Prices

Cash paid for Horses, Cattle and Niggers.

Douglas for President

George W. Jones, Agent for Iowa

By the mid-1850s the anti-slavery movement was strong enough to play a significant role in Iowa's politics (Sibley, 1957).

Some black Dubuquers also actively participated in the anti-slavery movement. The most prominent activists were Charlotte and Henry Pyles who came to Dubuque in 1853. Charlotte Pyles was well known among antislavery leaders for her fundraising efforts in Eastern Iowa (Hill, 1981-82:292).

The city residents' support of the anti-slavery movement and their relative show of solidarity with blacks in the 1850s can be related to Dubuque's state of the economy. During the 1850-56 period Dubuque experienced an enormous growth in economic activities that in turn contributed to the city's impressive urban development. Portraying Dubuque's rapid economic and urban growth one local paper reported on the extent of housing construction in town and high demand for them, since they were " all engaged long before they are complete." (*Miners' Express,* October 23, 1850, cf. Oldt, 1910:90)

Dubuque continued to prosper, and by the mid-1850s it was one of the major urban centers of commerce in the Midwest. Reflecting the prevalent mood of Dubuquers, Oldt(1910:111) summarizes the city's prosperous age and predictions by *Express* and *Herald*, that by 1870 "Dubuque was certain to become one of the greatest, if not the greatest, cities in the United States"(Oldt,1910:111). Newspaper accounts of changes in Dubuque's urban landscape during the 1850s were also indicative of the city's transition from a small frontier town to a relatively large urban center with considerable economic significance for the region. In an editorial, the *Express* commented that "Our city is crowded at this time with strangers. Every other man we meet on the street, nearly, is a stranger. Many of them are seeking locations for business" (*Express,* May 18, 1853, cf. Oldt, 1910:98). In light of economic prosperity and increasing job opportunities, workers in Dubuque felt less threatened by an influx of migrant workers, including some free southern blacks into the city's job market. For instance, in a strong show of solidarity in 1855 all other political parties and tendencies were united to oppose the Democrats' pro-slavery stance in Dubuque. According to Oldt

(1910:337), "Whigs, Know-Nothings, Native Americans, Free Soilers, Abolitionists, Maine Lawists, etc." banded together and called their ticket the "Peoples." One contentious issue that was challenged by some Dubuque residents was the infamous Fugitive Slave Act of 1850.[9] In its February 18, 1855 editorial, the *Tribune critically* refuted the act and argued that in its present form it "makes bloodhounds of us or incarcerates us in a common jail if we refuse to be put on the track of the fleeing slave."(cf. Oldt, 1910:336)

By the late 1850s things started to change when Dubuque's impressive urban growth and economic prosperity came to a halt. As a frontier town, Dubuque had to face the inevitable as jobs started to disappear and businesses closed down. The "panic of 1857" in Dubuque, referring to the city's economic collapse, was a reflection of much greater economic crisis at the regional and national levels. Historians trace the roots of the crisis to "the collapse of the Ohio Life Insurance Company in August 1857," which in turn forced eastern seaboard manufacturers and wholesalers to demand immediate payment from Dubuque merchants for products shipped on credit. But like in many other cities, either "the goods were still on shelves in Dubuque," or "they had been sold to farmers, miners, mechanics, and others on credit." The crop failure in 1858 also compounded the problem, when many farmers failed to meet their debt to local businesses and banks (Johnson, 1996: 79). By the fall of 1858 there was a big reduction in rents in Dubuque, and "Dwelling houses that a year or eighteen months ago would rent from $300 to $400, can now be rented for less than half the amount, and in many instances go begging at these rates for tenants" (*Express & Herlad,* September 12, 1858, cf. Oldt, 1910:126). Dubuque appeared to have run its course and reached the end of its prosperity.

Dubuque's involvement in mining and regional trade also made her highly susceptible to changing preferences for raw material, market fluctuations and shifts in spatial preferences for urban locations and transportation nodes.[10] As a frontier town,

Dubuque grew as an "instant city," to borrow Gunther Barth's term, where "vast number of people from many different places were thrown together, unified only by their desire to find gold or other precious metal or to provide services for those who were engaged in this quest."(cf. Hamer, 1990:10-11)

With worsening economic conditions there was also a noticeable change in public's attitude toward strangers, outsiders or any one who appeared to pose a threat to one's job or job security. Blacks were particularly affected by Dubuque's economic downturn, as the city became increasingly inhospitable to African Americans. A comparison of the census data for 1840 and 1860 indicates that despite a sixteen-fold increase in the city's population there was a sharp proportionate decline in black population, from 8.6 percent to a meager 0.5 percent, respectively.[11] This was at a time when black population was on the rise in Iowa, as between 1850 and 1860 the African American population tripled in the state (Bergmann, 1948:15).[12]

RACE RELATIONS DURING THE CIVIL WAR PERIOD

As the north was preparing for a head-on confrontation with the South, Dubuque residents were trying to cope with the city's battered economy and its grim prospects for future growth. An economy in shambles, the news of imminent war, prospects of an end to slavery and the possibility of secession by southern states frightened many Dubuque residents. For one thing, Dubuque's economy was intertwined with that of the South through dealings with St. Louis, New Orleans and other southern markets. In the words of one historian, "much of the grain and flour had usually been consigned to New Orleans houses, but now it was deemed unsafe and all was chaos." Contrasting "the flush times of 1856-57 and the dullness of 1861-62," a *Herald* editorial made note of "empty buildings once filled with goods or occupied four or five years ago (*Herald,* August 10, 1861, cf. Oldt, 1910:139).

By 1860, public sentiments in Dubuque started to change. For example, when Stephen Douglas, the prominent senator from Florida and the sponsor of the Kansas-Nebraska Bill came to Dubuque in 1860, his reception was outstanding by all standards of the time. According to some reports, he was well received by a large crowd followed by a procession that was composed of both Dubuque residents and outsiders numbering from 15,000 to 20,000 (*Herald,* October 12, 1860, cf. Oldt, 1910:349).

The onslaught of the Civil War affected Dubuquers in both direct and indirect ways, and residents were ideologically torn between the support for the Union and sympathies for the southern Confederates. This was partly due to the composition of Dubuque's population. Whereas the earliest settlers came from the South, immigrants arriving in the late 1840s and 1850s were heavily from New York, Pennsylvania and the New England states (Datisman, n.d.:12). Southern sympathizers probably reflected the ideas and secessionist activities of George Wallace Jones, a former U.S. senator from the Iowa Territory. Jones was an ardent supporter of Jefferson Davis, the president of the Confederacy and his long-time friend and college classmate. Because of his southern sympathies, Jones was arrested and briefly imprisoned in 1861 by the direct order of President Lincoln. However, he received a hero's welcome in Dubuque after being released from jail (ibid.). Another prominent Copperhead in Dubuque was Dennis A. Mahoney, editor of the influential newspaper the *Dubuque Herald.*[13] He also was briefly imprisoned for his pro-Confederate activities and editorials (Mercer, 1982:58; Bergmann, 1948:39).[14] The extent of support for the southern cause in Dubuque is hard to document. The *Times,* the pro-Union paper in town, downplayed these tendencies and reported that "there was a small squad of secessionists here" (April 16, 1861, cf. Oldt, 1910:259). In general, there are indications that Dubuque residents supported President Lincoln and the war efforts. Lincoln's call for volunteers for the Union army not only got the approval of all Republicans, but also many Democrats who shifted their alliances on this matter.

The city's two major papers also represented opposing ideological and political tendencies on the war efforts. With the advent of the war the *Herald* became increasingly pro-confederate and the voice of Democrats, while the *Times* represented the views of Lincoln supporters and the Republican Party. The *Herald's* support of the southern cause was derived from its opposition to "the privileged economic position of the East" in the Midwest than its desire to create a social system in Iowa that was in line with the southern economic reality. The *Herald* and Dennis Mahoney as its editor represented a populist position that opposed the privileged class and defended "the people" in general and the working class in particular. Mahoney opposed the war not necessarily in support of the south, but in arguing that the south's efforts for secession and the Republicans' lopsided management of the crisis were equally detrimental to the future of the Union (Johnson, 1996:163). The *Herald* also reflected the anti-abolitionist sentiments of all southerners residing in Dubuque County, as for many of them "the Negro was regarded as an animal, nothing more" (Oldt, 1910:277). The paper's pages were periodically filled with anti-black slogans and statements. In particular, the *Herald*'s anti-black rhetoric was intensified in 1863 when Stilson Hutchins, a staunch Copperhead briefly became the acting editor in Mahoney's absence. His language was harsher than Mahoney's, and he made race an important issue in Dubuque during the war years. For example, in an editorial he assured that Dubuque would never relinquish old traditions as "She is copperheaded, copperbottomed, and copper fastened. She is, in short, the white man's country, and we glory in it and will labor to keep her so"(cf. Johnson, 1996:188). On the question of slavery and abolitionism, the April 5, 1863 issue of the *Dubuque Herald* also editorialized "who wants to vote the nigger emancipation ticket? Who wants Iowa covered with indolent blacks? Answer at the polls." The editorial then advised readers that "it is far better to crush them at the ballot box than to be obliged to meet them with the cartridge box" (cf. Oldt, 1910:358).[15] The *Herald's* harsh language represented more the sentiments of working class and poor residents, many of Irish heritage, who had to cope with future uncertainties and their own ethnic- and class-based insecurities.

By 1860 Dubuque's economy was still dominated by mining and commercial capitalism. As a result, in the absence of industries the bulk of its working class population was engaged in manual labor. About three-quarters of Dubuque's workers were immigrants, mostly of German and Irish descent. Most German workers were artisans, while the majority of the Irish were unskilled workers (Johnson, 1996:128-29). This inevitably divided workers and can be considered as the prototype of a "segmented working class."[16] In addition to occupational and skill-level differences, there was also a gap in the value of property ownership among Dubuque workers of German and Irish origins. For example, Johnson (1996:117, 130) estimates the average property value for Dubuque workers in 1860 at about $379, while artisans and unskilled workers' property ownership value averaged at about $732 and $163, respectively. This was at a time when the elite business class in Dubuque had an average property value of $4,534.

In general, the stereotype that refers to poor, working class and mostly Catholic Irish was the outcome of massive immigration of the Irish during the 1845-55 period, who were predominantly poor and were driven out of their famine-stricken homeland (Ignatiev, 1995:41). Those who came to America during the late 18th and early 19th centuries were mostly Protestants and did not have to cope with their "Irishness" as a race in the New World. Early Irish immigrants also did not come from the poorest strata of the Irish society either. By some estimates only 20 percent of Irish immigrants in 1820 were laborers (Miller, cf. Ignatiev, 1995:38).

In his book *How the Irish Became White,* Noel Ignatiev (1995) provides an interesting historical account of Irish immigrants and their struggle to come to grips with their subordinate status both in Ireland and in the New World. Back home, British colonizers ruled the Irish under a series of codes that are known as "Penal Laws." These laws put pressure on Irish Catholics and effectively excluded them from participating in social-economic, political, and military activities. In Ignatiev's words, during the 18th century "Irish Catholics formed an oppressed race," a created social reality that was even acknowledged by the oppressed Irish themselves (34-35).

Once in America, the poor Irish "were thrown together with black people on jobs and in neighborhoods." Joined together in the eastern and southern states due to their poverty, the two groups inevitably socialized with each other, resulting in a new category of mulatto population. According to Ignatiev, census enumerators in the 1850s identified 406,000 mulattoes nationwide. As a result of their intermingling with blacks the Irish were often called "niggers turned inside out," while blacks were sometimes referred to as "smoked Irish" (40-41). This second wave of Irish immigrants were oppressed by British colonialists back home; and once in the New World, they were also thrown to the lowest rungs of the American stratification system and forced to wrestle with their identity as "white Americans." As Ignatiev points out, "while the white skin made the Irish eligible for membership in the white race, it did not guarantee their admission; they had to earn it" (59).

In understanding the nature of race and ethnic relations in Dubuque, specifically white-on-black racism, we have to take the Irish ethnic factor into consideration. As was discussed earlier, the predominant majority of Dubuque's Irish were poor, still carrying their bitter memories of oppression back home and the way they were treated on the East coast. Irish Dubuquers thus defended the southern cause and joined the Democrats in order to establish themselves as white ethnics on the western urban frontier. John Finch, a British Owenite who traveled the United States in 1843, made the following observation:[17]

> It is a curious fact that the Democratic Party, and particularly the poorer class of Irish immigrants in America, are greater enemies to the negro population, and greater advocates for the continuance of negro slavery, than any portion of the population in the free states. (Finch, cf. Ignatiev, 1995:97)

Irish dislike of blacks and opposition to their cause was more the result of competition in the labor market than racist attitudes. In fact, the poor Irish immigrants entered a sector of the American labor force that was already occupied by free blacks in the north. Thus they had to compete with blacks for increasingly scarce menial employment positions as porters, dock workers, waiters and the like.[18] Being mostly poor and belonging to the unskilled sector of the working class in Dubuque, Irish residents' fear of an influx of freed blacks from the south was therefore a real one.[19]

Dubuque's two major newspapers played a significant role in representing divergent perspectives on the issue of black emancipation. While the *Herald* became the mouthpiece of the Democrats who supported the southern cause in various degrees, the *Times* represented pro-Union Republicans who at times supported the war not to set the southern blacks free but to keep them in the South. For instance, in 1862 G.T. Stewart, the *Times* new editor argued that continuation of slavery only degrades "white free labor" that is forced to compete with "black slave labor." He also argued that by joining the South and making Iowa a slave state the Democrats would also "drive away the Irish, German and American laborers." The *Times* also editorialized that "the Republican Party is directly opposed to the introduction of Negroes, either free or slave, into the North"(Stewart, cf. Johnson, 1996;197-98). Thus by supporting the Union, Republicans argued that freed black slaves in the South would cherish their freedom and be induced to stay there. Johnson provides a compelling argument for Republicans' political motives during the war in Iowa and Dubuque, thus challenging historians who see them as supporters of black civil rights: they believed by abolishing slavery black and white workers will be "placed on an equal footing," whereby "white labor would surely dominate." (Johnson, 1996:199)

Mostly represented by political party affiliation the "social class card" also played a significant role during the War years, as Dubuque residents contemplated the extent of their contribution to the war efforts. By the 1860s Dubuque had a coherent upper class that was comprised of two generations of business elite. Johnson (1996:109-121) identifies them as "patricians" and "entrepreneurs." The former included the early miners who earned their wealth through hard physical labor and their political power through "citizenship and public service." In contrast, as the second generation of elite Dubuquers the latter were "professionally-educated, commercially oriented men, who thrived in the up-tempo life of 'metropolitan Dubuque'" (110). The upper class in Dubuque's early days were mostly miners who joined the Democratic Party. But as the new business class increasingly dominated Dubuque's economy in the 1850s and 1860s, the political preferences and alliances also began to change related to national politics. Thus in the late-1850s the Republican Party became the party of property owners and the business class. On the other hand, while there were significant numbers of the old ruling elite who belonged to the Democratic Party, workers and new immigrants comprised the bulk of its membership.

During the Civil War years the Democratic Party increasingly became the political voice of the southern cause and drew a large membership from among artisans and workers, while at the same time it started to lose its upper class members to the Republican side (Johnson, 1996:132-34). In assessing Dubuquers' class alliances and party affiliations in 1860, Johnson (155-56) estimates that the business class comprised 73 percent of the Republican Party leadership vs. 57 percent for the Democratic Party. In contrast, 17 percent of Republican leaders came from the working class compared to 34 percent for the Democratic

Party. Although hard to document, it appears that differences in skill levels and earnings between workers of German and Irish origin also divided them along political lines.

A contentious issue for Iowans and Dubuque residents during the Civil War period was the manner of response to the federal government's call to recruit volunteers for the war efforts. As the war intensified, each state within the Union was required to fill its quota in recruiting men for the Union army. But recruiting efforts were apparently not very successful in Dubuque. Dubuque residents' strong support of the southern cause was manifested in a poor record of recruitment in the early 1860s. In one editorial, the *Herald* reported that "Dubuque was the only backward county in the state and has done nothing as yet toward filling her quota, offering bounties, or kindling a patriotic fire" (August 5, 1862, cf. Holdt, 1910:281). The *Herald* and its editor, Mahoney, initially supported a voluntary-based army and assumed that "drafting would be partial, one-sided and of Democrats only" (Ibid.). At the time, Mahoney also believed that if the sons of the rich elite were not going to the front, they should at least be required to make some "pecuniary sacrifice." Thus in an editorial in September 1861 the *Herald* admonished the elite and demanded their monetary contribution to the war effort (cf. Johnson, 1996:178).

As pressure mounted on cities and counties to fill the war quota, the number of volunteers began to dwindle. Recruitment efforts brought to the fore the question of social class and unequal representation of the rich and the poor in the Union Army. This was certainly the case in Dubuque, and the *Herald* recognized the importance of social class and status by arguing that the war machine is in the business of recruiting the poor.[20] But as the war lingered, Mahoney changed his position and supported the draft as a workable alternative to minimize the recruitment of southern sympathizers and put the patriotism of the privileged class to test. He scolded the city elite Republicans such as "Stouts, Langworthys, Allisons, Adamses and others" for not volunteering for the draft, while "urging every Democrat to go to war." (*Herald*, cf. Holdt, 1910:280). In 1863 the Democratic-dominated Dubuque County Board passed a resolution that poor men should be exempt from the draft. The resolution also stipulated that since the rich are provided to do for themselves, the county should pay $300 to "purchase the freedom of each poor white man who may be drafted in Iowa and upon whose labor a family may be dependent for support" (Johnson, 1996:292). The resolution was apparently supported by a sizable majority, which approved securing the needed funds through issuing bonds to pay volunteers who will substitute for the exempted draftees. Of course, this was opposed by Republicans who called commutation "unconstitutional" and "abominable" (ibid), and became a campaign issue in local elections.[21]

In sum, to portray Democrats as "pro-Confederacy" and the Republicans as "pro-Union" related to race relations and the question of black emancipation would be an overgeneralization. As Johnson (1996:163) points out, although business and working classes and their parties were on opposite ends related to the war objectives, the Democrats' anti-black sentiments and racism "had plenty of company" among Republicans who supported the Union and later the abolition of slavery.

Finally, one should not overlook the role of Dubuque's black residents in supporting the Abolitionists and their recruiting efforts for the Union army. In one reported case, the *Herald* described black Iowans' active participation and support of the Union and the government's efforts to recruit volunteers in detail. Although efforts by a "Negro from one of the interior towns" and his willingness to volunteer was commended, the paper nonetheless referred to him as a "darky," while using the occasion to scold white upper class Abolitionists who tried to stay away from the war front (*Herald*, October 15, 1864, cf. Oldt, 1910:311-12).[22]

PERSISTENCE OF WHITE RACISM AND BLACKS' RESISTANCE IN THE POST-CIVIL WAR PERIOD

After the Civil War support for racial equality and blacks' civil rights gradually changed Iowa's race relations. This was both due to white Iowans' increasing support for blacks' equal legal status and challenges made by blacks themselves to change discriminatory laws. The first major change came in 1868 when Iowans supported a referendum that altered the state constitution, thus allowing blacks to vote. Next was the removal of the word "white" for qualification to serve as a state legislator in 1880. Finally, the passage of the Civil Rights acts in 1884 that entitled blacks "to the full and equal enjoyment of the accommodations, advantages, facilities and privileges of inns, public conveyances, barber shops, theatres and other places of amusement." This was followed by the 1892 legislation that desegregated public eateries and bathhouses (Schwieder et. al., 1987:19).

As a result of the challenges to racial discriminatory practices, Iowans' reaction to the presence of blacks started to change. With blacks' increasing collective assertiveness and their demands for equal treatment during the Reconstruction period, race relations in Dubuque and the rest of the nation started to take a different path. That is, racist ideology became more subtle and, in order to exclude and suppress blacks, prejudiced whites became more active in the political arena. Anti-black sentiments specifically ran high in Dubuque after the Civil War. For example, when in 1868 Iowans approved five constitutional amendments regarding blacks' voting rights, Dubuque County voters overwhelmingly voted against all five.[23] Following the passage of the amendments, the Dubuque *Herald* commented that "Iowa has undoubtedly elected the nigger. It is triumph of which to be proud. In Dubuque the nigger runs ahead of Allison [a pro-South prominent public figure]. In the state the nigger is but little behind the other radical candidates" (November 7, 1868, cf. Oldt, 1910:367).

One manifestation of changes in strategy to contain blacks in Dubuque was the public's reaction to the question of schooling and education for black children. Dubuque residents' opposition to integration of black students into public schools continued, and there were little changes in public opinion on this issue by the war's conclusion. According to newspaper accounts, in January of 1866 a petition was signed by a group of white residents and presented to the Dubuque school board to establish a separate school for "colored people." In March 1866 the school board approved a plan to establish a separate school for "Negro children" in the basement of the Methodist Church. While city politicians were busy with legalizing segregated schools, editorial comments in the *Dubuque Daily Herald* continued to reflect the concerns of residents who even opposed having segregated schools for black children. Commenting on a growing anxiety about educating blacks in Dubuque and making the city a haven for the "Negro," a *Herald* editorial concluded that "If such a school is established here, niggers will flock here in swarms to get 'larnin,' and the gas will have to be kept lighted all day to enable one to find his way through town" (*Herald*, February 2, 1866, cf. Oldt, 1910:921).

In another report on the newly opened Negro school, the paper focused on black children's physical features who "numbered seventeen" and came in "all sizes, ages, and shades of complexion, *straight hair, curly hair, and wool*" (March 7, 1866, cf. Oldt, 1910: 921)(italics mine).

Later, in 1870, the continuation of a separate school system for "colored" children and its economic feasibility for the city was questioned and scrutinized by the Board of Education. From a purely economic standpoint, the board passed a resolution to disband the school and admit "colored" students in ward schools. However, faced with a fierce opposition from white residents, both rich and poor, members of the board of education unanimously voted to repeal their earlier decision. As a justification for the reversal, during a board meeting in 1870 the president of Dubuque's board of education stated that "probably a majority of our citizens are strongly opposed to the discontinuance of the colored school," and that "a mingling of races" will lead to "discord in the schools, and a virtual exclusion of the colored children" (The Public Schools of Dubuque, 1878:74-75). In an editorial the *Dubuque Herald* portrayed white residents' opposition to desegregated public schools as a reflection of their patriarchal and benign concerns, who genuinely did not want to see any harm done to "colored children" in public schools (*The Daily Herald*, 1877).

Another discriminatory practice affecting black families in Dubuque was the existence of institutionalized two-tiered school tuition fees. Based on the figures for 1877 released by the Dubuque Public School System, black students had to pay $5.00 per month for attending the "colored school" compared to an average of $1.22 for white students in public schools (The Public Schools of Dubuque, 1878:10). From 1866 to 1877 the Dubuque "colored school" had an average of 20 students per school year. Had they been admitted to public schools, they would have comprised only 0.7 percent of the student population for all Dubuque schools (Ibid, 36).[24] Thus for eleven years white residents fiercely opposed racial integration in public schools for the fear of an almost nonexistent black student population.

Black residents in Dubuque did not have any organization or access to legal means to challenge segregated schools. There is almost no documentation of the African American community's position on separate schooling. The only report on black residents' dissatisfaction with the segregated school system is from 1875, when a petition was submitted to the board of education by "fifteen colored citizens" asking to disband the colored school. Commenting on the petition drive, the *Dubuque Daily Herald* (1875) stated that only fifteen people have signed the petition and that many other "colored citizens" are "understood to be opposed to it." The "colored school" was eventually discontinued in 1877, and black children were admitted to ward schools. However, this did not mean they were welcomed to public schools by white students. Racial hatred continued to plague Dubuque schools in the late 19th and early 20th centuries.

CONCLUSION

As a frontier town, Dubuque's record of race relations and treatment of its black residents during its first century of urban development contains both high and low points. This historical journey has witnessed unpleasant incidents of lynching but also admirable moments when Dubuque residents rushed to help fugitive slaves, as in the case of Ralph. Despite continued support for the southern lifestyle and slavery by a contingent of Dubuque residents, many of them poor and mostly of Irish origins, there were also strong anti-slavery voices in the community that at times united the entire city against bigotry. Dubuque's economic barometer, however, can measure the intensity of white-on-black racism, as Dubuque residents were more tolerant of blacks during the periods of economic prosperity. Thus the rise in anti-black sentiments, especially among the white working class during the Civil War, was a reflection of the city's stagnating economy and an imminent possibility of an influx of freed blacks into Dubuque's already battered and diminished labor force. But even in the absence of blacks, the midwestern frontier-town mentality from the outset epitomized racial, ethnic and linguistic conflicts and ensuing negative sentiments between first-generation European immigrants and Americanized European immigrants of earlier periods. Uprooted from their homelands and rejected by the older generation of immigrants on the east coast, frontier-town settlers in the midwest at times had to resort to force and violence in order to assert their ethnic presence on the western frontier. In *New Towns in the New World,* David Hamer (1990:7) argues that the American westward expansion and creation of frontier towns was "complicated by the fact that there was already the experience of two centuries of settlement on the eastern seaboard, and that experience created strong tradition both of subduing 'the wilderness' and of establishing new towns."

In comparing the growth and development of 19th century frontier towns in the United States, Canada, Australia, and New Zealand, Hamer also argues that in many ways the urban frontiers faced similar obstacles and challenges and hence shared similar features. Most significantly, high levels of transience forced settlers to make a commitment "to improvement of one's family's prospects rather than to the subordination of self-interest involved in building a community." This was particularly true for mining towns like Dubuque, "where suddenly swollen populations could vanish just as suddenly"(10). Thus in addition to racist culture generated by a long history of slavery, anti-black sentiments in Dubuque were also rooted in economic uncertainties because working class residents considered blacks a serious threat as potential contenders in the job market. Preventing blacks from getting settled in Dubuque during the 19th century was clearly justified by white workers and the poor with uncertain economic prospects, who understandably pursued their own selfish individual interests in a volatile urban environment.

The African American presence in Dubuque remained numerically insignificant throughout the 19th century. But during and after the Reconstruction era, African Americans kept asserting themselves in the fight against prejudice and racial inequality despite their minority status both in terms of numbers and political power. For example, black parents played a significant role in petitioning the Dubuque board of education for school desegregation in the 1870s. After the Civil War, black residents also held annual meetings and gatherings in celebration of the Emancipation Day. Except for occasional brief reports in the local papers, there is no documentation of the social, political and economic conditions and status of African Americans in Dubuque during and after the Reconstruction period. In general, newspaper accounts of African Americans in Iowa were always related to their criminal records such as murder, rape or theft.

In the words of one historian, "if colored groups engaged in worthwhile education or social projects — and certainly they did — newspaper readers were not often apprised of it" (Bergmann, 1948:45).[25] The only viable institution that brought Dubuque blacks together and provided some leadership seems to have been the African Methodist Episcopal Church (AME). In one case, the *Dubuque Telegraph Herald* (1903) reported on a club formed by the AME to establish a lodge of colored Masons in Dubuque.[26] However, the AME's role was mainly to assimilate blacks into the mainstream community and make their presence in Dubuque more acceptable for white residents.

Notes

1. Germans' superiority in the political and economic areas however remained a basis for Irish resentment.
2. An article published in the *Annals of Iowa* titled "Slaves in Iowa"(1903:66) states, "From this we learn that sixteen slaves, old and young, were owned by parties in Dubuque County. Whether the owners were permanent residents, or temporary sojourners, we have been unable to ascertain. But the fact is thus officially published in the 6th U.S. census, that slavery existed in Iowa territory."
3. The Congress made an exception for Missouri.
4. In the 1850s there were about 115,000 slaves living south of the Iowa borders in the state of Missouri alone (Dykstra, 1993:VIII).
5. For an historical account of the Iowa Underground Railroad movement see Berrier (2001).
6. For a detailed account of the Ralph's case see Parish, 1908; Petersen, 1957-1959; Swisher, 1926; and *Des Moines Register*, 1938.
7. Most of the aggressive measures against black settlement and their immigration into the state were brought to the Iowa legislature by politicians such as Edward Langworthy from Dubuque County. See Bergmann (1948:13-14) for details.
8. Sponsored by Senator Stephen Douglas, the Kansas-Nebraska Bill contained the provision that the question of slavery should be left to the decision of the territorial settlers themselves. See Ray (1965,

cf. The Columbia Encyclopedia (2001, sixth Edition), Columbia University Press.

9. According to the provisions of this act, all the citizens were obliged to assist federal marshals to apprehend fugitive slaves, and heavy penalties were imposed on those who assisted slaves to escape from bondage.
10. As a frontier town established on the western banks of the Mississippi river, Dubuque served as a hub for distribution of goods and services for new settlers in the region. But the city was also highly vulnerable to shifts in regional trade and population movement. See Mahoney (1990, Chapters 6 & 7) for an excellent account of the structure of regional urban system. In an epilogue he also discusses Dubuque's volatile economic status in the mid-1800s due to shifts in transportation routes, particularly the railroad networks.
11. See Dykstra (1982:71) and the *1860 U.S. Census-Iowa, Dubuque County*, the National Archives of the United States (1939).
12. The drastic increase in the state's African American population might have been the outcome of a failed racist policy. In 1851 the Iowa General Assembly passed an act which prohibited the new settlement of free blacks and mulattoes in Iowa, with the provision of hefty fines for those violating the act's rules. But the measure was never enforced, because the pro-Union editor of the Mount Pleasant *True Democrat,* the official newspaper to publish the measures, claimed "defective publication" and did not publish the racist measure (Bergmann, 1948:15).
13. The term "Copperhead" refers to individuals in the northern states who sympathized with the South during the Civil War.
14. Mahoney was an Irish Catholic who was elected twice to the Iowa state house in 1848 and 1858.
15. As pro-Confederacy sentiments became stronger in Dubuque city and County, there was also a growing resentment in Iowa toward the city's pro-slavery position. Statewide efforts to put an end to pro-South tendencies eventually forced the *Herald* to modify and soften its tone (Oldt, 1910:294).
16. I will discuss the issue in the 20th century Dubuque in chapter 8. For a theoretical discussion of what is better known as the "split labor market" theory, see Bonacich (1972).

17. 'Owenites' adhered to "the political and social scheme of Robert Owen, of Montgomeryshire, who in 1816 published a work to show that society was in a wretched condition, and all its institutions and religious systems were based on wrong principles. The prevailing system is competition, but Owen maintained that the proper principle is co-operation; he therefore advocated a community of property and the abolition of degrees of rank"(Brewer, 1898).
18. On this point see Ignatiev (1995:99).
19. See John Finch (cf. Ignatiev, 1995:99) for a description of the Irish immigrants' mindset and their opposition to black emancipation.
20. Some historians have disputed the "rich man's war and the poor man's fight" argument as was suggested by the *Herald* and its editor Dennis Mahoney. For example, Johnson (1996) applies interpretations by James Mcpherson and James Geary to Dubuque, and concludes that among the recruits the members of business class (the elite) were overrepresented while recruits from working class backgrounds were underrepresented (see chapter 4). However, his analysis is partially flawed, as his conclusion is only based on the 1860 data, or the period that the war efforts have just begun (chapter 5, see discussion of Table 5.1, p.315). His analysis for subsequent war years however indicates that as the war continued, more soldiers of the poor and working class origins were recruited into the Union army. This was also true for the reenlisted veterans toward the end of war (333, 347).
21. See the *Herald* editorial (October 11, 1863, cf. Oldt, 1910:301).
22. One can assess the presence of a more positive attitude of Iowans residing in the "interior towns" toward blacks and emancipation, as the black recruiter mentioned above was both trusted to carry large sums of money to buy recruits, and to represent his predominantly white town in Dubuque.
23. The five constitutional amendments were, "1) Negroes to vote in Iowa; 2) Negroes to be enrolled as militia; 3)Negroes to be counted in the census; 4) Negroes to be counted in the apportionment for senators and representatives; and 5) Negroes to occupy any office in the state"(cf. Oldt, 1910:367).
24. The figure excludes high school students.

25. The situation does not seem to have changed much, as even in the 1990s African Americans are mostly represented in the local newspaper for their alleged criminal activities and/or criminality (see Bagsarian, 1993a). This issue will be discussed in detail in the following chapters.
26. Except for the article cited above, the author could not find other reports on the black lodge and its fate.

CHAPTER 4

PERSISTENCE OF WHITE RACISM IN DUBUQUE: THE SECOND CENTURY

By 1890 the frontier had disappeared, Native Americans had been moved to reservations beyond the reach of the white frontier, and the United States was on her way to pursuing imperial interests in the continent and beyond. Industrialization was well on its way, bringing with it the rise of organized labor. From 1870 to 1900 Dubuque citizens saw their city grow and prosper, and at the turn of the 20th century Dubuque was a well-established midwestern metropolis in its own terms. But social and economic developments after WWI dashed any hopes Dubuquers had for their city's future growth. During the post-depression years, a persistently stagnant economy stalled the city's economic development and contributed to the flight of Dubuquers in search of better jobs and opportunities.

Racial tensions and the overt racism that plagued the city for a long time subsided in the post-WWII period. There are two reasons for this relative calm on the race relations front. First, due to factors discussed earlier, Dubuque's inhospitable environment forced some black residents to leave and discouraged others from moving in, leading to a virtual elimination of the minority population.[1] Second, although relatively insignificant at local level, civil rights victories for the minority populations in the 1960s also resulted in improvements in Dubuque's race relations. But civil rights gains were short lived, and many of the liberal policies of the earlier decades such as Affirmative Action came under attack by conservative politicians during the two Reagan administrations.

The 1980s was also a decade of economic downturn at the national level, and a period of devastating defeats for organized labor as a result of austerity measures taken by the government. In particular, by cutting production costs to maintain an acceptable rate of profit for investors, the private sector resorted to the well-known process of industrial and economic restructuring. This in turn effectively streamlined and weakened the labor force.[2] In particular, mid-size urban communities with industrial and manufacturing bases as well as small towns in rural areas were hit hard by the 1980s' recession and massive layoffs. With a strong industrial base, Dubuque was also not spared. Thousands of high-paying industrial jobs, mostly in Dubuque's corporate sector, were lost as a result of restructuring.[3]

As was the case during the 19th century, economic cycles and subsequent changes in employment and job opportunities continued to affect race and ethnic relations in the 20th century. This chapter documents the nature and extent of racial prejudice and discrimination during various economic cycles and political periods in the past century. In particular, I focus on the extent of white-on-black racism in connection with historical changes in the city's political economy.

PERPETUATION OF WHITE RACISM IN DUBUQUE (1900-1960)

As a northern state Iowa did not support Jim Crow measures by legal means. But like in many other northern states race relations after the Civil War were still shaky, though qualitatively different from those in the South. For instance, in 1884 the Iowa legislature passed a Civil Rights Act that declared all discrimination illegal in hotels, restaurants, theaters, barber shops and public transportation. But in practice the civil rights measures were mostly ignored, and discrimination continued in the next century in many communities including Dubuque. In the absence of human rights and minority advocacy groups, most cases of discrimination against nonwhites were not reported and went undocumented. The only available sources are local newspapers that periodically reported on blacks, mostly those who were visiting Dubuque on certain occasions. Two incidents at the turn of the 20th century provide vivid examples of prejudice and racism in the community.

The first reported incident involved a football team from Savannah, Georgia, which visited Dubuque in 1906. According to newspaper accounts, the team consisted of sixteen players, fifteen white and one "Negro." Staying in a local hotel, the hotel management refused to serve the "Negro" in the main dining hall with the rest of the team. Instead, he proposed that "his dinner would be served to him privately in an upper apartment," and that "he could order everything on the bill-of-fare." Initially, the white team members accepted the proposal, but when the teachers found out about the deal they asked the team to leave unless the "Negro" be allowed to join them in the dining room. Management stood firm on this issue, "Knowing that their regular patrons had far more claim upon their consideration than these youth who were to be here for the one day," and the team left the hotel and dined at another local restaurant (*Galena Gazette*, 1906:3).

The second reported incident took place in 1907, when the seven member Dixie Jubilee Singers, all African Americans, were invited to perform at St. Joseph College (present day Loras College). In an account of the incident, the *Dubuque Telegraph Herald* (1907) reported that once in town, "they were not able to find a hotel which had a vacant room, or at least they were told that." Anticipating the problem, the college organizers tried to make arrangements in advance, but apparently all but two hotel-keepers "flatly refused to accept the colored people as guests." One of the hotel keepers who initially agreed to take them in later on changed his mind, and apparently fearing public reaction he stated that "under no consideration would he house the colored singers." Eventually the company was fed and housed at the college facilities. Upon their departure, the group's leader commented "This is the first time we have ever been unable to secure hotel accommodations in a northern town, we have experienced difficulty in the South, but never in the North" (ibid.).

Another prevalent anti-black sentiment of the time was a deep-rooted fear of miscegenation, particularly between black men and white women. The occurrence of an adulterous relationship between a black man and a married white woman and the birth of their child in the first decade of the past century became a scandalous event in town. Reporting the incident, the *Dubuque Telegraph Herald* stated that "the awful story of 'the Clansman' and 'Leopard's Spots' was brought home in Dubuque."[4] The paper then commented, "the community in general is incensed" for the scandalous birth of a bi-racial baby, as "the leopard cannot change his spots," and consequently the white woman's husband reportedly "*commanded that the wife be taken from his home, never again to darken its doors*" (*Dubuque Telegraph Herald*, 1906)(italics mine). With a subtitle that read "Have Fear of Black Evil," the report continued to describe the malice brought on by the black presence in the community, especially those who were "in company with white girls." Finally, the report reflected on public opinion that "the shame of it lies with the woman," but the "Negro" male should also be kept "where he belongs." The birth of the "mixed breed" child was apparently the third within a few weeks, causing "hostile spirit toward blacks similar to that of the South."

The 1920s witnessed the resurgence of the Ku Klux Klan both in Iowa and Dubuque that negatively affected many Dubuque residents including the Germans, Catholics and to some extent African Americans.[5] A persistent prejudice toward African-Americans, combined with Dubuque's localized ethnocentrism continued to affect the tiny nonwhite minority who were politically passive for the most part, and hence vulnerable to discrimination. Although before WWII individual African-Americans were in communication with the National Association for the Advancement of Colored People's national headquarters (NAACP), Dubuque's black residents in most part were legally unprotected (Brigham and Wright, 2001:334). In the absence of a local NAACP chapter, discrimination cases involving blacks were handled by the organization's branch in Waterloo, a city 90 miles to the west. In most cases, the NAACP lawyers were very effective in defending blacks. In 1930, for example, a white woman in Dubuque "sought the arrest of a young black teenager who allegedly bumped into her while running." This incident coincided with the killing of a 12-year-old white boy in which Dubuque residents suspected the involvement of a black culprit. The black teenager was sentenced to seven years, to be served in a state training school. Since the boy's father was unemployed, he sought legal help and eventually the Waterloo NAACP branch got involved. Efforts by many Dubuque residents and the boy's NAACP attorney eventually led to his release (323).

A recurring problem for African Americans who came to Dubuque in the 1930s, either as visitors or migrant workers, was discrimination in housing and public accommodation. Occasional statements made by longtime Dubuque residents confirm that this indeed was the case. One example, is the recollection of several workers who, as members of the local unions, were interviewed for the Iowa Labor History Oral Project. A business agent for the American Federation of Musicians (AFM), who worked with union bands, remembered the way even the nationally known Duke Ellington black band was denied public accommodation in the 1930s Dubuque.[6] In another occasion, a John Deere worker who in his youth worked at his uncle's Dubuque bar in the 1930s, also stated in an interview that when "a colored person came there and he wanted a shot of whiskey, he got it in a colored glass and he drank it outside the door." He also remembered that "colored people" were advised to "not to stop for anything" and "not to let the sun set on them" while in town.[7]

In the absence of advocacy groups such as the Human Rights Commission to monitor and document discriminatory practices by landlords and realtors in the 1930s, individual accounts and observations are required. Chapter 2 used census data for various city wards to examine the presence and extent of segregation in housing. Confirming a racially segregated environment, Joe Blaser, a typographer for a local paper who was interviewed for the Iowa Labor History Project recalled segregated black residences in town: "There used to be a few black families living up on Rock Street, right up Eight Street. They were all segregated in that one place."[8] In fact, there were so few blacks in town that they were often remembered as "novelty." The following comment by a worker is more indicative of white residents' limited social and cultural experience than their prejudice toward blacks:

> When I was just a kid ..., see, a colored person in the town, hey, about the only time you seen one was when a carnival or a circus come to town. Other than that you didn't see them. We didn't have minorities in this town. This was a prejudistic town. There's no doubt about that.[9]

Also of note, is the role of the local police in the 1930s to keep blacks out of Dubuque. Unlike in metropolitan areas with large African American population, where whites took the law in their own hands to "keep blacks in their place," the police in Dubuque were actively involved in preventing blacks from coming in.[10] When in an interview a Dubuque worker was asked about the presence of "a kind of policy in Dubuque in the Depression times to keep blacks out," he remembered that "there were two policemen that strolled the beat downtown" and "whenever a colored person would land in the city of Dubuque and walk up that main street" they were warned by the policemen "we don't want to see you here after sundown."[11] A black railroad maintenance worker for the Chicago-Dubuque line remembered how in the 1950s the "police officers would greet disembarking black passengers [in Dubuque] and tell them to get back on train" (James Sutton, quoted in McAllister, 1991).[12]

Blacks continued to be discriminated against during and after WWII. A longtime resident recalled in retrospect how overt discrimination was rampant in 1940s Dubuque, as some stores had signs that read "We do not patronize Negroes." An African American resident also remembered "late-night phone calls from the Dubuque Police Department asking if her family could take in a black who had been turned away at the hotels and needed a place to stay" (Pat Scott, quoted in Kraske, 1983b). Racial discrimination in public accommodations was also a normal practice in the 1950s Dubuque. But not all the residents conformed to segregation. For example, a teacher at the Immaculate Conception Academy, a Catholic boarding school, remembers how her students used to challenge discrimination and prejudice in the late 1950s:

> I had charge of some 80 "boarders," several of them African Americans from Chicago. When their parents came to visit or to pick them up, the Dubuque restaurants and hotels would not admit them. So it was routine for blacks to sleep and eat at the academy. Sometimes a large group of white girls would deliberately take a black friend to a restaurant. On being told the eating place did not serve blacks, the girls would move out en-masse, to the restaurant's dismay.[13]

RACE RELATIONS IN DUBUQUE SINCE THE CIVIL RIGHTS ERA

The advent of the Civil Rights movement during the early 1960s also affected Dubuque—as committees were formed to deal with civil rights violations, hotels and restaurants were forced to open their doors to black patrons, and employers were required to hire blacks and other ethnic minorities under Affirmative Action provisions (Kraske, 1983b). But as in many other communities, civil rights measures did not change people's hearts and minds and prejudicial attitudes remained strong in Dubuque. A longtime Dubuque resident who has since moved to Florida remembered a bus ride to Dubuque in 1968, when a group of young white army draftees from Dubuque cheered the news of the assassination of Martin Luther King as it came over the radio (Arnold, 1991).

Aside from prejudicial attitudes, blacks were greatly inconvenienced and disadvantaged when it came to jobs, housing, and public accommodation in town. For instance, an African American who moved to Dubuque in the mid-1960s complained about difficulties she had in finding a job. After several unsuccessful attempts on her own she finally got a job by filling out the application brought by a friend in order to conceal her skin color and ethnic identity (cf. Burns Schuster, 1965). When and if hired, black workers had to cope with workplace harassment and their coworkers' prejudice. Ruby Sutton, a black Dubuque resident and long-time activist recalls how in the 1960s white coworkers at the Illinois Central Railroad Station in Dubuque harassed her husband and "put rocks and dirt in his lunch pail" in order to force him quit his job (Ruby Sutton, cf. Barnes, 2001:106). She also remembered that before the passage of Equal Rights laws in Dubuque in the 1960s landlords "could say they weren't going to rent to you," and when it became a law "they would say it was already rented." As late as 1969 Sutton recalls the experience when she and two other white coworkers went to a restaurant but were denied "public accommodation" because of her race.[14] A Catholic nun and a long-time Dubuque peace activist also shared her recollection of an incident of discrimination in public accommodation in the early 1960s, when she and other nuns "phoned one Dubuque restaurant after another" to find out if the Chicago African American parents of several students would be allowed to eat there. In the end, only one restaurant in town accommodated them.[15]

Overall, the media in Dubuque do not seem to have paid much attention to the Civil Rights movement's objectives, particularly related to local problems. The only critical report on the life and times of Dubuque's ethnic and racial minorities in the 1960s is a series of articles by Peter Anderson entitled "*The*

Invisible Man," which were published in the *Dubuque Telegraph Herald* in 1969. Anderson (1969b) acknowledged persisting racism and discrimination practiced by Dubuque businesses and employers, real estate agencies, the police and "even the children on the streets" whose prejudicial attitudes and discriminatory acts took varied forms such as "the snub, the sneer, the look of disdain, the crude word, the aggressive act." His report ends with his concluding remarks that racism can be seen "everywhere, even in church." Anderson noticed that while African Americans comprised only 1/10 of 1 percent, white racism kept blacks segregated in a "sordid, cloistral neighborhood" (Anderson, 1969a). In one case, plans to build an apartment complex for low income families in 1968 were met with fierce opposition. Perceiving low income housing as a potential factor for attracting blacks to Dubuque, the plan's caretaker received a life-threatening phone call from a Dubuquer who stated that "if you keep on building that nigger heaven, you'll wind up in heaven yourself a lot sooner than you think" (Anderson, 1969b). Blacks were also ignored by Dubuque churches in the 1960s, and attempts by a few congregations to invite blacks to their churches were met by strong opposition from some church members (Anderson, 1969d). In an interesting commentary on Dubuquers' fear of blacks, Anderson scolds city residents for their negative attitudes toward blacks and their fear of losing jobs to a "minimal 94 black residents" in town. He then questions the validity of this "faulty folklore" and "the numerical absurdity inherent in the 90,000 to 94 odds"(1969b).

Despite some gains during the 1960s, racial prejudice and discrimination against African Americans in Dubuque continued into the next decade. One incident in particular reveals the depth of racial strife in Dubuque and that civil rights gains of the 1960s in the rest of the nation had little bearing on this city. In 1970 the president of the University of Dubuque, a four-year college affiliated with the Presbyterian Church, was forced to resign his post after his plans to establish a "Culture Center" for African American students were made public.[16] In an interview with a local reporter the president stated that immediately after his announcement, there was a "crescendo of racist attitudes among some members of the administration, students and the community that built to crisis proportions," which forced him to offer his resignation (William G. Chalmers, quoted in Anderson, 1970).

Later on, when black students from the city's colleges planned to stage a "Black Art Experience," an anonymous note was sent to them threatening to "blow up" the black "Culture Center" at the University of Dubuque, if they put on the show. SPONGE, which stood for Society for the Prevention of Niggers Getting Everything, signed the note (*Dubuque Telegraph Herald*, 1970).[17]

Black educators did not fare any better than black students. In rare occasions they were hired by the Dubuque school system, but they had a hard time finding a rental unit or house to buy. In one of its first reports of racial discrimination, the newly formed Human Rights Commission noted that in 1969 a school teacher was "unable to find an apartment and was forced to stay with a family while teaching in the public school" (*Dubuque Telegraph Herald,* 1969).[18] As a consequence, after a year the teacher moved out of town.

During the 1980s the already critical state of race relations in Dubuque further deteriorated, as after two decades of prosperity the city's economy began to slow down while the unemployed scrambled for scarce jobs in town. The 1980s also witnessed a resurgence of racism and hate crimes ranging from blatant acts of hate to dissemination of demeaning material and offensive racial and ethnic jokes. The first notable hate crime took place in June 1982, when someone poured gasoline onto the lawn of an elderly Asian couple. The carefully poured fuel burned the grass spelling out the word "Chink." The incident forced the couple out of Dubuque, and they subsequently moved to California (Kraske, 1982a). In another apparent case of racial hatred the lawn of the United Pentecostal Church in Dubuque was burned in the shape of a cross. A nontraditional and "noisy" church, the hundred and twenty members usually prayed out loud together, which according to newspaper reports included singing and "fervent worship" resembling the worship style of black churches. [19] Perhaps out of the fear of retribution the church pastor reportedly stated that he believed the cross burning was not racially motivated (Gabe, 1983).

The third serious case in 1982 was a cross burned in a black family's yard. In this last case a white male was allegedly angered because "spics and niggers" were getting jobs at FDL Foods, Inc.[20] He was also upset because several blacks had been seen in the company of white women in Dubuque (Kraske, 1982b).[21] According to the Human Rights Commission director, after the massive layoffs at the city's two major employers, namely, John Deere and FDL Foods, blacks on the city's working class "North side" were warned that "if they are employed in some city factories there could be trouble" (Mat Lorenz, quoted in Kraske, op. cit.).

The above-mentioned incidents and alleged job discrimination charges against FDL (formerly Dubuque Packing Company) in its manner of hiring African Americans, Asians and older workers angered the progressive elements in the community. A coalition of about twenty organizations was formed in defense of human rights, and 250 people demonstrated to protest the persistence of race-based discrimination in the work place and other social situations in Dubuque. The charges were not substantiated beyond street protests, but there are indications that racial prejudice particularly against African Americans was prevalent among both workers and members of the city's old ruling elite. Each group had its own reason. While industrial workers found black workers' entry into a depressed job market to be a threat to their job security, employers were apprehensive of new investments by outside capital and its inflationary effects on wages due to increased employment opportunities. Related to the latter group's argument, in the early 1980s there was a widespread belief among Dubuque residents that outside industries were discouraged to come to Dubuque "because local power brokers feared the low wage scale would be threatened and that new industries would bring in black people" (Hendricks, 1983). To document the extent of prejudicial attitudes and racist beliefs held by the members of the ruling elite in town is difficult. But this was accomplished in the early 1980s during an informal conversation between Jonathan Raban, a British traveler and novelist, and R.C. Wahlert, the Chief Executive Officer of FDL Foods, a major meat packing facility in town. In response to Raban's curiosity of "why there are no blacks in town," Wahlert responded:

> I don't know why that is. *I guess they just don't like the climate around here.* I don't blame them. I don't like the climate. The winters here, they'd freeze the ass off you. Hell, it's a goddamn awful climate. But it's a wonderful climate for hogs. You know we've got ten times as many hogs as people? *Two million people in this region; twenty million hogs.....no blacks, and let's hope it stays that way.* (cf. Raban, 1981:152)(italics mine)

Minorities continued to be harassed, discriminated against and subjected to indignation and insults in the 1980s. A 1983 article in the *Dubuque Telegraph Herald* reflected on various ethnic minorities' experience of living in an all white community: Arnold Neely, an African American who worked in the city's Water Department complained of "being stared at as he walks downtown." Patty Perez, a Hispanic, was "conscious of keeping her hands in view" whenever she was in a store so that "she is not suspected of shoplifting." Another black female resident was told by a beauty parlor owner that "if I have you as a customer, I will lose other business"(Kraske, 1983b).

Perhaps one of the most controversial events related to the state of race relations and human rights in the 1980s was the election of Clarence Duffy to the Dubuque Human Rights Commission in 1982. A WWII veteran and a chef in Dubuque restaurants Duffy was also the editor of a newsletter, the *Little Dublin News* which claimed to be the voice of the Irish in Dubuque. First published in 1980, this monthly newsletter took a "nostalgic look at the good old days on Dubuque's south side" where most of the Irish Dubuquers resided. Gradually the newsletter also became the unofficial voice of certain factions within the working class who were adversely affected by the 1980s' economic restructuring in Dubuque. For instance, in addition to its nostalgic narratives of the bygone past the newsletter also published ethnic and sexist jokes that poked fun at African Americans, Jews, German Americans, migrant workers and women. African Americans were subjected to the newsletter's harsh racist attacks who on occasions were referred to as "jungle bunnies" and other derogatory labels (Pins, 1983a). Compared to Germans, blacks seem to have been considered as "the lesser of the two evils" by the newsletter. This is a class-based and selective prejudice, as the former symbolically represented upper-class power and money.[22] As a powerless group blacks served as a reference point for all nonwhite workers who threatened white workers' jobs and economic security. Thus in the newsletter the editor let both Germans and blacks know their real social status and place in town.[23]

Under the "illegal alien" rubric, the *Little Dublin*'s editor also attacked migrant laborers and anyone who seemed not to belong to a "white European Dubuque." For instance, showing a picture of three women who seemed to be Asians the newsletter commented "we are hiding out these illegal aliens and will raffle them off at our St. Pat's dance" (Ibid). The newsletter also revived the stereotype of a migrant laborer as a lazy individual who is taking advantage of American welfare (*The Little Dublin News*, June 1981: 8).

Finally, women were also targets of sexist jokes in the newsletter. The following one-line anecdote appeared in the June 1982 issue: "What does a woman have two and a cow four? Feet.[sic]" In 1984, another anecdote blamed a slowdown in out-of-town mail delivery on "all those stupid broads they have working in the post office now"(*Little Dublin News*, April 1984). Immediately, the American Postal Workers Union representing Dubuque postal workers demanded Clarence Duffy's resignation from the Human Rights Commission. In addition, outraged by the racist and sexist tone of the newsletter and insensitivity of city officials to Duffy's election to the Human Rights Commission, a multi-ethnic coalition of concerned Dubuque citizens asked Duffy to resign or otherwise be removed from the post (Kraske, 1983a).[24] But apparently Duffy had the support of many Dubuque residents. For instance, in an almost unanimous show of support, the city council voted 6-1 to retain Duffy on the Human Rights Commission. In Duffy's support, John Klauer, a city council member stated that "if members of a coalition fighting the appointment of Clarence Duffy don't like it in Dubuque, they can leave" (John Klauer, quoted in Pins, 1983b). Another council member reacted to the coalition's persistence in its demand for Duffy's removal by commenting that after listening to coalition members' arguments, he can understand "a lot of reasons behind the prejudice toward black people" (Don Deich, quoted in Pins, 1983c). The city mayor also contributed to the debate on Clarence Duffy's membership in the HRC. In one of the city council meetings he scolded the coalition members for their opposition to Duffy's appointment, and stated that "I am ashamed of you for having used this forum to divide our city" (James Brady, quoted in Pins, op. cit.). Klauer was later forced out of office by a 99 percent vote (Pins, 1983d), and James Brady and Don Deich made public apologies for their actions at the council meetings (Kraske, 1983c). Duffy later toned down his attacks on ethnic groups and, following the above incidents and several other hate crimes between 1989 and 1991, he made reconciliatory remarks in one of his editorials, concluding "we know that all are created by God to be equal before him.... and, too, how often has it been the Irish Catholics who have been the object of hate and prejudice?" (December 1991:8). The newsletter's attacks on migrant workers and women in the 1980s ought to be appreciated within the context of a depressed economy with a relatively strong but highly vulnerable organized labor. Faced with massive layoffs and high rates of unemployment many workers considered the two groups both as potential strikebreakers and competitors in a tight market for seasonal and minimum wage jobs.

Dubuque's image as a quaint midwestern city was shattered in 1989 when a charred cross was found in the debris of an African American family's garage. This and bitter memories of cross burning incidents in the early 1980s led to the mobilization of Dubuque's African Americans, who were also supported by a small but resolved contingent of community activists. In response to these hate crimes, in mid-1989 the Dubuque Human Rights Commission issued a policy statement entitled "Strategies to Improve Race Relations in Dubuque." The policy statement later led to the formation of a task force that formulated the controversial Constructive Integration Plan (CIP) to bring in hundred "families of color" to Dubuque. The ensuing community reaction to the Constructive Integration Plan, both positive and negative; including the involvement of the Ku Klux Klan; and steps taken by Dubuque officials to address its dismal record of racial diversity merits a more careful attention and analysis. Because of the historical significance and intensity of racial tensions in the late 1980s and early 1990s, I discuss these events and the CIP's objectives in more detail in chapters 5 and 6.

CONCLUSION

Historical accounts of race relations in Dubuque in this and the preceding chapter should not be construed as an indictment of all Dubuque residents for their alleged racist beliefs and deeds, as many Dubuquers in numerous occasions have effectively opposed racism by confronting racist elements in their town. The apparent disdain for African Americans and continued efforts by a contingent of Dubuque residents to exclude them from city's social life in the last two centuries have been based on deep-rooted racist beliefs developed historically, revised occasionally and disseminated and promoted at the national level. Even the homegrown and selective prejudice toward Dubuque residents of German descent in the 1920s was influenced by a nationally promoted anti-German propaganda during and after WWI. One has to consider active white racist elements in Dubuque, or victimizers, as also being victims of a social process and a political economy that has a life bigger and a reality much beyond their immediate community. At this juncture, the important question both at local and national levels is whether or not there is a link between abrupt periods of racial and ethnic intolerance and historical changes in the nature and overall state of economy.

Dubuque represents a typical midwestern urban community. Its residents have striven to improve their lot, and at times have struggled to survive through harsh economic periods. Related to Dubuque, two periods of intense racial and ethnic strife and resurgence of white supremacist activities stand out: the 1920s and the 1980s. These were also periods during which the city was hit hard by a local and national economy mired in economic crises. In both periods subsequent organizational restructuring by most corporate entities resulted in high rates of unemployment and inflicted many in this working class community.

Continuing the historical journey reveals that extreme ethnocentrist beliefs and racist attitudes do not develop independent of other social, economic and political factors; and that their extent and intensity seem to be adversely correlated with the communities' overall social and economic well-being.[25] Also, an historical examination of racism in Dubuque supports the proposition that a racist ideology developed and sanctioned at the national level can survive and even thrive where targeted racial minority groups, in this case African Americans, have minimal or no representation in the community.

Notes

1. For a comparison of data pertaining to minority population between 1920 and 1950, see chapter 2, Tables 5 and 6.
2. On this issue see Bluestone and Harrison (1982).
3. Chapter 8 discusses in detail the outcomes of industrial restructuring and its effects on race relations in Dubuque.

4. This was apparently in reference to the popular novel of the time, *The Leopard's Spot* by Thomas Dixon (1902), in which he fantasized on the evils of inter-racial intercourse during the Reconstruction period.
5. Historical documentation of the Klan's presence in the 1920s indicates that blacks were not the main targets of the white supremacists' agenda. Since during the two periods of 1920s and 1980-1990s the Klan played a significant role in Dubuque's race relations, I will discuss it in more detail in chapter 5.
6. Gavin, Mark, Dubuque. Interview by Paul Kelso, October 27, 1977. *Iowa Labor History Oral Project*, Iowa Federation of Labor, AFL-CIO. State Historical Society of Iowa, Iowa City, p. 32.
7. Grimes, Donald, Dubuque. Interview by Merle O. Davis, April 30, 1982. *Iowa Labor History Oral Project*, Iowa Federation of Labor, AFL-CIO. State Historical Society of Iowa, Iowa City, p. 49-50.
8. Blaser, Joe, Dubuque. Interview by Paul Kelso, October 17, 1977. *Iowa Labor History Oral Project*, Iowa Federation of Labor, AFL-CIO. State Historical Society of Iowa, Iowa City, p. 31.
9. Donald Grimes, interview, ibid, p. 49.
10. See the introductory chapter for a comparative analysis of the treatment of blacks in the pre- and post-civil rights era.
11. Mark Gavin, Interview, Ibid, p. 33. Paul Kelso, the interviewer, kept pressing the interviewees from Dubuque on their knowledge of a vigilante group known as the "Yellow Hats," who allegedly helped the police and the unions in keeping blacks out of Dubuque in the 1930s. None of the interviewees acknowledged the existence of such a group, and /or the union's role in supporting them. See, for example, Paul Kelso's interviews with Mark Gavin, Ibid, p. 33; and Elmer Vorweld, September 8, 1977, *Iowa Labor History Oral Project*, Iowa Federation of Labor, AFL-CIO, State Historical Society of Iowa, Iowa City, p. 23.
12. For a historical and sociological investigation of this practice see James Loewen's recent book (2005) in which he traces the origins of all-white "Sundown towns" to the post-Civil War period.
13. Sister Dorothy Hennessey, personal correspondence, November 7, 1993.

14. The incident prompted her to contact Dubuque's city manager and eventually establish Dubuque's Human Rights Commission. The HRC then began to send white "testers" out to see whether rental properties were available for black would-be tenants (Ibid, 105-106).
15. Sister Dorothy Hennessey, personal correspondence, November 7, 1993.
16. In 1970, there were a total of 75 African American students registered in the city's three colleges: 37 at the University of Dubuque, 30 at Loras College, and 8 at Clarke College (Ryder, 1970). According to the census data, there were a total of 100 African Americans residing in Dubuque in the same year (see Table 14).
17. Ignoring the threat, however, the Black Art Experience went on as planned, but the FBI was called in for investigation (ibid.).
18. The Dubuque Human Rights Commission was established in 1969.
19. The church only had one black family among its members.
20. At the time, the FDL Foods, Inc. was a corporate meat packing plant and one of the two major employers in town.
21. The fear of inter-racial socialization and miscegenation are still alive in this community. As late as 1991, several white female students who socialized with African Americans talked to the author about being harassed and insulted by their neighbors, receiving obscene phone calls, and being labeled as "Nigger lovers."
22. See chapter 1 for the newsletter's racist attacks on Dubuquers of German and Jewish background.
23. See for example *the Little Dublin News* (January 1982:4).
24. After several meetings with the Mayor and City Council members, the coalition modified its position by dropping its demand for Duffy's removal, contingent upon his attendance in a cultural sensitivity workshop (Kraske, 1983d).
25. That is, economic growth and prosperity contribute to a higher degree of racial and ethnic tolerance.

CHAPTER 5

CHOOSING THE SCAPEGOATS: PRESENCE OF THE KLAN IN RACIAL AND ETHNIC CONFLICTS

Race and ethnic relations in Dubuque during WWI and the 1920s took a sharp twist in terms of the nature and scope of prejudice and discrimination. The American government's involvement in WWI and its siding with England stirred strong anti-German sentiments all over the nation, but more so in communities with heavy concentrations of German Americans. The anti-German hysteria hit Iowa in general and Dubuque in particular during the war years. The crisis was intensified by some of the war proclamations issued in 1917 and 1918 by Iowa's Governor Harding. One of the most controversial was the Language Proclamation, which made English the official language of the United States and the State of Iowa. The proclamation also condemned foreign languages as being disruptive of the "peace and quiet" of communities. The Language Proclamation was meant mainly for Germans, or at least in Dubuque it was used to harass German Americans and suppress their German cultural roots and identity (Rapp, 1991). Based on some estimates, Dubuque's four German newspapers in 1917 had a circulation of 12,000 or so, but by 1925 "such newspapers were hard to find" (ibid.).

Anti German sentiments during the 1920s were also inflamed by the strong presence of the Ku Klux Klan in Dubuque with its clear anti-Catholic slogans in a predominantly Catholic town. While the first wave of the Klan activities during the Reconstruction Era aimed at maintaining the southern way of life by suppressing newly freed blacks, the second wave in the 1920s had different and far more ambitious ideals of white supremacy.

In the absence of an all-out migration of southern blacks to the northern states, the Klan revival of the 1920s had to resort to new strategies and find new scapegoats to promote "purity," "Protestantism," and "nativity" to support its slogan of "one-hundred-percent Americanism." In Iowa, the Klan's focus shifted from blacks to Roman Catholics, Jews, foreigners and organized labor during the 1920s. In the words of one chronicler of the Klan activities in Iowa, various groups became handy scapegoats for the Klan, including "... Catholics, whose church hierarchy sought to control the United States from abroad; Jews, who dominated the finance of the country; [and] immigrants, who come here for what they can get out of the country" (Johnson, 1967:45).

The Klan in the 1920s was more concerned with local social problems, which it attributed to certain groups and social classes. In the Midwest, the Klan targeted "the commercial and industrial elite" as the "villains" who, representing an emerging corporate capitalist sector "had taken control of state and local governments in the years after 1900." This was at a time when American capitalism was making a transition from the late 19th century competitive era into a new era of corporate-monopoly capitalism in the early 20th century.[1] At the same time the new era signaled the end of the Midwest's "Golden Age of Agriculture" and its political clout in Washington, making it the nation's economic backwater. Subsequently, the Ku Klux Klan did not target members of the old ruling elite who represented the competitive sector, many of whom were Klan members themselves. Rather, its members vented their anger at the "new elite" who, "under the guise of boosterism and economic progress," undermined traditional values and compromised ethics for more profit (Neymeyer, 1995:59-60).

Estimates of Klan membership in Iowa during the 1920s vary from 75,000 to 250,000, and Iowa ranked twelfth in the nation in terms of Klan membership. Even assuming the low estimate to be correct, this is impressive since the state's population at the time totaled less than 2.5 million (Johnson, 1967:33-34).[2] Klan activities and rhetoric during the 1920s were not aimed at blacks and, in the case of the Dubuque Klan Chapter, none of the local black residents were direct targets of Klan activities.

Similar to many other Iowa communities the Ku Klux Klan became active and highly visible in Dubuque during the 1924-1926 period. This was the result of a combination of efforts by the local Klan chapter that facilitated Klan activities in the city, and the national Klan organization, which used Dubuque as a regional platform to propagate its ideology.[3] Many who have lived the 1920s have testified that the Dubuque area Klan chapters "ranged from ultra-patriotic social clubs to vehement anti-Catholic organizations" (McCormick, 1975).

Some believe the conflict between Klan members and their opponents in Dubuque only involved "Caucasians" (Rapp, 1991). A pamphlet titled *100 percent American Songs* and distributed by the *Dubuque Kounty Klan Kuartette* in the 1920s supports Rapp's claim, as out of seven songs in the pamphlet three are specifically about Catholics, and in another song there are references to the "Jew," the "bootlegger" and the "weak-kneed man." The Dubuque Klan's attacks on Roman Catholics were nasty and direct. Song number four in the pamphlet titled *Kluxing 'round the Romans* starts with the following lines:

> Kluxing 'round the Romans in Dubuque makes life
> worthwhile,
> Kluxing 'round the Romans gives us all a healthy smile.
> We lick them as they come, for they're always full of
> Rum,
> Dubuquers like to Klux around the Romans.

Spreading the fear that Catholics have taken over America, under the title *Oh, He Ain't Gonna Rule No More*, song number three starts with:

> Oh, I'd rather be a Klansman,
> In a robe of snowy white,
> Than be a Roman Catholic priest,
> In a robe as dark as night.

At the local level the Klan was apparently apprehensive of Catholics dominating the city's educational system. Some have interpreted the Dubuque community school board's infighting between 1924 and 1926 as a reflection of an internal struggle between supporters of the Klan and Catholic members (McCormick, 1975:44). An excerpt from the *100 percent American Songs* pamphlet sheds some light on the Klan's concerns over the question of education. Titled *Keep our Public School Bells Ringing*, song number four ends with the following:

> We must put our men in office,
> Who will keep our laws enforced,
> Or our school bell will cease ringing,
> And the Parochial school endorsed.

Although varied in tone the city's two leading papers, *The Dubuque Times Journal* and *The Dubuque Telegraph Herald* also reported on the Klan's presence in positive terms, with the latter being the most supportive. The first Klan gathering (Klonklave) was held in August 1925 on a private farm north of city boundaries.[4] One underground anti-Klan Catholic newspaper claimed that J.A. Loetscher, a prominent industrialist of the time, leased the farm to the Klan (*Tolerance,* 1924b). A day before the scheduled Klonklave the *Dubuque Times Journal* reported the Klan prediction that between 50,000 and 75,000 Klan members are expected to come to Dubuque, and that "all highways leading into Dubuque will be filled with a veritable stream of motor caravans bearing placards reading "100 percent Americanism," "KIGY," "on to Dubuque," "KKK," etc." (*Dubuque Times Journal,* 1925b).[5] According to Klan officials, an estimated crowd of 56,000 people "the majority of them being Klan men" paid admission fees to attend the Dubuque rally (*Dubuque Telegraph Herald*, 1925c:10; *Dubuque Times Journal,* 1925d).[6] The gathering was in fact a district Klonklave for the states of Iowa, Illinois and Wisconsin. The *Dubuque Times Journal* reported that "invitations have been sent from Dubuque to every Klan organization in Iowa, Illinois,

Indiana, Wisconsin and Minnesota, and local headquarters state that letters which they have received indicate that a large crowd will be in attendance"(1925a).

Although there was no official representation of the Dubuque Klan organization in the 1925 gathering, the *Dubuque Times Journal* reported that "the crowd included several thousand Dubuquers, members of the hooded order as well as visitors and sightseers"(1925c). But there are indications that the Dubuque Klan organization was actively involved in planning and organizing the event. The paper also reported that railroad fares "have been reduced one-fourth for visitors wishing to attend the Klonklave." Similarly, the Dubuque Electric Company, the city's major transportation firm ran special bus services between downtown and the Peru Road in the city's outskirts, where the Klonklave was held (1925a). In describing the scheduled events for the Klonklave, the *Times* reported that in addition to speakers, airplane stunts, community singers and concerts, the organization was negotiating "for the services of a performer, who, it is declared, will slide down a cable with his clothes aflame, representing a human fiery cross"(Ibid.). The entertainment included "a ladies team from Davenport, a male quartet from Muscatine, and a band from Waterloo" (Johnson, 1967:51, 71).

While the public was allowed to hear the speeches and take part in the festivities, it was excluded from initiation ceremonies for new members. Many were attracted to the Klan gathering by its highly publicized promise of "fun and entertainment for all." For instance, in addition to the adult participants, the paper reported that "between 15,000 and 17,000 children under the age of 15 years" were also admitted free of charge. Based on the Klan official claims, the report concluded that the KlonKlave "was the largest public gathering in the city in its history" (ibid.). For the record, both prior to and after the Klonklave none of the two papers published editorials in condemnation of the Klan or the City officials who allowed the gathering. Also, there were no letters to the editors by Dubuque residents who might have found the event questionable.

The second Klan gathering was held in August 1926, also on the same farm located on Peru Road north of town. Compared to the first rally attendance was significantly lower, as reportedly around 30,000 participated in the second tri-state Klonklave (*the Dubuque Telegraph Herald*, 1926d: 18). Estimates by the *Des Moines Register* (1926) were far below the attendance figures furnished to the local paper by Klan members, as it estimated that somewhere between 5,000 to 20,000 participated in the event (cf. Johnson, 1967:74). Even that is an impressive figure, considering the fact that Dubuque's population at the time was around 40,000.

Obtaining the parade permit in 1926, a Dubuque Klan representative claimed that around 1,000 Dubuquers were Klan members, excluding the women's auxiliary organization of the Dubuque County (*Dubuque Times Journal,* 1926b). Similar to the previous year, the Dubuque Electric Company operated special bus services between downtown and the farm where the Klonklave was held (*Dubuque Times Journal, 1926c).* According to a local Klan spokesperson, many Dubuque organizations also helped them to organize the rally. For instance, he described in detail the logistics of food provision at the rally that "will be operated by various Protestant churches throughout the city and by several of the most prominent fraternal organizations" (*The Dubuque Telegraph Herald*, 1925c:2).

The *Dubuque Times Journal* reported "it was a memorable day for the Klan, men and women, and the thousands who joined them in their celebration." The report then praised the Klan for their organizational skills and stated "the manner in which the thousands of automobiles were handled without serious congestion of traffic speaks extremely well for the Dubuque Klan"(1926d). There are no specific records of religious institutions and fraternal organizations that allegedly sponsored or took part in the Klan activities in Dubuque. But in her study of the Klan in Iowa, Johnson (1967:53) states that among the Protestant denominations the Methodist, Baptist, and Presbyterian churches provided both members and logistical support for the hooded organization. Fraternal organizations also appeared to have no conflict of ideals and objectives with those of the Klan in the 1920s. According to Johnson (op. cit.: 52), "so many Masons joined the Klan that the Grand Master of the Iowa Lodge felt compelled to make a statement warning his Iowa brethren against the Klan." Similarly, many Legionnaires also joined the Klan, even when the Iowa American Legion was publicly denouncing the Ku Klux Klan in 1923.

In conjunction with the two public rallies in 1925 and 1926, Klan members also petitioned the City Council for a parade permit. A 1925 petition signed by Dr. E.R. Young, the "Exalted Cyclops of Klan Number 20 of the Realm of Iowa," stated that if approved "the Klan members would parade in regalia but with their masks up and their faces uncovered" (*The Dubuque Telegraph Herald*, 1925a:2).[7] It was also indicated in the petition that would-be participants will "mostly come from a territory within a radius of one hundred to one hundred and fifty miles of Dubuque" (*The Dubuque Telegraph Herald*, 1925b:5). The 1925 petition was denied twice by the unanimous vote of the city council members on the grounds that "if the paraders were Dubuquers that it might be a different matter."

The Klan put the Dubuque membership figures "in the thousands" in 1925 and about 1,000 in 1926, but no estimate could be verified for accuracy. However, the fact that the city council members in 1925 were unanimous in denying the petition and that the majority of participants were out-of-town Klan members and sympathizers are an indication that the Klan did not have a large local contingent. Nor did it have strong political clout in the city government to support its activities. But that seems to have changed altogether by 1926, as the second petition submitted to city hall was quickly endorsed by the city manager and the police chief. Nevertheless, they preferred to have the city council's approval on this matter, which was eventually gained after a considerable debate among council members (*The Dubuque Telegraph Herald*, 1926a:2). The city council granted the parade permit on condition that "the marchers wear no masks and that all the placards and banners which they intended to carry through the streets be submitted to the chief of police for approval" (*Des Moines Register*, 1926). Several factors indicate the increasing power of and support for the Klan in Dubuque. First, the police chief and the city manager immediately endorsed its petition for a parade. Second, unlike the case in 1925 where the petition for Klan parade was unanimously denied, in 1926 the council members were divided on this issue. Third, the parade was led by a contingent of "mounted Klansmen" from the Dubuque County Klan Number 20 (*The Dubuque Telegraph Herald*, 1926d: 18).[8] Finally, the Dubuque Klan was also represented by "an all-Klan band, a Klan drill team, and a ladies drill team," all in Klan regalia and with uncovered faces (*The Dubuque Telegraph Herald*, 1926b:1).

Newspaper reports on the parade are also indicative of considerable public support for the Klan at the local level. Anticipating the Klan gathering, the *Dubuque Telegraph Herald* (1926b) declared that "this year the residents of the city will have the opportunity of spectacular demonstration of a parade." Reporting on the parade, the paper claimed "the parade was one of the most colorful and impressive ever witnessed in Dubuque"(*The Dubuque Telegraph Herald*, 1926d: 18). Assuming the report's relative accuracy, many Dubuque residents greeted the Klan with open arms. But this is hard to accept for a predominantly Catholic town. Also difficult to determine is what percentage of the crowd were Dubuque residents and how many of them were out-of-towners. Nonetheless, in 1926 there existed a considerable pro-Klan contingent in Dubuque. The city residents' apparent reception of the parade; the commending tone of the newspaper's reports; the fact that no editorials condemning the Klan activities appeared in the two leading papers on the following days; and that no counter-demonstrations ever took place in Dubuque all support this conclusion. However, the absence of anti-Klan protests may also suggest the Dubuque public's fear of retribution by Klan supporters, had there been a counter-demonstration in town.[9]

Aside from alleged "peaceful" and "nonviolent" parades and public rallies, the Klan was also active in cross burning activities. On three occasions during the 1923-1924 period crosses were burnt on the bluffs facing the north end of town, where most Dubuquers of German descent resided (*the Dubuque Telegraph Herald*, 1923b; 1924a). In another incident not reported in the newspapers of the time, an out-of-town contingent of the Klan allegedly put up a cross on top of Kelly's Bluff, which overlooked the south end of town where most of the Irish Americans were residing (*Little Dublin news*, 1985:2).[10] Two crosses were also reportedly burnt as a part of the Klan ceremonies in the 1926 Klonklave rally. In all, between 1924 and 1926 the Klan held two public meetings (Klonklaves) and one parade and burned crosses at least on four recorded occasions.

Since the Klan always wrapped its members in a shroud of secrecy, there are no membership lists or minutes of the Dubuque County Klan meetings. This makes any accurate assessment of the extent of their influence in Dubuque almost impossible. The only documentation of the Klan membership is a list published in 1924 by *Tolerance*, a Chicago-based underground Catholic newspaper actively fighting the Klan in the region. The newspaper's list included the names of twenty-eight alleged KKK members in Dubuque. The list also revealed the occupation and place of work for nineteen of the individuals (*Tolerance*, 1924a). Dubuque dignitaries whose names appeared on it apparently disputed the *Tolerance* list and set a $5,000 reward for proof of the list's authenticity. In a follow-up report, *Tolerance* ridiculed Dubuque Klan members for denying their Klan affiliation by letting out "a mighty squawk" (*Tolerance*: 1924b).[11] Assuming the *Tolerance* list to be authentic, an interesting aspect of it is that it had representation from the middle and working classes across white ethnic lines yet also from local entrepreneurs who belonged to Dubuque's old traditional ruling elite. For example, out of nineteen members whose occupations were identified, five members were either business owners or had management positions. The rest represented the middle and working classes in both the manufacturing and service sectors. The first name on the *Tolerance* list is A.E. Loetscher, identified as sales manager for the Farley-Loetscher Company. In the same article, the paper also reported that J.A. Loetscher "leases the Isborn Farm west of Dubuque when the Kluxers held their meetings" (*Tolerance*, 1924b). If this is the case, it requires the addition of J.A. Loetscher, the prominent industrialist and staunch enemy of organized labor in Dubuque to the list of Klan membership. In addition, among traditional upper-class members of the Klan, J.F. Stampfer stands out with a reported net worth of $200,000 in wealth and assets. Stampfer was the founder of J.F. Stampfer and Company, one of Midwest's most successful clothing enterprises at the time (Lyon, 1991:420), and was among 141 Dubuquers who were identified in 1913 as having $100,000 or more in total wealth (*Dubuque Telegraph Herald*, 1913).[12]

Clearly segments of the working class in Dubuque sympathized with the hooded organization. One strong voice in the city's politics was organized labor, whose membership at the time included almost two thirds of Dubuque's work force (Scahrnau, 1993:55). Organized labor's position on the Klan and their agenda is hard to be evaluated. There are no indications that the unions in Dubuque opposed the Klan in public, and labor seemed to have become reluctant allies of the Klan on the issue of immigration. For instance, the *Dubuque Leader*, the official newspaper of the Dubuque Federation of Labor, completely ignored the Klan's presence in town during the 1924-26 period, the peak years of the hooded organization's activities. One searches in vain to find a statement or an editorial in the pages of the *Leader* in condemnation of the Klan, even during the weeks that they had their two Klonklaves in 1925 and 1926. The official record of the unions' position on social and political issues was in the annual proceedings of the Iowa State Federation of Labor (ISFL), an affiliate of the American Federation of Labor (AFL). The ISFL documents for the 1920s, the peak period for Klan activities and presence in Iowa, never addressed the latter group's anti-Catholic and anti-German propaganda. In fact, in addition to the American Legion, the ISFL also seemed to be in agreement with the Klan on the issue of immigration, which in the 1920s was mostly from European countries. Throughout the 1920s the ISFL's Committee on Immigration submitted annual reports on European migrant workers in which it supported stricter immigration laws.[13] For instance, in its 1927 report to the ISFL convention delegates the Committee concluded "at this particular time there are more workers in America than there are jobs," and that "lifting of any of the restrictions in the immigration laws will mean a flooding of workers from the war torn countries of Europe who the workers of America will not be able to compete with" (Proceedings of the ISFL Annual Convention, 1927:29). Thus organized labor's position on the Klan in the 1920s could best be described as schizophrenic. On the one hand they were targets of the Klan's anti-labor, anti-Catholic and anti-German rhetoric, but on the other hand they found in the Klan an unholy ally on economic necessities, jobs and opposition to migrant workers in light of high rates of unemployment in the country and the state.

The Klan also had an active role and presence in the state and local politics. It was particularly at odds with the Catholic Church on the issue of parochial schools, since in the early decades of the 20th century there was a growing concern on the quality of rural education in Iowa and possible ways to improve it. One solution was school consolidation in rural districts, and between 1906 and 1925 about seventy requests for consolidation were appealed to the Iowa Supreme Court (Reynolds, 1999:85). Aside from economic reasons to oppose the idea, such as a possible increase in rural property taxes to support the new schools, parents were also concerned about the dangers of transporting their kids to other counties on "generally miserable back roads in the Iowa countryside"(88). In addition, Catholic parents became increasingly concerned about survival of parochial schools in the rural counties where they had a visible presence yet still remained as a numerical minority. Catholic families feared that proponents of consolidation plans would include predominantly Catholic neighborhoods in the proposal, since they needed their property taxes to build the new consolidated schools (192).

Both by public persuasion and political participation, the Klan rallied around this issue. Considering parochial education "un-American," they fought hard on school boards and at the state level to prevent "Catholics from taking over the educational system in Iowa." Yet the 1926 state elections were a fatal blow to the Klan's objectives of creating a "one-hundred percent American" educational system, when Mary Francis, the incumbent state superintendent of Iowa Schools, lost the race to her challenger Agnes Samuelson. Francis was a crowd pleaser at many of the Klan rallies and gatherings across Iowa. In 1926 she traveled from Des Moines to Dubuque, allegedly using public funds, to address the Klan at its District Klonklave. Delivering a three-minute speech, Francis declared "I am glad to meet a crowd of loyal Americans. I am glad to meet people who are interested in public school education" (*New Sharon*, 1926). Her challenger won the election using a campaign that was based on constant attacks on the incumbent's Klan connections and her misuse of public money.

Increasing public pressure and subsequent defeats in the 1926 state elections eroded the Klan's social base. As elsewhere in Iowa, the Klan in Dubuque started to languish for the rest of 1926 and most of 1927. Local Klavern meetings became less frequent and there were no reports of Klan parades in Iowa. The downfall of the Iowa Klan was hastened by its defeats in the 1926 elections. Faced with dwindling membership and increasing operational costs, Ralph Hoyt, the Iowa Grand Dragon unexpectedly deserted his post in 1927. According to Johnson (1967:74-75), an ideologically disillusioned and economically bankrupt Hoyt "gathered all the robes and the papers he could find around the headquarters, closed his offices, and returned to his home in Greenfield."[14]

Despite the relatively strong presence of the Ku Klux Klan in Dubuque, to assume that the organization ruled the city with an iron fist and without any opposition would be erroneous and historically inaccurate. The anti-Catholic position of the Klan in a predominantly Catholic town could not have had strong local support. However, it appears that in particular the influential paper of 1920s Dubuque, *The Telegraph Herald*, did provide subtle but effective support for Klan sympathizers. By and large, if not active supporters, Dubuquers were passive observers of the Klan's presence in town.

The only organization that openly disapproved Klan activities in Dubuque was the American Legion. For instance, there was a report in a local paper on the Dubuque post as going on record for "disapproving of the Ku Klux Klan and urging its members to strive to effect its destruction"(*The Dubuque Telegraph Herald*, 1923a). The Legion's action was apparently part of a concerted effort at the state level to introduce bills in the legislature which "would make organizations operating like the Ku Klux Klan illegal and give the state authority to dissolve them" (ibid.). While the legionnaires were denouncing the Klan, an anti-mask bill was introduced into the Iowa house. In March, 1923 the Iowa house passed the Yenter Anti-Mask Bill as a new amendment to the Iowa constitution.[15] Although not directly aimed at the Klan, the Bill made it a misdemeanor for any person wearing a mask in order to "prowl, travel, ride, or walk within this state to the disturbance of the people or to the intimidation of any person" (Murray, 1951:156; Johnson, 1967:57). But the Bill's passage did not deter Klan supporters in Iowa. At the same time that the American Legion of Iowa was supporting the passage of the Yenter Bill in the state general assembly, good numbers of the legionnaires were joining the Klan across the state (Johnson, 1967:37-38). The American Legion's anti-Klan stance was not a matter of ideological discord, but rather a disagreement on the tactics used to promote its peculiar brand of patriotism. Otherwise, both organizations promoted "one-hundred percent Americanism" and supported restrictive immigration measures to drive out the undesirable foreigners.

Some Catholic organizations were secretly fighting against the Klan presence in Dubuque and the region. For instance, in a correspondence between two officers of the Knights of Columbus, a patriotic Catholic organization, the Grand Knight of Council #510 in Dubuque supported the work done by *Tolerance* in publishing the Klan list in Dubuque but questioned the list's authenticity. He then gave some advice to the Knights' officer in Clinton, Iowa, on appropriate strategies to deal with the Klan (Hoffman, 1924).[16] This is a significant piece of evidence on anti-Klan sentiments in Dubuque. But similar to the American Legion the Knights of Columbus was also a patriotic organization with about 1,200 members at the time, and had a strong social and political presence in the community (Williams, N.D.: P.1 of 41).[17]

Although Klan opposition in Dubuque and other parts of Iowa was mostly nonviolent and within the confines of law and order, there were also occasional violent clashes between the anti-Klan forces and members of the hooded organization. The only recorded incident for the Dubuque area occurred in 1924, when anti-Klan forces attacked a Klan meeting in a field in the nearby town of Center Grove. Several people from both sides were reportedly injured and the police arrested several anti-Klan individuals (*Des Moines Register*, 1924).[18]

Events of WWI and the Klan's ideological tenets of "Americanism" and "patriotism" temporarily shifted the focus in Dubuque from blacks to Catholics, German Americans and Jews. But this temporary lapse did not spare blacks from being afflicted by white racism, and they continued to be subjected to prejudicial attitudes and discriminatory practices. At the national level, civil rights activities in the South during the 1950s and 1960s led to revival of white supremacist groups, but mostly in the South. For one thing, a strong post-WWII economy was not conducive for their activities, and most white supremacist groups were marginalized in the North during this period.

THE RESURGENCE OF WHITE SUPTREMACIST ACTIVITIES IN DUBUQUE DURING THE 1980S

After almost three decades of growth, the post-War economic boom came to a halt with the economic crisis of the mid-1970s that had both national and global repercussions. The economic downturn of the late 1970s and early 1980s also had negative effects in Iowa. As one of Iowa's major urban centers Dubuque's economy was hit hard, and by 1982 high unemployment rates in the city and a shattered farm economy in its hinterland devastated Dubuque and surrounding rural communities. The economic uncertainties and massive lay offs in the early 1980s once again provided a social context for the revival of the Klan and other white supremacist groups and resumption of their activities, both in the nation and in economically depressed urban centers like Dubuque.[19] By the late 1970s the Klan had about 10,000 members nationwide and, though on a smaller scale compared with the 1920s, by 1980 Klan activities were again in full swing (Chalmers, 1987:406). After decades of relative calm white supremacist activities resurfaced in Dubuque with three reported incidents of hate crimes in 1982.[20] As the economy recovered slowly in the mid-1980s, there seemed to be a lapse in the occurrence of violent hate crimes. But this was all changed when again in 1988 two crosses were burned in Dubuque. Later in 1989, another charred cross was found in the debris of a black family's garage that was destroyed by an arsonist's fire. The last incident became an impetus for Dubuque's African Americans to initiate the formation of a local chapter of the National Association for the Advancement of Colored People (NAACP).[21] The newly organized NAACP successfully mobilized the community—a public rally was organized and pressure was put on law enforcement agencies to identify and prosecute hate crime perpetrators. Unprecedented in city's race relations history, for the first time a seventeen-year-old youth was arrested, charged for the 1989 cross burning and sentenced to ten years in prison. According to the prosecutors, the actions of the accused were triggered by a fight between a black high school student and a white friend of the accused when "the black student got the better of the white student" (Rodgers, 1990).

At this juncture the Human Rights Commission initiated an effort to form a task force for the planning and implementation of a program for racial and cultural diversification in Dubuque. Chapter six will discuss the task force's proposed Constructive Integration Plan (CIP), that called for sweeping programs to re-educate the citizenry and asked the city to recruit one hundred minority families by 1995.[22] The nature and intensity of the proposed plan created an uproar of dissent and protest, and incidents of hate crime skyrocketed overnight. From October 1989 to December 1991 twenty-two crosses were burnt, and eleven other race-related incidents occurred ranging from arson to painting racist remarks and graffiti on buildings and walls.[23]

Events reached their climax in early 1992, when the leaders of two white supremacist groups appeared in Dubuque and organized marches and rallies in a city agitated by the clash of ideas for and against racial diversity and harmony. The first showdown was by the Mississippi-based Nationalist Movement, a white supremacist group which in early 1992 organized a "Whites' Rights" march in downtown Dubuque. Upon the urging of the NAACP, the HRC and civic leaders, Dubuque citizens were encouraged to show their disapproval of the Klan rally by gathering in a far removed location in order to avoid confrontation. While a handful of white supremacists marched downtown, more than 600 people attended a rally celebrating Martin Luther

King's birthday in a city park (Bagsarian, 1992a). The "Whites' Rights" march was followed by a Klan rally in 1992, organized and led by Thomas Robb, the National Director of the Knights of the Ku Klux Klan. Again, while about 30 to 50 robed members and supporters of the Klan rallied in a downtown park, about 500 protesters chanted and waved anti-Klan slogans behind police barricades. On the other end of town, between 3,000 to 5,000 people also attended a rally to peacefully celebrate diversity in Dubuque (Wiley and Hovelson, 1992; *The Dubuque Telegraph Herald*, 1992).

Faced with strong public opposition and costly law suits by anti-Klan organizations and civil rights activists, since the 1980s the Klan have tried to look more civil and deliver a generic message of justice and welfare for white Protestant Americans. This new image was initially promoted by David Duke, a young, college-educated and well-dressed new leader who opted for a modernized Klan organization by changing its negative image into a more positive and civilized one. At one point he stated, "People expect you to have cow manure on the bottom of your shoes, chewing tobacco in your mouth, and be unintelligent and rough and mean and discourteous. It's just terrible" (David Duke, cf. Sims, 1996:166).

White supremacists' rallies in Dubuque therefore followed new guidelines adopted by the Klan and some other hate groups. For instance, when Rob Thomas, the Grand Wizard of the Knights of the Ku Klux Klan came to Dubuque, instead of donning Klan robes and wearing white hoods, he was "dressed in a gray suit, white shirt and red tie." He did not use strong racist and anti-Semitic rhetoric, told a crowd of about 200 people that the Klan "had nothing to do with those violent incidents," and stressed that "he doesn't support the cross burnings" in town. He furthermore claimed that the Klan "existed to make sure that the white race continued to receive its due in a country increasingly becoming dominated by minority groups" (Bagsarian, 1991b: 11B).

LAW ENFORCEMENT AGENCIES AND RACIAL DISCRIMINATION

The Ku Klux Klan rally and presence in Dubuque polarized the community in two ways. While people rallied behind anti-Klan or pro-white supremacist slogans and sentiments, anti-Klan protesters were also divided on adopting a strategy to protest the Klan's presence in town. For example, a newly organized group called Citizens United for Respect and Equality (CURE), which became active after the 1991 cross burnings, advocated and planned a face-to-face anti-Klan protest on the day of the rally. The group did not get overwhelming support from the community as civic and business leaders and the local chapter of the NAACP advocated an alternative, more peaceful form of protest. Trying to avoid confrontation and potential violence, the latter groups organized "A Night to Unite" party and vigil to "celebrate diversity" in a city park far removed from the KKK rally. In fact, there was an orchestrated effort by the media, law enforcement agencies and business leaders to persuade the public to ignore the Klan rally and show their disgust by attending the Night to Unite gathering. This non-confrontational strategy was harshly criticized by CURE and other human rights activists who argued that hate groups ought to be confronted directly and that ignoring them will only encourage more hate crimes and will implicitly condone racism.[24]

CURE supporters argued that while the police department assured the rights to free speech and demonstration for the white supremacist groups and their supporters, similar rights for their opponents were clearly ignored and citizens were strongly dissuaded from confronting the Klan. In response to CURE's accusations, the Dubuque assistant police chief acknowledged that "both people have first amendment rights," but added that in preventing a potentially violent confrontation between Klan members and protesters their first priority was public safety (Terry Lambert quoted in the *Des Moines Register*, 1992).

Related to the Klan rally, CURE conducted a content analysis of public statements made by law enforcement agencies and the local newspaper about their handling of the first amendment rights of the Klan supporters and those of the anti-Klan protesters. CURE leaders argued that while the police and the local paper emphasized the Klan's rights to free speech, similar rights were not extended to anti-Klan protesters (CURE, 1992).[25] CURE's analysis, however, should not be used to indict the Dubuque police department and label its members as being Klan supporters. City officials and the police were understandably cautious on matters of public safety, and sought to avoid confrontation. Nonetheless, at the height of racial crisis in the early 1990s there were some accusations of racial bias and brutality made against an all-white police force by several members of the local chapter of the NAACP and other local activists. Serious charges were brought up against the police in early 1993, when Dubuque police officers arrested four blacks that allegedly interfered with the arrest of a black teen-ager in front of a downtown bar. The arrested individuals accused the police of rough treatment and harassment, and one of them, a black female who was six-months pregnant, claimed the police "used unnecessary force when they took her into custody" (Dubuque Telegraph Herald, 1993). The lack of resolve by the local NAACP leadership to investigate the incident divided the African American community, as a group of them picketed outside the Dubuque Law Enforcement Center to protest against the police brutality and the NAACP's inaction. These events led to an investigation by the Iowa NAACP, and eventually the issue was put to rest after an informal agreement between the police department and the NAACP was made to form a "community advisory panel" to monitor future incidents (Bagsarian, 1993c). While the NAACP lawyer did not find enough evidence to press charges against the Dubuque police department, he nonetheless expressed his concerns about an all-white police force in town.[26] Police officials claimed that in their attempts to arrest suspects they are always color blind, and that they are not targeting blacks *per se* but crime and criminals (Bagsarian, 1993b). In the end, an internal investigation by the police chief cleared the officers involved in the scuffle of any wrongdoing.

Lack of sensitivity was also manifested in the newspaper accounts of the African Americans' presence and role in crime-related activities in Dubuque. This was the case when the city's newspaper interviewed the young leader of a group of African Americans who accused the police of brutality in the above-mentioned incident. Instead of concentrating on the charges of police brutality and mistreatment of blacks, the reporter focused on the youth's criminal background as well as his childhood experience, noting "he grew up in a rough Chicago neighborhood" (Bagsarian, 1993a). In another report, the pregnant woman who accused the police for the use of unnecessary force in her arrest was portrayed as a repeat offender. In both cases blacks' socio-economic status and past criminal records were used to justify their mistreatment by the police (*Dubuque Telegraph Herald*, 1993).

Although charges of police brutality against blacks in Dubuque are hard to prove, statistics on the number of arrests made in Dubuque are indicative of the existence of racial bias. Based on census data and the justice department's records, a much higher proportion of African Americans are arrested for various crimes compared to whites. For instance, while in the early 1990s one in every 177 Dubuque residents was black, one in every 17 people arrested in town was African American (see Table 8).

Dubuque is not an exception, but rather a typical Iowa community where there is an unequivocal statewide racial bias in the criminal justice system. For instance, by the end of 1992 only 1.7 percent of Iowa's population was black, yet African Americans comprised 24 percent of state's prison population (Bagsarian, 1993b). The numbers remained steady throughout the last decade of the 20th century. According to the Iowa Commission on the Status of African Americans, in 2000 blacks comprised only 2 percent of Iowa's population but filled almost a quarter of the state's prison cells (Associated Press, 2000).

Table 8: Ethnic Breakdown of the Individuals Arrested in Dubuque, 1992

Ethnic Group	Population (1990) #	Population (1990) %Total	Arrests Made (1992) #	Arrests Made (1992) % Total	Per Capita In-Group Arrests Made
White	57,546	98.4	4,000	93.4	0.07
African American	331	0.6	269	6.3	0.81
Asian American	368	0.6			
Native American	69	0.1	15	0.4	0.02
Hispanic	370	0.6			

Source: Table constructed based on information in Bagsarian(1993b).

Much higher rates of arrest and incarceration for African Americans than whites can not be used as an automatic proof of a racist criminal justice system in Dubuque and Iowa: criminal behavior is determined by many factors such as class position, level of education and level of poverty among particular social groups. Furthermore, the continuing social significance of race and ethnicity as a determining factor for economic and political gains also translates into higher rates of poverty and unemployment among blacks, for which the law enforcement agencies can not be held directly responsible. But socialized in a culture that is rooted in racial classification and selective stigmatization of certain groups, the police often act on these internalized cultural values. For instance, despite repeated disclaimers by the Dubuque police department, there were indications of prevalent prejudicial attitudes and discrimination explicitly aimed at African Americans in the community. One can find hints of a subtle form of racial profiling and bias in statements made by Dubuque police officers about local gangs, and the police department's strategies to keep them out of town. For example, during an interview with a local paper the police officer in charge of the "gang problem" stated that the police have "noticed a lot of new faces on city streets," and have concluded that "typical [gang] members in Dubuque are black" and in their mid-20s (Dan Avenarius, quoted in Batio, 1992:2). Later on, interviewed by *Argot*, a grassroots monthly newsletter, the same officer admitted that the police conduct routine background checks on African American "targets" in certain neighborhoods where drug transactions take place. But he backed away from his earlier statements and commented "*I'm sure in large cities the police don't treat them with the kid gloves we do.* We go strictly by the book" (Batio, 1992:2)(italics mine). He also blamed a recent increase in dealings of crack cocaine in town on new black arrivals by concluding that "he is not a racist, but if these sons-of-bitches hadn't come here it wouldn't have happened" (ibid.).[27] Finally, important to note is that at the peak of the cross burning controversy in Dubuque, most cross burners and their youthful supporters appear to have been part of "white" gangs in town. For example, authors of a biographical report on hate crime offenders in town explained how most cross burners had previous records of criminal and violent behavior, and how most of their fights were with "a group of white males" who often finished off the beatings with "baseball bats"(Arnold and Jaspen: 1991). However, they were never perceived or labeled by the police as gangs or a serious threat to the community.

CONCLUSION

In the 1920s the Klan spared blacks and capitalized both on Germans and Catholics to recruit sympathizers and advance its agenda in Dubuque. It fueled patriotic sentiments by portraying Dubuquers of German descent as external enemies, while attacking Catholics for being a threat to preservation of American values in rural Iowa.[28] In a historical context, the Klan and other white supremacist groups in most cases react to significant cyclical shifts in the American economy only at times of crisis. The rise of the Ku Klux Klan in the Midwest in the 1920s is interpreted by some historians as "an anti-modernist reaction against increasing urbanization and the apparent destruction of rural values," and that the Klan's appeal to rural population in the region was their "promise of preserving rural values" (Reynolds, 1999:185). This was also a period during which the American economy completed the transition from a competitive to corporate-monopoly stage.

This historic shift in turn affected industrial planning as well as production and distribution of commodities. A new corporate capitalist economy was detrimental to small scale farming and local industries with limited capital, and small businesses that could not compete with the newly emerging industrial and commercial conglomerates. Thus the Klan in 1920s Dubuque and elsewhere in Iowa became the voice of disillusioned local capitalists and entrepreneurs; the middle class; petty land owners and farmers; and a working class that had to grapple with a depressed economy, lay offs, and future uncertainties.

Resurgence of hate crimes in Dubuque in the 1980s also coincided with a depressed economy in the nation and in Iowa. But unlike the 1920s when the Klan had a broad based social support, in the 1990s it was the members of the white working class, both union and non-union, the unemployed, and the poor who opposed the Constructive Integration Plan (CIP), with some even actively supporting the Klan's presence in town. The following chapter will discuss how business leaders neither supported nor opposed hate crimes and the Klan in public. They intervened only when the city's image was badly tarnished and their boosterist objectives for economic development and tourism were endangered. Also, while the Klan spared African Americans from their racist attacks in the 1920s, during the 1990s they targeted blacks and to certain extent other "nonwhite" residents, since the latter groups were perceived as formidable contenders at all levels of employment in Dubuque's shrinking labor force.

Aside from a deep-rooted white-on-black racism which is historically embedded in American society, choosing African Americans as a "scapegoat" and a target for hate crimes during the 1980s Dubuque was a historically specific case. Although the Constructive Integration Plan did not single out blacks as the only minority "people of color" to be recruited, many Dubuquers nonetheless perceived the CIP's plan as a "black recruitment" blueprint. In addition, the active involvement of the local chapter of the NAACP, especially during initial stages of the

CIP, left no doubt in the average citizen's mind that "blacks will be brought into Dubuque."[29]

One indication of the historical specificity of scapegoating blacks is that opponents of the CIP in Dubuque were not concerned about other "minority" groups or people with darker skin complexion in general. For instance, in addition to African Americans, there were other ethnic groups such as Asians and Hispanics. Although in relative terms, both groups had a numerical majority over blacks, except in few minor cases they were by and large spared from racist attacks and overt prejudice.[30] Also, among Asian residents in Dubuque, there was a small but visible contingent of Asian Indians who were first or second generation immigrants. In a color-conscious culture where people are classified and treated based on their skin color, Asian Indians could easily fall under the "people of color" category.[31] But none of the 50 or so Asian Indian residents (or about 12 families) in Dubuque were targets of hate crimes or overt prejudice during the 1980s.[32] This could have been due to their middle and upper class status, as all the heads of households were highly educated professionals such as physicians, engineers and college teachers, with no representation among the working class. [ag] Thus at least in Dubuque, the poor and working class individuals did not perceive Asian Indians as a threat to their jobs and economic well being.[34]

Finally, after the 1960s a significant change took place in the nature of relations between whites and nonwhites. While prior to the civil rights era white residents directly confronted what they perceived as "undesirable" nonwhites and blacks in northern urban communities, in the post-1960s the police have been delegated by white residents as institutional proxies to keep nonwhites in check. Treatment of blacks by the Dubuque police and countless other cases of racial profiling nationwide should be understood within the context of this significant historical change.

Notes

1. See chapter 7 for a discussion of this issue.
2. National membership in the Ku Klux Klan in the 1920s reached 5 million (Feagin and Vera, 1995:5).
3. In line with the national Klan ideology and agenda, in the 1920s the local branch of the Ku Klux Klan also declared its position on certain undesirable groups, which included blacks, Jews and Catholics in a statement printed in the pages of the *Dubuque Telegraph Herald* (1925).
4. Also known as "Klaverns," Klonklaves were regular weekly meetings of a Klan, held at a local Klan headquarters.
5. "KIGY" is an acronym for "Klansmen I Greet You."
6. The newspaper accounts of Klan activities were often prepared and furnished to the papers by Klan members. Hence one may question their accuracy and validity.
7. This was imposed upon the Ku Klux Klan by the passage of the Yenter anti-mask Bill into law in 1923, which I will discuss it in the following pages.
8. Another possibility is the defeat of anti-Klan activists by court rulings in several states such as Kansas, where the judge ruled that the Klan had constitutional rights to demonstrate, as long as they did it in an orderly fashion.
9. The *Dubuque Telegraph Herald* has a conspicuous record of reporting Klan activities in Dubuque in favorable terms. By the same token, reports on negatively perceived Klan activities by the paper were also conspicuously low key and casual. For instance, the paper's report on the third cross burning incident in 1924 appeared on page 24 and in the "Boy Scouts" section. See the *Dubuque Telegraph Herald* (1924).
10. The report by the *Little Dublin News* is more anecdotal, and the author was unable to verify its accuracy.
11. In addition to the above list, Dr. E.R. Young and G.C. Hoch, and William Roschie signed the two petitions presented to the city council for parade permits in 1925 and 1926, respectively.
12. Klan membership representation across social class and occupation lines was a common feature in many other Iowa urban communities as well. A "dues ledger and account book" for the Waterloo-area Klavern, for example, lists 198 members for the 1925-28

period with occupations ranging "from farmer and machinist to physician and manager" (Neymeyer, 1995:56).

13. In the 1920s migrant workers from Mexico were not yet the main concern for labor unions. In Iowa, for the first time the IFSL adopted a resolution in 1929 submitted by its "Committee on Immigration" that demanded "total exclusion of foreign labor including that from Mexico, until such time as American labor can find a proper and equitable adjustment to new conditions brought about by the so-called machine age." (Proceedings of the ISFL Annual Convention, 1929:21).
14. With a population of less than two thousand at the time, the small town of Greenfield was a stronghold of the Ku Klux Klan in rural Iowa.
15. Yenter was a state representative from Johnson County, Iowa.
16. We have to remember that Clinton was the birthplace of the American Protective Association in Iowa. Founded in 1887 by a group of Protestant businesses, the APA gained strength in the area by spreading the fear of a "Catholic menace" in a community where Catholics comprised forty percent of the population. See Johnson (1967:34-35).
17. Originally established as an Eastern Catholic organization, the Knights of Columbus was a fraternal order which had three divisions or "Degrees" representing "Charity, Unity and Fraternity." A fourth degree representing "Patriotism" was later added in 1900, and the order started to gain significant support in the Western states. The ideological roots of the fourth degree were based upon "an exalted concept of American patriotism; ...an enduring appreciation of our American institutions; ...and a realization of the outstanding part our Catholic ancestry played in the discovery, exploration, evangelization and development of America" (Williams, n.d.b:1). As a secret organizational branch of the Knights of Columbus, the fourth degree's program was declared as opposing "the spread of communistic and other pernicious doctrines so at variance with our American concept of the dignity and liberty of man" (op. cit.,p.3).
18. A report by the *Dubuque Times Journal* in 1926 contradicts that of the *Des Moines Register*. According to the *Times,* the first reported attack on Klan members in Iowa took place in the city of Corning,

when on July 24, 1926 "a hostile group of about 75 persons armed with pitchforks, hammers, crowbars, and other rude weapons attempted to stop Klansmen on their way to a county Klan meeting" on the city's outskirts." Reportedly, the police arrived on time to avert a violent confrontation (*Dubuque times Journal,* 1926c).

19. I will discuss Dubuque's state of the economy in more detail in chapter 7.
20. For details see chapter 4.
21. The Dubuque chapter of the NAACP was organized in early 1989.
22. The task force is also known as the "Constructive Integration Task Force," and its plan is titled "We Want to Change." See chapter 6 for a detailed discussion of the task force's efforts and the plan's objectives.
23. See the *Dubuque Telegraph Herald (1991),* Gabe(1983), Jaspen and Webber (1991), and Kraske(1928a).
24. CURE was joined by several other anti-Klan groups from the midwest and across Iowa, including *the Midwest Network to Stop the Klan, Anti-Racist Mobilization* (ARM) from Iowa City, *Humans Unlearning Racism Together* (HURT) from Des Moines, and *the Iowa Peace Network* (the CURE Prescription, 1992). The "Night to Unite" peace rally was organized by *the Council for Diversity*, the local chapter of the *NAACP*, the *Dubuque Area Chamber of Commerce*, and the *Dubuque Area Peace Coalition* (Bagsarian, 1992b).
25. In its analysis CURE tallied the frequency of comments made by Dubuque's Police Department and the *Dubuque Telegraph Herald* in support of the free speech rights of the Klan and their opponents as 6 and 1, respectively.
26. The Dubuque police have repeatedly denied any intentional discrimination in their hiring practices and have claimed that they have not been successful in attracting minority candidates to Dubuque. The three new recruits for the police forces in 1992 were also white (ibid.).
27. The police department never repudiated the statements made by the above officer about African Americans in Dubuque (see Hanson, 1993).
28. On this issue see also Mecklin (1924).

29. Dubuque residents' reaction to the CIP was reflected in many of the letters sent to the city's newspaper. Many of those opposed to the plan expressed their concerns about "minorities brought to Dubuque by force." See for example Williams (1991).
30. According to the 1990 census there were 331 blacks, 357 Asians and 370 Hispanics in Dubuque. The Asian minority in Dubuque included 60 Chinese, 56 Filipinos, 81 Japanese, 41 Asian Indians, 48 Koreans, 28 Vietnamese, 5 Cambodians, 5 Thai and 33 residents from other ethnic nationalities. Hispanic ethnic group included 166 Mexicans, 45 Puerto Ricans, 19 Cubans and the rest were categorized as "other Hispanics" (Charvat and Goudy, 1991).
31. This has been the case in many British colonies where Asian Indians have been classified as "colored." The most vivid example was the status of Indians in South Africa's system of apartheid.
32. According to the 1990 census, in 1989 there were 41 Asian Indians residing in the Dubuque County.
33. Information on the Asian Indian community was obtained in my interview with Dr. Krishnasamy Savidamuthu in Dubuque (September 1993).
34. Under different social and economic circumstances this same ethnic group has also been subjected to brutal acts of hatred and racism. As an example, in the early 1990s upper class members of an Asian Indian community in Jersey City, New Jersey were subjected to constant harassment by white, black, and Hispanic youth, mostly from working-class families (Marger, 1991:346; Marriott, 1987).

CHAPTER 6

FAILURE OF A DREAM: DUBUQUE'S BLUEPRINT FOR RACIAL HARMONY[1]

This journey to Dubuque's past presents periodic social and economic crises that seem to correlate with intensification of racial and ethnic prejudice. But in relative terms race related incidents were neither frequent nor excessively violent, and especially after the 1960s prejudicial attitudes mostly remained beneath the surface of urban civility. This changed when in 1989 a charred cross was found in the debris of an African American family's garage destroyed by an arson fire. The incident was in fact a turning point in Dubuque's recent history of race relations, as concerned citizens, local activists, the newly formed NAACP and the Human Rights Commission (HRC) became more active and gathered their strength to deal with a resurgent racism in town.

For the first time in the city's history, the Federal Bureau of Investigation became involved in investigation of the cross burning cases, and the Justice Department dispatched mediators to Dubuque in order to meet with the NAACP leaders and city officials (Stanley, 1989). According to Justice Department records, between November 1988 and July 1990 fourteen race-related incidents in Dubuque were reported to its Kansas City branch (Whitcomb, 1992:68-69). In response to these hate crimes, in mid-1989 the Dubuque HRC issued a policy statement entitled "Strategies to Improve Race Relations in Dubuque." The Commission formulated a statement that envisioned strategies and specific plans in order to change people's attitudes toward minorities; promote a multicultural, nonsexist education; increase exposure to different races and cultures; advocate and enforce equal treatment of all; and establish broad-based community support in order to sustain a successful program to resolve racial problems (Iowa Advisory Committee to the U.S. Commission on Civil Rights, 1993:5).

Following the release of its policy statement, the Commission sent out an invitation letter to about 240 Dubuque residents to take part in a citizens' group and implement the formulated strategy. Out of this selective list only about 20 residents responded, most of whom later became the core of a task force that wrote the *Constructive Integration Plan* document. Titled "We Want to Change," the Constructive Integration Plan document (hereafter designated as CIP) proposed a strategy to improve race relations in Dubuque and enhance its ethnic diversity. The CIP's mission was two-fold — as its short-term objective the plan sought to "recruit, relocate, integrate and retain twenty new families of diverse color in Dubuque each year" until 100 new minority families resided there by 1995. The mission's long-range goal was that Dubuquers "will provide such a hospitable environment that these minority families will enjoy their permanent homes in Dubuque." The task force clearly emphasized that the plan did not advocate the "preferential employment of incompetent candidates" but rather sought to promote "an aggressive recruitment and employment of highly qualified and productive applicants of color"(*We Want to Change*, 1991:1). One important but controversial aspect of the CIP was its nontraditional approach to minority recruitment and the way it aspired to guarantee long term employment for the newly arrived "families of color":

> Potential *new residents of Dubuque will need the assurance of long-term employment* on which they can build their family's stability. This will require secure employment for the primary provider and in many cases for a secondary provider. *Such an assurance is often compromised by a seniority system that requires that the last hired be the first fired*; labor and man-

> agement together will be challenged to address and resolve this issue (Ibid: 4) (italics mine).

The above policy statement required commitment on the part of business and industries to secure employment for prospective black workers and demanded that labor leaders and white workers make costly sacrifices. The plan also emphasized the importance of a multicultural, nonsexist educational process both for children and adults, as well as the formation of a welcoming committee to facilitate the move for the newly recruited minority families. After a series of meetings that were open to the public, in March 1991 the task force approved the final draft of the "We Want to Change" document. It was then approved by the Human Rights Commission and finally endorsed by the city council by a 6-1 vote (Hansen, 1992:42-46). This ended the planning phase of the CIP, and in June 1991 the task force moved to the next phase for the plan's implementation. From its very inception, as a strategy for social change the CIP did not get residents' enthusiastic support and citizen participation remained at an extremely low level during the task force's open meetings.[2]

During its planning phase the citizenry did not take the CIP seriously, and many tried to ignore it by assuming that support for its final implementation would somehow die down. But once the plan entered its implementation phase the opponents quickly realized the project's seriousness. While a series of public meetings were held to discuss strategies for CIP's implementation, a rash of cross burnings and other hate crimes scarred the Dubuque community and stunned concerned citizens. A closer look at the timing of hate crimes committed in 1991 reveals a positive correlation between the finalization of the CIP and frequency of hate crimes. For instance, by the end of June 1991 the CIP task force completed its planning phase, gained the approval of the city council and moved to implement the plan. A few days later the first cross was burned, followed by 17 other cross burnings throughout the year. Many residents who opposed the CIP did not openly express their views until the plan entered the implementation phase, and most of the dissenting letters sent to the local newspaper were submitted during the September-November 1991 period. The following discussion is an assessment of city residents' response to the CIP and plans for improving racial and cultural diversity.[3]

COMMUNITY REACTION TO THE CONSTRUCTION INTEGRATION PLAN

After the plan's approval by the city council there was an immediate backlash, and a *Herald* report noted that "false rumors were spread by people who had not even read the plan" (Maiers, 1992:438). In an editorial, the *Dubuque Telegraph Herald* summarized Dubuque residents' reactions to the plan:

> 1) How did such an unacceptable plan get cooked up in the first place?
> 2) I am not opposed to minorities, but why stir up the pot? If they do not want to come here, why push it? We are getting along just fine the way we are, are we not?
> 3) Let us get all Dubuquers back to work first. Why hire outsiders before our own local people?
> 4) I get tired of being called racist. I never hurt anyone. What makes Dubuque worse than any other city our size? (Quoted in the Iowa Advisory Committee to the U.S. Civil Rights Commission, 1993:6).

Citizens were clearly divided on the integration plan, and those who voiced their opinions and concerns could be placed into three broad categories. First, there were a minority of vocal residents who unconditionally opposed the idea of recruiting minorities and any attempts to promote racial harmony. The most common themes in their letters to the city's newspaper editor were the fear of whites losing jobs to blacks and a concern for an increase in crimes and drug-related problems if "minorities were brought in."[4] Furthermore, in some of the letters the writers tried to appeal to the sympathetic public by using examples of biological differences between blacks and whites. For instance, a long-time resident and a former city council member wrote a lengthy letter to the editor in which he argued "livestock are not human but they do have genes that determine their color and it so happens that white and black livestock have different behaviors." He further accused an alleged "elite gang" for involving Dubuquers in "social engineering" in order to bring about racial diversity (Pfohl, 1993). Others disguised their opposition by demanding that the plan should be put to a public vote (Mueller, 1991). This appeal to the "public" or "majority vote" was also used as a convincing weapon in a petition drive to have a public referendum on the issue.

On the other extreme were the "unconditional" supporters of the CIP who were either actively involved in the formulation of the plan or were the plan's ardent sympathizers. This second group also included liberal-minded residents who were dismayed by the deep-rooted racist sentiments in the community. Several themes ran through all their letters in support of the CIP, including appealing to people's senses to fight racism; criticizing the "uneducated" people who were causing problems; seeing racism as an expression of fear or as an individual problem; and feeling of shame and guilt as a "Dubuquer."[5]

The third group included those who were opposed to the plan and its adherence to affirmative action policies but believed in the equality of opportunity ideal and tried to convince the public that blacks should decide on their own whether or not they wanted to come to Dubuque. One resident commented "they should not be recruited here by a task force of people who feel they need to teach residents of Dubuque a lesson in racism" (Williams, 1991)

As was the case for citizen's reaction and response to the Constructive Integration Plan at the grass-roots level, community leaders and organizations were also slow to react and respond to the CIP. Various groups acted on their own self-interest and at times provided the rationale for their response, or lack thereof. In general, business leaders and labor organizations did not openly support the CIP because it did not serve their interests.

The business community initially remained neutral in public. But once the plan was approved by the city council and the task force launched the first implementation phase, a few business leaders began to mobilize the city in order to derail the plan. In September 1991, for instance, an anonymous group identifying itself as the "Concerned Citizens for Fair Employment Opportunity" placed a $200/day newspaper advertisement challenging the objectives of the CIP. The advertisement stated that the plan was unfair, and that "it was not the proper function of local government to assist in attracting, soliciting, or relocating minority or other persons or groups from outside Dubuque County into the city for employment purposes." It also urged the city residents to petition for a citywide referendum for the approval of the integration plan (Arnold, 1991b). For a few days nobody seemed to know who the advertisement's supporters were. The *Dubuque Telegraph Herald* which published it claimed that its policy required it to keep the identity of the person(s) who placed the ad confidential (Arnold, 1991a). However, several days later a local businessman and a member of the city's zoning commission identified himself as the person who is "part of a group" which spearheaded the petition drive. He also claimed that he represented "a substantial number of Dubuquers" who were upset about the plan and its alleged use of city funds to recruit minorities (Arnold, 1991b). According to one report, more than 2,000 residents signed the petition opposing the integration plan (Hull, 1991:40).[6]

Business and industry leaders were clearly alarmed by hate crime incidents in town. But their concerns about the crisis were not so much about violations of "nonwhite" residents' human rights but about the negative effects hate crimes could have on community economic development plans and the ability to attract people and new business ventures into town. Thus as the collective voice of big business, the Chamber of Commerce expressed its concerns only after more than seven crosses were burnt and the city began to get negative publicity by the national media. At this time and on behalf of the business community the Chamber offered a $5,000 reward for "any information leading to the arrest or conviction of persons committing hate crimes in the city." Referring to recurring race-related incidents, a representative of the city's corporate interests commented in a news conference that "cross burnings and racial violence could bankrupt Dubuque morally and economically" (Arnold, 1991d). One member of the business coalition further added that "if this [$5,000 reward] doesn't get results, maybe we'll have to add a $1,000, and then another $1,000" (Eldon Herrig, quoted in Arnold, op. cit.).[7]

On the other side of the fence, organized labor had its own rationale not to endorse the CIP. Union leaders remained silent throughout the planning stage of the CIP and opposed the plan because of its recruitment strategy that disregarded the seniority clause in labor contracts (Giunta, 1992:202-203). At the time, a weakened organized labor was participating in the newly formed Labor-Management Council (LMC), when in the aftermath of the 1980s economic restructuring it had lost most of its bargaining power and political clout. Representing 21 labor unions, 31 employers and over 12,000 workers the LMC remained tight lipped on the Constructive Integration Plan's objectives, while deploring racism and prejudice in principle. Without referring to the CIP, the LMC eventually sent a belated, brief and general letter of support to the *Telegraph Herald* editor. In the letter the LMC co-chairs deplored "incidents of racism and intolerance whenever and wherever they occur," affirmed the "value of multi-cultural and multi-racial diversity" and pledged "to support social justice and honor the human rights of all people" (Maas and Stohlmyer, 1991).

Politicians and lawmakers at both the state and local levels also responded to the race related disturbances in Dubuque.

In one of his weekly meetings with reporters, Terry Branstad, the Iowa Governor at the time stated that he was "deeply saddened" by recent cross burnings in Dubuque, and that he would "strongly support the most severe penalties for those involved in these kinds of acts"(Terry Branstad, quoted in Fogarty, 1991). At the state house, two congressmen from Dubuque were for the most part quiet. But in two separate interviews they stated that while they were "troubled" by events in Dubuque, they "did not want to interfere with local officials' attempts to deal with race-related problems" (David Nagle and Jim Nussle, quoted in Norman, 1991).

Local politicians also responded to the crisis with varying degrees of intensity. In a joint statement of condemnation of racial intolerance, the chairpersons of the Dubuque County Democratic and Republican Parties wrote to the *Telegraph Herald*'s editor and indicated that by putting aside their differences on political issues they have come forward together to speak against "the cowardice that has manifested itself in senseless acts of vandalism, cross burnings, racial smears, and other acts of violence that have shrouded our community like a pall" (Flynn and Takes, 1991). The majority of the city council members supported the CIP and its implementation, and the Dubuque City Council approved the initial plan by a 6-1 vote. In an interview with the *New York Times* the only council member who opposed the plan commented "they can bring in 200 of them [minorities] as long as we don't have to pay for it," and as long as they [blacks] behave themselves and don't bring a bunch of ragtag relatives that cause trouble" (Don Deich, quoted in Wilkerson, 1991:30).

As a member of the city council the mayor remained a staunch supporter of the CIP all along and vehemently confronted Dubuque "racists" and cross burners in public rallies and on nationally broadcast television interviews. However, as the crisis intensified and the Ku Klux Klan began to capitalize on Dubuque's racial problems, he suddenly changed his position and came up with a new hypothesis on the root causes of the problem. Racial problems in Dubuque were not "homegrown," said the mayor, but were somehow "imported" and influenced by national politics to "draw attention away from the Louisiana race that features NAAWP founder and former Ku Klux Klan Grand Wizard David Duke" (James Brady, quoted in Arnold, 1991e).[8]

Religious institutions remained mostly on the margins of community social action front. In particular, with its strong economic and political clout and as the most influential religious entity in town, the Catholic Church was slow to respond to the crisis, and the Archdiocese of Dubuque remained conspicuously silent during the 1989-1991 period. The church reacted only when other power brokers sensed the potential threat of economic loss to big business in town. After two years of racial tensions in town Dubuque's Archbishop finally made a public statement, challenging the city's Catholics to "shun racism and open their souls to people of all colors" (Jaspen, 1991).[9]

Naturally black organizations in Dubuque had a vested interest in the CIP and its anticipated outcomes. Some black community leaders were actively involved in the planning and implementation phases of the CIP. But their collective voice, namely, the National Association for the Advancement of Colored People (NAACP), remained mostly on the sidelines when the crisis escalated in Dubuque. The NAACP was one of the major political forces for social change and promotion of racial and ethnic diversity in Dubuque during the late 1980s and early 1990s. It also played an instrumental role during the CIP's planning phase. But a change in leadership in 1990 was followed by a change in strategies to cope with race problems as well. The Dubuque chapter thus became a reluctant player and latecomer in the fight against civil rights violations and hate crimes. Later on, the Dubuque NAACP leadership was harshly criticized by some of its members and local activists for its inaction and ineffectiveness in coping with Dubuque's racial problems including allegations of police brutality against African Americans.[10]

Finally, a few neighborhood groups and organizations also got involved in community mobilization efforts but mostly to dismantle the CIP. Among 5 officially recognized neighborhood councils in Dubuque, only one, namely the *Washington Neighborhood Association* (WNA), was politically active at the time of racial crisis. WNA represented the "North End" residents, who lived in one of the oldest neighborhoods in town. Parts of this historical neighborhood included working class residential areas which for the most part were well kept. But it also included the more deteriorated neighborhoods where the majority of residents were the working poor and unemployed and resided in rental properties. The area was devastated in the 1980s by the construction of a new highway that cut through the neighborhood and contributed to displacement of many residents.[11] Of all the public reactions to the CIP, probably the most passionate and socially relevant response came from the WNA's president, Elizabeth Mihalakis. In a forum organized by the Dubuque Area Peace Coalition and the Ecumenical Ministries of Iowa to address race problems in Dubuque, she made a powerful and impassioned speech that reflected the sentiments of many white working class and low income residents:

> The Constructive Integration Plan which proposes attracting 100 minority families to Dubuque sends a message that the city wants to bring new residents to a city where jobs and housing are already scarce. [People] are pleading: "Listen to us. We need help. Help us first!" But nobody seems to listen to that. All they hear is, "you are racists, you are full of hate." I don't believe that's true. (Elizabeth Mihalakis, quoted in Hanson, 1991)

Mihalakis represented the position of a segment of the white working class and poor residents who regarded affirmative action and any effort to diversify the Dubuque work force as a form of "reverse discrimination." In the last few decades expressions of patriotic sentiments and unfounded claims of reverse discrimination have been recurring themes among workers during tough economic periods. In Dubuque, these sentiments later surfaced in a letter to the *Telegraph Herald* in which Mihalakis blasted the objectives of the Constructive Integration Plan and the city's liberals for labeling any one opposed to the plan as "racist":

> In truth, I believe that black people are every bit as racist toward white people as white people are every bit as racist toward blacks. Recently, an insinuation was made that I was in some way responsible for the slavery of blacks, and that I owe black people because in the past a great injustice had been committed against them. No way will I be held responsible for something in which I had no say, something over which many white men fought a war to remedy, and I will not live my life to apologize. (Mihalakis, 1993)

FROM CONSTRUCTIVE INTEGRATION PLAN TO THE COUNCIL FOR DIVERSITY (CFD)

As the CIP task force continued to iron out details of the implementation process, grass roots opposition to the plan mounted. The public's reaction ranged from a rash of letters to the local newspaper editor to an increase in number and intensity of hate crimes and violent acts against minority groups. This put Dubuque on the national spotlight and created a great deal of negative publicity which upset the business community the most.

Up until early 1990s Dubuque was an obscure midwestern city and not even recognized by many at the national level. But after the rash of cross burnings in 1991, the city's racial problems caught the national media's attention. Aside from reports published in the regional print media, several articles also appeared in the *New York Times, Time* and *Newsweek*. A front page story in the *New York Times* ran with a picture of four young Dubuque men wearing T-shirts with the "NAAWP" logo, an acronym for *National Association for the Advancement of White People.*[12]

Dubuque also made it to the national television network news and talk shows. Phil Donohue, Oprah Winfrey and Larry King each broadcast special programs interviewing cross burners, civic leaders and activists in Dubuque.

At this juncture civil and business leaders began to appreciate the gravity of the situation and negative consequences of a race war for economic development in Dubuque. Overnight they became interested in helping to resolve the race problem in the community. From December 1991 to February 1992 the CIP task force met with representatives from the business community, labor organizations and educational institutions who indicated an interest in "becoming involved in the implementation of a program of diversity for their community" (Hansen, 1992:51-52). But what actually emerged from this new coalition was a quiet political *coup de grace* that promptly disarmed the original CIP task force, handed over the leadership responsibilities to business power brokers in the community and drastically altered the initial objectives and direction of the original integration plan. In March 1992 the formation of the new "Council for Diversity" (hereafter referred to as CFD) was announced at a news conference. This was also an unofficial statement of CIP's dissolution and the exclusion of its task force from the new council's deliberations: only two members from the defunct CIP task force were included in the new 12-member council (Wiley, 1992).[13] In addition, city employees were deliberately excluded from the new council in order to deflect opposition to the alleged use of city funds for minority recruitment, both in terms of actual tax dollars and city employees' time devoted to the plan.

A comparison of the membership makeup of the original CIP task force and that of the new CFD shows a clear shift in power base. While civil employees, intellectuals, educators and activists dominated the former, the latter was clearly taken over by the community's movers and shakers. Four of the 12-member council included two previous members of the CIP task force, a social worker and a seminary faculty member. The rest were comprised of the President of the First National Bank and the new CFD Chairperson; the Vice President and Director of Marketing for the American Trust and Savings Bank; the Plant Manager of John Deere, the largest employer in town; the Chairman of the Board and President of FDL, a meat packing plant and the second largest employer in town; the President of the Dubuque Federation of Labor; the Archbishop of the Dubuque Archdiocese, the dominant religious institution with immense economic and political clout in town; the President and CEO of Wm. C. Brown, a major book publisher and employer in town; and the President of a local college (Jaspen, 1992).[14]

The CFD replaced the twelve-page comprehensive "We Want to Change" document with a brief one-page "Mission Statement" that made no reference to recruiting minorities or using city funds for the program. It also replaced the concept of "racial diversity" advocated by the now defunct CIP with that of "cultural diversity":

> Our objectives are the promotion and enhancement of the cultural diversity of Dubuque... We will support the city government, civic, labor, business organizations, and other interested parties in their efforts to expand job opportunities for all. This cooperative effort will help ensure that all qualified present residents of Dubuque and qualified newcomers, regardless of color, will have reasonable assurance of stable employment. (The CFD Mission Statement)[15]

27 major Dubuque employers then quickly endorsed the new mission statement. Once the controversial seniority clause was taken out of the original CIP document, The Dubuque Federation of Labor representing the organized labor also supported the new CFD (Jaspen, 1992; Giunta, 1992:202-203). Firmly in control, the CFD secured a budget for the first two years of its operation through private money, hired an African American director and set up a campaign for educating the city residents on the issue of cultural diversity. As a private, nonprofit organiza-

tion, the CFD's meetings were not subjected to the Iowa open meeting law, and the CFD's chairperson made it clear that he "doubted all of the council's meetings would be open to public" (Meriwether, quoted in Jaspen, 1992). In retrospect, solving the town's race problems was not the intent of the CFD plan. Instead, the town's movers and shakers intended to take over an issue that seemed to have boiled in to an ugly community brawl, to cool it and to replace the liberals' racial diversity plan with something largely symbolic.

The community's reaction to the newly formed Council for Diversity (CFD) and its new mission statement ranged from endorsements by considerable number of business leaders and strong support by some known racist elements, to residents' overall indifference and apathy. After the CFD's formation, its chairperson published an article in the *Dubuque Telegraph Herald* to clarify the council's mission and to counter "some misperceptions" in the community about the CFD's objectives. In particular, he assured the public that the council did not intend to bring "people [of color] in," nor will it use the tax money to support the Council. He then concluded "the Council's purpose is not to 'tell people how to live,' but, instead, to facilitate growth of understanding and appreciation among all people" (Meriwether, 1993). The local NAACP president also praised the CFD's new mission statement for an "inclusiveness" that could "help Dubuque open doors to people of color and all people" (Ernestine Moss, quoted in Arnold, 1992a). James Brady, Dubuque's mayor who initially and strongly supported the defunct CIP and its task force, softened his position and also gave his blessings to the new plan. Acknowledging the differences in objectives between the CFD and the original CIP, the mayor concluded "I think you have to walk before you can run, and I applaud them for what they are doing" (James Brady, quoted in Arnold, 1992a).

Among strong supporters of the CFD was an admitted cross burner who in an interview stated that "he has not read the mission statement but was pleased that it makes no mention of quotas or the use of tax dollars." Referring to crosses burnt and other hate crimes committed by him and others, he commented that "he is glad the trouble they have got into wasn't for nothing" (Michael Lightfoot jr., quoted in Arnold, 1992a).[16]

In most part, Dubuque citizens received the CFD with little or no enthusiasm. But one can also interpret the public's non-response as a sign of relief and their tacit approval of the CFD for its successful derailment of the CIP. Those skeptical about this quick turn of events and drastic changes in the mission's objectives also remained silent. There were, however, a few vocal voices of opposition who criticized the politics involved in the formation of the CFD and implications of its revised mission statement. One of the opponents was Marty O'Shea, a member of the Human Rights Commission and former member of the CIP task force. O'Shea was also the only HRC member who abstained from voting on CFD's approval. While he admired the spirit of the CFD's message, he expressed concerns for the hasty process of imposing the CFD and the impact of its new mission statement on the community. He further questioned the CFD's "closed door" policy which he considered as a policy of exclusion (Marty O'Shea, quoted in Arnold, 1992b). Another former member of the original CIP task force also voiced his concerns about the new mission statement's change of direction, from being an "affirmative action plan" to an "equal opportunity statement" (Tobin, 1992:224). In response to this criticism and other concerns, the CFD chairperson assured the public that although the CFD was not an affirmative action document, monitoring a "growing population of people of color" in Dubuque would be addressed by the Council "in an affirmative action process, whether those words are in or not"(Meriwether, 1992:239).[17]

ASSESSING THE COMMUNITY'S REACTION TO THE CONSTRUCTIVE INTEGRATION PLAN

The common denominator of the debates over "attracting minorities" or "promoting cultural diversity" was the public's assumption that "minorities" meant "blacks." Although the CIP document made no reference to "blacks" but to the "people of color," people on both sides of the fence tried to make their case by referring to blacks as the only legitimate minority group, or "people of color."[18]

Business leaders' concern about maintaining a positive image for their town is endemic of many average-size American cities and, related to the Midwest, dates as far back as the mid-19th century, when many frontier towns were established. In *New Towns in the New World,* David Hamer (1990:12) argues that in the highly competitive process of establishing the western frontier towns, speculators often had to resort to "boosterism," which involved "newspaper editors, businessmen, real estate agents, politicians" and others who had vested interests in a town's economic development. Hamer also points out the crucial role the private enterprise sectors play in promoting their towns as "an ideal of urban community" and in furnishing "proof of their own town's inevitable destiny as the metropolis of its region"(12-14). This competitiveness at the regional level meant that frontier town developers tried to downplay negative features, such as spatial segregation of various social classes and ethnic groups, urban plight and the presence of any conflict arising out of social inequalities. Similarly, in the 1990s business leaders and the Chamber of Commerce in Dubuque used the old "boosterist" tactics of the frontier era in order to sell their town to outside businesses and to secure federal and state grants, while sweeping the community's social and racial problems under the rug.

Organized labor's response was also similar to that of the business community, but more as a subordinate voice from within the Labor-Management Council (LMC). Following massive layoffs in the 1980s, the LMC was spearheaded by local industries and corporate entities to ward off tensions between management and organized labor. Therefore, union leaders were mostly concerned with the high rate of unemployment among their rank and file, and were not in a position to have an independent and effective voice on this issue.

Urging city residents to practice racial tolerance, state and local politicians also echoed the business community's concerns. They were concerned about adverse effects on the community's positive image, likely economic setbacks for the city's boosterist objectives and losing business to other cities, while demanding an end to hate crimes and condoning harsh punishment for hate criminals (Flynn and Takes, 1991). Local churches did not play an effective role in resolving the crisis either, particularly the Catholic Church, the major religious and political voice in town. Without addressing the underlying reasons for racial conflict, the merits of the CIP, the controversies surrounding its stated objectives or strategies to deal with the crisis, the statement made by the Catholic Church was a general appeal to Dubuque faithful for their tolerance and compassion. However, according to the newspaper report, the Archbishop considered the church proclamation as "one of the most important statements in his eight years as Archbishop" (Jaspen, 1991).

The NAACP chapter in Dubuque did not provide an effective leadership for blacks and the rest of community. For instance, at the height of cross burnings and hate crimes in 1991 its only reaction was a declaration of war on racism by launching a ribbon wearing drive and asking citizens to wear black-and-white ribbons "until race relations in Dubuque improve" (Ernestine Moss, quoted in Bagsarian, 1991a). According to a local observer many of Dubuque's black residents did not join the NACCP since they considered the Dubuque branch as a "white ploy" to co-opt the nonwhite contingent in town. There were also rumors that in violation of the NACCP's national guidelines two top officers of the Dubuque branch were on city hall's payroll.[19]

Finally, among the leadership of various community groups representing economic, political and social entities only the white working class and low income residents appear to have been cognizant of the root causes of racial violence in Dubuque. Representing the Washington Neighborhood Association, Elizabeth Mihalakis correctly linked racism in Dubuque to lack of jobs and affordable housing, but she failed to strongly condemn racism and hate crimes in the city. Understandably, white workers' subordinate position in the community's political and economic decision making machine led them to look after their own immediate class interests, while ignoring those of a tiny contingent of a prospective "minority" working class.[20] The tactics used by white supremacists and their sympathizers to alert community planners and leaders about the plight of the working class in Dubuque should be examined within the above-indicated social context.

CONCLUSION: FAILURE OF A DREAM?

The Constructive Integration Plan was a sincere effort on the part of the Human Rights Commission, city hall, and local activists and intellectuals who were determined to improve the state of race relations in Dubuque. But from the start both the social class make up of the task force and the plan's objectives, strategies and intended policies were problematic. The task force members were mostly middle class civil servants, intellectuals and activists who seemed to be genuinely concerned with and committed to resolve racial problems in Dubuque. But as a middle class initiated social policy and strategy the CIP did not garner a broad-based social support. The task force members tried to impose their ideas of racial integration on the white working class, the underemployed and unemployed without even attempting to include them in the decision making, planning and implementation processes.[21] Furthermore, in fairness to public opinion, the HRC's initial list of invitees for the CIP left the majority of Dubuque citizenry out in the cold. One contributor and CIP supporter later contended that very few people from the areas affected by economic hardships of the 1980s and recent hate crimes were invited to participate (Hansen, 1992:57).[22] In his testimony before a fact-finding committee of the U.S. Civil Rights Commission, the president of the Dubuque Federation of Labor also reiterated that CIP task force members were "somewhat naive regarding what it takes to mobilize a community around an issue, and in particular, the issue of diversity," since "major segments of the community were noticeably missing from the task force" (Giunta, 1992:199-200). Finally, CIP supporters gave the impression that Dubuque "commoners" are "racists par excellence," all of which needed education and sensitivity training so that their racist and bigoted attitudes could be changed. Although well intended in their objectives, CIP supporters effectively ruled out any possibility of mass participation and overlooked the underlying economic and political reasons for the resurgence of racism in town.

As a working paper, the CIP's "We Want to Change" document was also deficient both in terms of conceptualizing the problem and the plan's implementation. First, by emphasizing the need to guarantee long term employment for prospective employees of "color," the plan intended to seek assurance from employers and labor unions to exclude the new recruits from the stipulations of the seniority system in hiring and firing procedures. Understandably, this made organized labor and its leaders extremely nervous, as they were put in an uncomfortable impasse. They could support the plan on the principle of racial equality and justice, but they could not compromise the seniority system as it was suggested in the CIP document (Giunta, 1992:196). Second, the CIP's stipulations about not providing "preferential employment of incompetent candidates" reveals their awareness of anti-affirmative action sentiments but hardly assuages it, since it still implies preferential treatment for the competent minorities. Finally, like many other well intentioned policy statements, the CIP aimed at eliminating racial prejudice which is a sociocultural symptom of a much greater problem, without attempting to understand the economic and political causes of a resurgent racism in Dubuque as well as in the nation. The task force members were hoping that by recruiting 100 "families of color" and therefore exposing Dubuque citizens to "racial diversity," the problem of racism and racial prejudice would miraculously be reduced or eliminated altogether. As an example, in his testimony before the Civil Rights Commission a member of the task force indicated that in addition to attitude change and education as one of several recommendations made by the group, "equally important was increased exposure to different races and cultures" (Maiers, 1992:352).

Clearly, the CIP was inspired by the ideals and objectives of the affirmative action policies initiated in the 1960s. Originally intended to offer a temporary remedy to members of racial and ethnic minority groups who had been victims of past discrimination, these policies had been supported and implemented by the federal government.[23] By going one step beyond the "equality of opportunity" ideal, affirmative action policies aimed to improve economic conditions and educational achievement of minority populations by guaranteeing "equality of results."

Proponents of affirmative action continue to believe that the use of preferential policies in employment and education is necessary if our goal is to reduce the socio-economic gap between the minority and majority groups.[24] Thus the resulting CIP policy statement required commitment on the part of business and industries to secure employment for prospective black workers and demanded that labor leaders and "white" workers make costly sacrifices. However, with increasing popularity of postmodern theories that emphasize inherent equality of diverse ideas and representations, another interpretation of affirmative action gained considerable support in the late 1980s: instead of advocating its original objectives of bringing about social and economic equality among diverse populations, the policy objectives were construed as a promotion of ethnic and racial diversity and proportional representation within institutions and communities. Thus, the CIP also emphasized the importance of a multicultural and nonsexist educational process both for children and adults, as well as the formation of a welcoming committee to facilitate the move for the newly recruited minority families.

CIP's opponents also used two arguments commonly espoused by those who oppose affirmative action policies. First, they argued that by giving minorities preference in employment and educational opportunities over whites, affirmative action programs had in fact become tools of reverse discrimination against the latter group.[25] Second, they criticized affirmative action policies aimed at distribution of social rewards based on group membership rather than individual merits (Gordon, 1981).

A careful study of this recent chain of events in Dubuque and the failure of a plan by a contingent of liberal minded and concerned citizens who envisioned a community devoid of prejudice and discrimination raises more questions than it actually answers. Many of those who opposed the plan — from frustrated workers, the poor, and cross burners who acted on their prejudice to the members of the business community who worked behind the scenes to derail the plan — called the CIP's objectives "social engineering." In particular, the latter group further argued that the plan went against all the principles "that America stands for," that people should be free to live wherever they want to, and that federal and local governments or citizens' groups have no business and right to interfere in the "natural order" of social relations, including those pertaining to race and ethnicity.

Opponents of the CIP may have had a legitimate point by arguing that the CIP aimed at "social engineering." However, in most cases powerful groups and the ruling class have often utilized "social engineering" in order to protect their own social, economic and political power and privileges. The historical plight of Native Americans and confining the surviving population in isolated reservations; as well as enslavement of African Americans and their exclusion from economic and political processes long after the Emancipation Proclamation and conclusion of the Civil War are two examples. Supporters of the Constructive Integration Plan had a "dream" of transforming an all white city to one which would more resemble to a microcosm of an ideal racially integrated community. Although short sighted and impractical, Dubuque's liberals at least had a plan and a vision to improve the state of race relations, for which they should be rightfully recognized.

Notes

1. An abridged version of this chapter has been published in *Proteus (2005, 22:1).*
2. See the testimony by Jack Hansen (1992:43-45).
3. The reader is cautioned on the limited validity of the analysis due to the selective nature of news items and letters published by the only newspaper in town, the *Telegraph Herald.*
4. There was a prevalent perception that if implemented, the CIP would bring minorities, or, as it was widely believed "blacks," into Dubuque. But most of those opposed did not seem to have read the document in its entirety.
5. See for example, Hanson, 1991; Hanson and Braig, 1991; Schmidt, 1991; Shaffer, 1991; and Webster, 1991.
6. However, the findings of an unscientific opinion poll conducted in Dubuque indicated that 85 percent of residents favored integration and diversity.
7. The Chamber's strategy sought to resolve a crisis by attacking and/or eliminating the symptoms, in this case a few cross burners. But in reality it reflected their desire to protect the interests of the business community. Furthermore, the Chamber's offer of $5,000 reward(or more, if needed) to identify cross burners could have had an unintentional consequence of dividing the city's poor and working class, as the would-be informers most likely resided in the same neighborhoods as the culprits.
8. The Mayor's record of support for human rights is not outstanding. As chapter 8 will discuss, James Brady scolded the members of multi-ethnic coalition who opposed the election of Clarence Duffy (also with questionable human rights record) to the Human Rights Commission in 1982. A champion of the working class and strongly supported by organized labor, James Brady won the 1989 mayoral race over his challenger through a strong anti-gay

and lesbian campaign. Brady was outvoted by his challenger in the 1993 mayoral elections.

9. This was his only public statement since the outbreak of racial tensions in town.
10. This eventually led to an internal investigation by the Iowa NAACP division and a call for reelection in November 1993.
11. Chapter 8 will discuss the effects of highway construction on the city's working class neighborhoods in detail.
12. The NAAWP is a white supremacist group founded by David Duke, a well-known ex-Klansman and politician in Louisiana.
13. The two members were Jack Hansen, a free-lance writer and Claudette Carter-Thomas, a probation officer in Dubuque.
14. First National Bank was merged with another financial institution in 1992, and changed its name to the Hawkeye Bank of Dubuque.
15. At its face value, it is difficult to dispute this carefully worded statement in its present form. But without any historical reference to the city's economic crisis and racial tensions that culminated in the creation of the CFD, the above statement did not do justice to the reality of a multi faceted problem and persistent racism.
16. The Nationalist Movement, a white supremacist group that held a rally in downtown Dubuque in opposition to the original CIP proposal later on summarized its victory and the CIP's defeat on its web site:

> The mayor of Dubuque, Iowa had announced that the city would pay to import inner-city minorities as permanent residents because Dubuque was a minority-free metropolis. The Nationalist Movement scheduled a parade, rally and petition-drive against the *Destructive Immigration Plan.* An ordinance required an insurance bond and indemnification agreement as a condition for the parade. When the Nationalists refused to agree to the terms of the ordinance, the city backed down and the parade took place. Lesbians who attacked the march were arrested. The ordinance became uncomfortable, the immigration plan was scrapped, the *Pro-Majority Plan* was adopted and the mayor was hounded from office." (The Nationalist Movement, N.D.)

17. The preceding remarks were made during a fact-finding conference organized by the U.S. Commission on Civil Rights in Dubuque.
18. This is the case of perceiving blacks as a "point of reference" at the local level, an issue that is discussed in the introductory chapter.
19. Karen O'Rourke, former Director of the Center for Public Ministry in Dubuque, interviewed by the author.
20. Chapter 7 will discuss in more detail the attitudes of white workers within a divided working class on the issues of equal employment opportunity and affirmative action policies.
21. Except for an unemployed person, a wage laborer, a housewife and a priest, the rest of the 21-member task force was comprised of middle class civil servants, intellectuals and college educators and administrators (Hansen, 1992:47).
22. Chapter 7 will discuss how economic development, or lack thereof, and racial prejudice and discrimination have been closely related in Dubuque.
23. Although "race' is a socially created concept, I am nonetheless using it here to represent the conventional wisdom. The term "minority" is also used here in terms of certain social groups and populations that have little or no control over economic resources and political power. Needless to say, affirmative action policies later included women to the list of minority groups.
24. See for example, Kennedy, 1994, and Taylor, 1995.
25. Although theoretically speaking it is impossible to conceptualize reverse discrimination of a "white" majority, who control and dominate the economic and political spheres, by a more-or-less economically and politically disenfranchised 'minority population,' this theory has gained considerable currency particularly among working class "whites."(see Glazer, 1975; Yates, 1994)

CHAPTER 7
ORGANIZED LABOR, BLACK WORKERS AND DISCRIMINATION

Up until the WWI black workers in the North were employed in low-status, low-paying, and mostly menial jobs, as was also the case in Iowa and Dubuque. If and when blacks were employed in industries, they had to work in segregated environments and tolerate prejudice and discrimination in the work place. The post-WWI immigration of blacks to the northern states increased the number of black industrial workers, but they still ended up at the lowest rungs of industrial work force. Although less significant in numbers, black workers were also employed in Iowa industries, particularly in Waterloo, Des Moines and the Quad Cities area. Certain industries in Iowa hired blacks in significant numbers. For example, blacks were employed in meatpacking plants across Iowa, and as early as 1900 black workers accounted for about 13 percent of the work force at the John Morrell and Company meatpacking plant in Ottumwa (Scharnau, 2001:228). According to an Iowa labor historian,

> In Iowa packinghouses and farm equipment plants, black workers were consigned to the dirtiest, lowest skilled jobs. They joined the new industrial unions, but they remained largely out of the benefits of promotion and free movement between jobs based on seniority that unions had won for their members.(Stromquist, 1993: 243)

In general, labor unions regarded black workers as potential unskilled cheap laborers who were used by employers to suppress wages. In addition, blacks and other members of the working poor, mostly "nonwhite," have been occasionally used by Iowa employers as strike breakers (Scahrnau, 2001:226-229; Stromquist, 1993:244). Thus, a long history of white-on-black prejudice and discrimination separated white and black workers in the work place and, as a matter of survival, organized labor also had its own economic reasons not to accommodate black workers. White workers' negative attitudes toward their fellow black workers were reinforced by discriminatory practices of Iowa employers. According to a local labor historian "employers confined male and female black workers to race and gender stereotyped jobs that required low skill and received low pages," who often worked harder than their white coworkers, and were seldom qualified for overtime pay or job promotions. These discriminatory practices in turn "increased profit margins for employers and maintained preferred jobs and pay advantages for white employees." (Scharnau, 2001:237)

Organized labor's active presence in Iowa dates back to the last decades of the 19th century. Up until the 1930s the Iowa State Federation of Labor (ISFL), an affiliate of the American Federation of Labor (AFL), was the main voice and legal agent of the organized labor in Iowa and Dubuque. One source of information related to ISFL's position on black workers is the proceedings of its annual conventions. A survey of the ISFL's annual proceedings from 1895, when the first convention was held, to the conclusion of the Second World War yielded no reference to black workers and their rights, either as a general statement or in committee reports and proposed resolutions to convention delegates. The only statement that supports "equity to all men regardless of class, race, creed, or color" was made in a 1930 resolution adopted by ISFL delegates in support of Tom Mooney, a white labor leader in California, demanding his immediate release from prison (ISFL, 1930:33).[1]

During the post-WWI period the ISFL's major concern was rising unemployment rates and the threat posed by migrant workers, mostly of European origin. In Dubuque, the *Dubuque*

Leader, a weekly publication of the Dubuque Federation of Labor, voiced labor concerns about European migrant workers both at local and state levels. For instance, in 1922 the *Leader* reprinted an article by William Roberts, Chairman of the AFL's Labor Legislative Committee who condemned the government's lax immigration laws to let millions of Europeans in, at a time when half a million American workers were unemployed (*Dubuque Leader,* 1922:1). Later, concerns about unchecked immigration and its effect on local employment were reflected in a front page editorial that warned, "America can't let down the bars without paying a price." The price would be paid in unemployment, depression, lowered standards of living and lowered purchasing power, concluded the editorial (The *Dubuque Leader,* 1923:1). In the meantime, the *Leader* completely ignored the active presence of the Ku Klux Klan and their anti-organized labor and anti-black position during the 1920s.[2] For instance, as the Klan prepared for their big rally in August 1925, the *Leader* published no articles or editorials in condemnation of their presence in town.[3] Instead, the paper published articles asking black workers not to attend the American Negro Labor Congress (ANLC) in Chicago which was organized by the Third International and the Workers' Party, both labeled by the AFL and the *Dubuque Leader* as "Communistic" and supported by Russian "Bolsheviks" (Wise, 1925:1).[4]

With the presence and influence of the Congress of Industrial Organizations (CIO) in Iowa and post-WWII political developments in support of African Americans and civil rights at the national level, The ISFL's position also slowly started to change. Of note is the first resolution on protection of civil rights that considered "any group of individuals, or organizations, which creates, or fosters racial, religious or class strife among our people" to be "un-American, a menace to our liberties, and destructive to our fundamental law" (Resolution No. 27, ISFL, 1950:39).[5]

With the coming of the CIO to Dubuque in 1935, part of the city's organized labor became at least exposed to debates on the question of racial equality in the work place and the need for the passage of Fair Employment Practices law (FEP). Furthermore, the CIO became more active in the 1950s particularly related to racial segregation and discrimination in public places. For instance, the Iowa CIO's Human Rights Committee for the Elimination of Segregation and Discrimination introduced a lengthy resolution at the 1952 convention, demanding the passage of a Federal Fair Employment Practices Act and several other civil rights laws (Iowa State Industrial Union Council, CIO, 1952:202-205). The following year, the Anti-Discrimination Committee submitted a report that was highly progressive for its time. The report reiterated that

> The struggle against discrimination is not something to do in your spare time. It belongs at the top of the agenda of every local union, because the Iowa State CIO Council owes its entire existence, and its strength, to the solidarity of all workers, regardless of race, religion, color or national origin. (Iowa State Industrial Union Council, 1953:123½)

The report then recommended the "breakdown of all segregation in all organized CIO plants;" support of initiatives to help the "passage of FEPC legislation;" participation of the CIO members in community and civic meetings that address discrimination; and finally a boycott of eating places that use the sign "We Reserve the Right to Refuse Service"(Ibid.). Convention proceedings indicate that there was a lengthy and lively debate of the report among delegates, who in several occasions discussed the extent of racial discrimination in different parts of Iowa. Frank Ross, a delegate from the Cedar Rapids local talked about the national dimensions of discrimination and stated "Not only in our White House or in Des Moines at our State Capital, but I find it [discrimination] in the rank and file itself." He then explained how discrimination is rampant in his city, where

Quaker Oats, a major employer in town, will not hire "colored women" because "they do not want a colored woman in that plant to go into the women's dressing room and dress with the white ones." (Frank Ross, cf. Iowa State Industrial Council, CIO, 1953:128-129)

Continuing to report on persistent racial segregation and discrimination in public accommodation and in the work place, the Iowa CIO pressed for the passage of FEP laws in the state. The CIO's Anti-Discrimination Committee also strongly supported the court ruling in the *Brown vs. Board of Education* case in 1954 (Iowa State Industrial Union Council, CIO, 1954:95).[6] A year later, commenting on the Supreme Court ruling's lack of clarity and indecisiveness the chairman of the CIO's Human Relations Committee stated, "it is the opinion of this committee that it did little good to pass this historical ruling, and then set no date for the ending of segregation." He then criticized Iowa's slow pace of progress in the human relations area and noted "the state [CIO] convention of a year ago went on record to push in every city for an FEPC Ordinance. To our knowledge, not one city in Iowa has passed such a law." He then concluded "this [human relations] is a program that receives a lot of talk and little action" (Fob Jones, cf. Iowa State Industrial Union Council, CIO, 1955:142). The 1955 convention was the Iowa CIO's last independent state meeting, as in 1956 it merged with the ISFL and held the first joint AFL-CIO convention. This ended two decades of the Iowa CIO's active and remarkable involvement in human relations issues, a track record which was in sharp contrast with that of the ISFL in more than half a century of supporting the organized labor's cause since its inception in 1895.

During its first decade, the Iowa AFL-CIO became more proactive and passed numerous resolutions dealing with human rights issues, racial discrimination and immigrant laborers' legal rights. Without doubt, the Civil Rights movement of the 1950s and 1960s, the role of the NAACP and other activist groups, and several milestone Supreme Court rulings contributed to the organization's level of commitment to press for improvements in race relations (see Table 9).[7]

Between 1968 and 1994 concerns for human rights and racial discrimination subsided within the organization, or at least one can not find any committee reports or resolutions pertaining to the above issues in the annual convention proceedings. The only notable action was a 1977 resolution on Affirmative Action that proposed to "adopt and implement an affirmative action program.[8] Unclear is why for almost a quarter of a century the organization abandoned the cause of racial equality and protection of human rights, or at least did not discuss them in public. But in light of the economy's slowdown and eventual recession in the 1970s and early 1980s, anti-discrimination concerns took the back seat when the organized labor was more concerned with "bread and butter" issues, such as high unemployment rates, plant closings, and reduced wages.[9] Only on rare occasions did the organization demonstrate its potential for having a more active role in race-related politics. For example, in 1995 the IFL, AFL-CIO passed a resolution that strongly supported the NAACP and recognized it as "The premier civil rights organization in our country," and further encouraged all of its locals "to work more closely with the local chapters of the NAACP"(IFL, AFL-CIO, Resolution #17, 1995:48).

While in the post-WWI period the Iowa AFL-CIO took on certain human rights issues, unions at the local level were mostly preoccupied with immediate concerns about contracts and wage negotiations, increasing union membership, and economic issues. The turning point in Dubuque's post-war history of labor relations was the coming of John Deere into town in 1946, that put the city's industrialists on the defensive. In an interview a worker recalled the 1940s and the effect John Deere had on labor relations when Dubuque's "home owned businesses" had locked up the city's economy and labor force, and "did not want a business to come in here with high wages" (cf. Stromquist, 1993:170-71). Several unions, including the FE-CIO (the United Farm Equip-

Table 9: Resolutions and Committee Reports Related to Human Rights and Racial Discrimination Submitted at the IFL, AFL-CIO Annual Conventions, 1956-67

Resolution/ Committee Report	Issue	Convention/ Year/ Page #
Resolution # 15 (A)*	Condemning the Ku Klux Klan and racial discrimination.	1st/1956/38-39
Resolution #16(A)	Condemning segregated housing in Des Moines	1st/1956/39
Resolution # 6 (A)	Condemning racial quotas in admitting immigrants and to fight school segregation.	2nd/1957/46
Resolution #16(A)	To enforce FEP and support Supreme Court's decision in outlawing segregated schools.	2nd/1957/18-19
Resolution #51(A)	Support the passage of FEP legislation in nation and in Des Moines.	2nd/1957/46
Resolution #52(A)	Support Civil Rights and school integration.	2nd/1957/47
Resolution #67(A)	Anti-discrimination policy	2nd/1957/47
Human Rights Committee Report	Urging the organization to act on the 1957 Resolutions #16 & 51	3rd/1958/90
Resolution #66	Supporting & endorsing the upcoming Human Relations Conference.	5th/1960/9
Report	On race, prejudice and discrimination	5th/1960/4-5
Human Rights committee Report	Supporting human rights & FEP	7th/1962/2
Resolution (A, 1961)	Enforcing human rights concerns	7th/1962/3
Resolution # 10	Urging all labor unions to establish civil rights committees	9th/1964/27
Human Rights Committee Report	General statement in support of workers rights in a broad sense.	12th/1967/23-24
Resolution #28	Condemning the right-wing extremist groups such as the John Birch Society.	12th/1967/39

* "A" denotes resolutions adopted by convention delegates.

Sources: Various proceedings of the Iowa Federation of Labor, AFL-CIO annual conventions. Iowa City: State Historical Society of Iowa archives.

ment Workers), the AFL and the UAW (United Auto Workers) began dispatching organizers into the plant. When the dust settled, in 1947 John Deere workers voted for FE-CIO to be their legal voice in collective bargaining efforts. A year later after another election at John Deere, workers declared the Local 94-UAW-CIO as their bargaining agent.[10]

In the absence of black workers at the plant, Local 94 appears to have been more concerned with contracts, wages, and benefits than with human rights issues. For instance, in the late 1970s the local published a booklet to commemorate its 30th anniversary. In reviewing the 30-year track record of the local's activities one finds no references to black workers, human rights, or concerns for discrimination in the work place or public accommodation. These issues are also conspicuously absent in a table that outlined the local's accomplishments during three decades of its presence in Dubuque (UAW Local 94, ca 1978:121). Lack of documentation at the local level makes an evaluation of the local's actions concerning the protection of human rights at the plant almost impossible. But considering the overall attitude of the community toward nonwhites, to assume that both workers and the union officials lacked sensitivity about this issue is plausible. For instance, in the UAW local's 30th anniversary booklet there is a picture of a black-faced individual with a trumpet in his hands, most likely a John Deere worker, who is apparently imitating black-faced white minstrels of the early 20th century. The caption above the image reads "Bozo's Band at 1950 Xmas party" (Ibid, 70).

Dubuque has never had a sizable black population, and black workers' entry into Dubuque industries that had an organized work force started at a slow pace only after the 1960s. Despite indications of an overall lack of sensitivity on the part of Dubuque's organized labor, there are few occasions when the leadership took a stand in opposing discrimination and bigotry. For instance, when Robert Runde, president of the Dubuque AFL, was interviewed in 1982, he explained the union's support of the local Human Rights Commission when its existence was threatened by local power brokers.[11] Also, when in 1992 Dubuque was dealing with cross burnings and racial tensions, the Dubuque Federation of Labor leadership asked the Labor Center, a non-profit educational entity affiliated with the University of Iowa, to conduct a workshop on racism and bigotry for its rank and file.[12] Nevertheless, union leaders in Dubuque did not actively take part in the community's efforts to support and guarantee civil rights for the minority population. Nor did they publicly lend support to the liberals' plan to promote racial diversity in town. The union leaders' inaction was a reflection of a rising intra-class prejudice toward blacks and minorities among white workers who were themselves divided by a peculiar two-tiered labor market in the last two decades of the 20th century. This new intra-class division of labor was the outcome of two inter-related processes. First, similar to other industrial cities the higher paid and unionized workers were faced with a persistent threat of further cuts in positions, wages and benefits by the actions of the management. Second, there was an increase in numbers of the lower paid and mostly non-union workers who were also faced with an ever-shrinking market for low-paying, entry-level, and manual jobs. White workers in each group had their own concerns for job security and adequate wages that was in turn in conflict with those of the other group.

Related to race relations and employment of blacks and other minority workers in Dubuque's work places, both groups of workers interpreted liberals' plan for minority recruitment (the CIP) as a threat to their own specific class interests. Organized labor was mainly nervous about the plan's disregard of workers' seniority status for hiring and firing. In addition, labor unions were wary of employers who had historically hired African American workers both as strike breakers and lower paid workers. Iowa's labor history provides numerous examples of this practice by employers, in railroad and meatpacking industries for example, where blacks had been hired to defeat the striking workers (Scharnau, 2001: 226-229).[13] At times, the higher paid workers became the force behind hostile actions aimed at curtailing the source of cheap labor, in this case African Americans. A *New York Times* story on Dubuque's racial tensions is a good example of a reaction by the first tier of Dubuque's working class, when a cross burner was reportedly greeted "enthusiastically" by his coworkers in the city's meat packing plant "with backslaps and a standing ovation" (Wilkerson, 1991:1, 30).

The second tier of Dubuque's working class also had reasons to oppose the integration plan. In a tight and literally brutal local job market recruiting even one worker from outside the community meant a threat to the growing number of job seekers who were scrambling for scarce jobs. What made the situation even worse was that many of the workers in the second tier were skilled workers who previously held high-paying manufacturing jobs but were laid off during the 1980s recession. This second tier of the working class was vehemently and sometimes violently opposed to the minority recruitment plan. As a reflection of these socioeconomic conditions and changes, in the early 1990s one could find traces of prejudice and racism among the members of the working class and the poor in town. They ranged from ethnocentrist beliefs in white supremacy to legitimization of violence toward blacks and other minority groups. For example, an admitted cross burner stated that "everything in town was just fine until this [integration plan]. We need to take care of the people here instead of bringing these other people in. It's us against blacks." (Michael Lightfoot Jr., quoted in Wilkerson, 1991) Feeding off a common racist ideology, another worker whose goal was to become an auto mechanic feared that incoming blacks could take jobs he could have, and expressed his feelings by stating, "it's bad enough to lose your job to a white guy, but a black guy? It would mean that you lost a job to someone that everybody knows is lower than you." (Steven Dunn, quoted in Wilkerson, 1991) Finally, predicting white workers' reaction if the recruitment plan proved successful in the future, another worker remarked that "they ain't seen nothing yet. Cross burning? That's minor.

Someone's going to end up being done in. That's the way it's going to be." (cf. Swinton, 1991:7A)

Union locals for the most part remained silent on the increasing levels of prejudice among their rank and file. Both in work places and within the community Dubuque unions have a dismal historical record of supporting efforts to guarantee civil rights for blacks and other workers of minority status or to improve race relations. Organized labor's syndicalism in focusing only on economic concerns is understandable, but not necessarily admirable. This is an issue that has to be studied and analyzed not only at the local level, but also at state and national levels as well.

Notes

1. A member of the Socialist Party, a known opponent of the American involvement in WWI, and an active member of the California Federation of Labor, Thomas Mooney was arrested and jailed in 1916 after a bomb killed 10 people during a march in San Francisco.

   Many believed the government framed Mooney for his anti-government, pro-labor and socialist inclinations. After serving 23 years in jail, in 1938 he was pardoned by California Governor Culbert Olson, but died three years later at the age of 50 (see Hunt, 1971).
2. See chapter 5 for a historical review of the Klan's presence in Iowa and Dubuque.
3. Similar to 1925, the *Leader* completely ignored the Klan rally in 1926.
4. The AFL's anti-communist position was often reflected in editorials and articles printed in the *Leader*. For instance, in a 1925 article the AFL president compared communism to "the Boll Weevil in the cotton fields," and then warned the "Negro" workers of their illusions that a strong ANLC will wipe out "all racial, political and economic discrimination" (The *Dubuque Leader*, 1925:1).
5. Although not adopted by delegates, the resolution should be considered as a significant milestone in IFSL's history. Following the AFL's lead four years later ISFL delegates adopted a resolu-

tion in support of the Iowa's pending Fair Employment Practices (FEP) law (ISFL, 1954:70-71). This was the only positive race-related resolution passed by the ISFL before its merger with the CIO took place in 1956. Clearly, the ISFL had a conservative approach to race relations. For instance, in 1954 its Immigration Committee endorsed a discriminatory policy by urging the government to "enforce all immigration laws," and that "the quota of entrants be on an equal racial percentage basis to be set and determined by the needs and demands of agriculture and industrial employment."(ISFL, 1955:58) However, in 1957 the newly merged Iowa AFL-CIO passed a resolution on racial discrimination and pledged to bring about an "American immigration and citizenship policy and law free from discriminatory provisions such as the invidious national origins quota system." (see Resolution #6, IFL/AFL-CIO, 1957:47)

6. The *Brown vs. Board of Education of Topeka* case in 1954 is considered as one of the most important court cases in the U.S. race relations history. The core question in this case was "whether 'separate' but 'equal' schooling provide educationally equal opportunities." Rejecting the "separate but equal" education the Supreme Court ruled that not only segregated schools do not provide equal education for white and nonwhite students, they also violate the "equal protection" clause of the 14th Amendment. For a detailed discussion of the case see McLemore, 1991:335-37; and Tussman, 1963.
7. The Iowa AFL-CIO's efforts to educate the rank and file on the human rights issues has to be recognized. Of note is a discussion of race, prejudice and discrimination that was published in the 1960 annual convention proceedings. In rejecting race as a determining factor for discrimination, the report drew on the prevalent debates at the time and in particular emphasized the role of social factors in the learning process:

> It is a scientific fact, established by biologists, sociologists and geneticists, that in biological inheritance, all races are alike in their ability to learn and are alike in their innate (or inborn) behavior patterns. All races show the same distribution of every kind of ability. All races behave in the same

way and at the same average speed *under the same conditions and circumstances*" (IFL, AFL-CIO, 1960:4-5)(emphasis in original text).

8. The resolution called for a plan of action that "will formulate a firm policy of equal participation in committees and convention procedures for all brothers and sisters and promote like programs in central bodies and affiliated local unions"(IFL, AFL-CIO, 1977:17).
9. Although in a different historical period and related to a different labor organization, the ISFL's lack of resolve for racial equality during the 1920s and 1930s also coincided with a period of economic recession.
10. Later in 1968 the Local 94-UAW disaffiliated itself from the CIO and since then has represented John Deere workers.
11. Robert Runde, interviewed by Merle O. Davis, 1982. *Iowa Labor History Oral Project*, Iowa Federation of Labor, AFL-CIO. State Historical Society of Iowa.
12. Personal communication with Roberta Till-Retz, Program Coordinator, Iowa Labor Center, University of Iowa, March 4, 2002.
13. However, partly due to a nonexistent minority population in the work force the organized labor in Dubuque has rarely expressed such concerns in the open. For a theoretical discussion of the unions' position on black workers see Bonacich (1976).

CHAPTER 8
POLITICAL ECONOMY OF RACISM: DUBUQUE AS "ANY TOWN USA"

From Dubuque's early days as a small frontier village it has not been devoid of racial and ethic prejudice, and various ethnic and racial groups in different historical circumstances have served as convenient scapegoats. In more than 150 years of Dubuque's urban history three periods clearly stand out as being negatively affected by deterioration of the city's economic health, employment levels and overall quality of life. Dubuque's first period of economic downturn dates back to the late 1850s and early 1860s.[1] Local economic hardships combined with external political and economic pressures during the Civil War led to a rise in anti-black prejudice and resentment among Dubuque workers who regarded prospective freed slaves as potential threats and competitors in the city's depressed job market.[2] As discussed earlier, the ideological defeat of the South in the post-bellum period resulted in the passage of several civil rights laws in Iowa. But particularly in Dubuque these laws did little to significantly reduce prejudice and discrimination. The second period of economic hardship in Dubuque was the post-WWI era that witnessed the resurgence of the Klan in the region. Finally, after several decades of economic growth following WWII, in the late 1970s and the 1980s Dubuque plunged into one of its worst economic recessions. This was also a period of rising prejudicial attitudes that culminated in the racial crisis of the early 1990s. A question for social historians is whether or not there is a link between the resurgence of otherwise dormant racism on the one hand, and deterioration of economic conditions on the other.

This chapter focuses on the last two periods in Dubuque's history and examines political and economic forces that contributed to the rise and intensification of racial and ethnic conflicts.

WHAT WENT WRONG IN THE 1920S DUBUQUE?

In general, the history of race relations in Dubuque revolves around the negative attitudes of whites toward blacks. But prevalent racism during the 1920s had a different focus as working and middle class residents, mostly Catholic and of German descent, became targets of prejudice and discrimination. In order to understand Dubuque's state of the economy during the 1920s and early 1930s a brief historical overview of the city's economy is helpful.

By the mid-1830s the lead mines and smelters became Dubuque's basic industries and the 1840s brought prosperity for lead mining and trade (Somner, 1975:5). The climax of Dubuque's economic and commercial growth in the 19th century was between 1847 and 1857, when land speculators and developers expanded the city limits and Dubuque's population quadrupled from 4,057 in 1852 to 16,000 in 1857 (Blocker, 1988:25). As the lead mining industry witnessed its decline during the 1850s lumbering and related industries gradually developed and became the main economic sector in town. After a brief period of economic stagnation during the Civil War period Dubuque once again set out on the road to recovery. The city's economic growth and urban development was accelerated by additional rail connections to Iowa and the West, which in turn helped old and new industries alike to flourish (Mahoney, 1990). In addition to lumber-related industries such as saw mills and wood working plants, wagon factories, meat packing and brewing industries also developed during this period (Scharnau, 1993:53; Somner, 1975:6).

The last two decades of the 19th century brought more prosperity and economic growth for Dubuque, as it became a center of manufacturing and industrial activities in the region. During this period the city ranked first in Iowa in terms of the number of manufacturing firms and the average number of wage earners (Scharnau, 1993:55). The process of industrialization in the late 19th century also increased workers' awareness about the problems created by a profit-oriented capitalist economy. By joining labor unions Dubuque workers began to protect their rights and ask for better working conditions and higher wages. At the turn of the 20th century Dubuque had the highest rate of union membership in Iowa, with about two-thirds of the city's work force belonging to the organized labor (Ibid).

At national and regional levels the years between 1890 and 1910 were an era of economic concentration for capitalist firms, whereby larger companies either bought up smaller competitive firms or drove them out of business altogether. This proved to be detrimental to Dubuque's economy, as the majority of the town's local family-owned enterprises and industries were either out-competed by stronger companies in the region and forced out of business, or were unable to expand beyond local and regional markets due to lack of sufficient capital. By 1910 most of the steamboat companies were out of business, and lumber industries declined due to a shift in business from the Mississippi Valley to northern Minnesota and the Pacific northwest. Several devastating fires also accelerated the process, thus ending the era of lumberyards and related industries in Dubuque. This led to the loss of jobs and reductions in work force, followed by an increased level of poverty in the community (Somner, 1975:7; Scharnau, 1993:59-60). Facing national competition from larger firms and strong organized labor in Dubuque local business leaders were mobilized to fight the unions in order to stay in business. One strategy was to hold organized labor responsible for the failure of local industries "to keep pace with Des Moines, Sioux City and Cedar Rapids and failure to attract new industry."(Lucy, 1982:35)

In contrast, the WWI years brought prosperity for Iowa farmers in the rural heartland as a war-ravaged and devastated

Europe could not satisfy the demands for food and agricultural products. This was a golden opportunity for Iowa farmers to meet the wartime needs and reap the benefits. As a result, by 1920 agricultural land values more than doubled in Iowa compared to a decade earlier. For example, the average value of a farm rose from $14,574 in 1910 to $34,662 in 1920, a 138-percent increase in a decade. But this was a short lived prosperity, as European countries soon began to recover from the war and increased their agricultural output. As a result, Iowa farmers were dealt a devastating blow and agricultural land values and prices for farm products dropped drastically between 1920 and 1925. The farm crises of the 1920s affected many Iowa farmers, as they were unable to meet mortgage payments, and were forced to sell their farms (Johnson, 1967:43-44).

The end of WWI was also the beginning of a new era for the American capitalist economy. During this period a shift from competitive to monopoly capitalist production and distribution took place. Furthermore, large companies with adequate capital began to drive their competitors out of business and buy up their suppliers and distributors in order to exert monopolized control over the production and distribution processes (Ford, 1988:116).[3] The 1920s were prosperous years for American corporations, but this was achieved at the expense of the organized labor. For instance, between 1920 and 1923 union membership in the United States dropped from over 5 million to a little more than 3.5 million (Cohen, 1970:99). As a microcosm of the American economy, Dubuque industries also had a period of relative prosperity and expansion during the 1920s. But unable to compete nationally they demonstrated a determined resistance to union expansion and legitimate demands by organized labor. Fueled by an upsurge of nationalism in the country, business leaders in the city labeled the labor unions as "un-American," and soon the Ku Klux Klan found a fertile ground in Dubuque to espouse their racist, anti-labor, and anti-Catholic ideology. Organized labor became the target of vicious attacks by an unholy alliance of local businesses, industries and Klan sympathizers in town, as many of the workers were Catholics and, even worse, a good number of them were German Americans who were labeled as "unpatriotic" and "un-American."

In Iowa's urban centers the Klan naturally attracted leaders of business communities and members of fraternal organizations (Johnson, 1967:52). Some of the local business leaders and power brokers in Dubuque provided financial support for Klan activities. Grass-roots support also came from sectors of the middle- and working class population. But the Klan members of the 1920s came mostly from middle class backgrounds. These were ordinary Americans who were "solid, respectable citizens, kind and loving husbands, [and] conscientious members of their churches" (New Republic, 1923). For one thing, the rural nature of social and economic life in Iowa was a fertile breeding ground for average farmers with a conservative "middle-class" mentality. These farmers were faced with a harsh economic reality and an unknown future and hence were scared of the prospects of rapid social change. Within this social environment and among this particular class of citizens, the Ku Klux Klan successfully recruited its rank-and-file members.

The business leaders' anti-union tactics of the 1920s and their strategies for restructuring the city's industrial work force during the recession years led to massive layoffs and a sharp reduction in the work force by the end of the 1920s. Based on some estimates between 1927 and 1934 more than 30 firms either closed down or left town, eliminating 2,200 manufacturing jobs, only to be replaced by 13 new businesses employing a meager 300 workers (Scharnau, 1993:63). Despite the Klan's anti-labor position the organization found considerable support and sympathy among Dubuque workers. One plausible explanation for this interesting social phenomenon is the Klan's opposition to the government's lenient immigration policies, a view shared by the majority of workers, who considered European immigrants as a real threat to their job security in Dubuque's tight labor market.[4]

DID HISTORY REPEAT ITSELF IN THE 1980S?

The 1980s and 1990s were turbulent years in Dubuque pertaining to race and ethnic relations. During the same period the city's economic conditions were also deteriorating. A slowdown in Dubuque's economic growth was the culmination of a series of structural changes that took place within the American economy during the 1930-1980 period. As the nation's economy recovered from the Depression years in the late 1930s Dubuque's economy also improved, though at a slower pace. For example, in its annual report for 1938 the Iowa State Federation of Labor (1938:115) characterized the "port of Dubuque" as the "gateway to the nation's greatest granary" and a major industrial center, where "a total of 106 factories operate, among them the two largest sash and door mills in the world." The report also noted Dubuquers' awareness of the "opportunities brought to their door by the drawing of a new era in commerce and industry." Notwithstanding high rates of economic growth and development, Dubuque's share of an emerging corporate economy remained limited to a handful of industries and businesses, mostly operating within the confines of a regional economy. Multinational corporations were represented in Dubuque only by John Deere, which has a production branch on the outskirts of the city. Established in 1946, the John Deere Dubuque Works manufactured heavy construction equipment and by 1980 was employing 8,157 workers. Another significant industry which later joined the ranks of the regional corporate structure was the Dubuque Packing Company, which established its meatpacking plant in 1931 with 60 employees, and by 1980 employed more than 2,700 workers.[5] Although much less significant than the other two, a third company, Flexsteel Industries also played an important role in the city's economic life. A furniture manufacturer, by 1980 Flexsteel had more than 700 employees on its payroll (Chaichian, 1991: Table 2). Workers in all three major industries were represented by trade unions and enjoyed higher wages and better benefits and working conditions than other workers in the non-unionized sector.

Along with relative population growth and spatial expansion, the number of industrial workers doubled between 1940 and 1980. Overall, the post-War years brought about prosperity and job security for Dubuque workers, and one local historian called it Dubuque's "Golden Age" when "the local economy surged ahead as inflation and unemployment remained low, jobs and productivity grew, and real wages and consumption increased." By 1980 industrial workers comprised 36 percent of total work force in Dubuque County, which put Dubuque far above the national and state averages of 23 percent. At the same time "Dubuquers enjoyed the second highest median income in the state" and the city "ranked tenth nationally in per-capita consumer goods spending."(Scharnau, 1993: 68)

After a period of economic growth during the 1960s and parts of the 1970s, the American economy came again to face sluggish growth on the domestic front and a renewed fierce competition in the international market. High costs of labor and failure to invest in new machinery and technologies forced corporate managers to devise strategies to cope with the problem in order to maintain acceptable rates of profit in the market. The outcome was what critics commonly describe as "deindustrialization." Faced with aging plants and machinery, high rates of inflation, and rising labor costs, American industrial managers had to resort to draconian measures in order to stay in business and maintain a reasonable rate of return. In order to remain competitive in a globalized market corporations resorted to wholesale rationalization and industrial restructuring, removed capital from domestic operations and reinvested in overseas operations, moved plants from union strongholds in the north to southern states, or shut down plants altogether (Bluestone and Harrison, 1982:35-36).

In line with the national corporate strategy of industrial restructuring, some of Dubuque's corporate industries laid off up to half of their workforce during the 1979-1982 period alone. Facing a strong organized labor and its demands for better wages and safer work places, others threatened to shut down their plants if workers did not cede to their demands. In all, between 1979 and 1982 about 7,500 jobs in Dubuque were lost to industrial restructuring, of which the share of manufacturing firms employing 100 or more workers was 4,953. Between 1979 and 1982 the three major industrial firms, namely, John Deere, Dubuque Packing Co. and Flexsteel were responsible for almost all manufacturing jobs lost to the recession, laying off 4,921 workers (Chaichian, 1991: Table 2). During that same period John Deere reduced its work force of about 8,700 by 3,400 workers, and the Dubuque Pack laid off 1,450 employees out of a total work force of 2,700. When in early 1982 John Deere temporarily shut the Dubuque plant down, the city's unemployment rate jumped as high as 23 percent. The city's average unemployment rate for 1982 was 14 percent, and based on a survey of 203 counties by the Federal Bureau of Statistics, in the same year Dubuque County had the highest rate of unemployment in Iowa (Pins, 1982a).

The Dubuque Packing Company's strategy to fight organized labor and reduce its work force in the 1980s is probably one of the most controversial episodes of labor-management relations in the city's recent labor history. The Dubuque "Pack," as it was called by workers, was the first American food company to export food products to foreign countries in post-WWII years. With its high paying jobs and organized labor the Dubuque Pack became the second largest employer in town. By 1978 the Pack was one of the largest private companies in the United States. But the recession of the late 1970s and early 1980s took its toll, and by 1981 the company claimed that since 1979 it had lost $25 million. Between 1979 and 1981 the Pack workers were forced to make concessions, from wage freezes in 1979 to a 16 percent wage cut in 1981 (O'Hara, 1999:11-14). In an apparent union-busting plan in early 1982 the plant's owners announced that they planned to shut down the operation. The Dubuque Pack was subsequently dissolved and the plant's former chairman bought the defunct enterprise and then changed the company's name to

FDL Foods. Despite much effort by the United Food and Commercial Workers Union (UFCW) to fight the company through court injunctions, in late 1982 the deal was closed (*Des Moines Register*, 1982). Union leaders argued that the plan was in retaliation for unfair labor practices charges pressed by the UFCW, and accused the plant owners of "union busting" and "selling the company to themselves" (Pins, 1982b; *Des Moines Register*, 1982). After the sale of the Dubuque Pack to FDL Foods the old management in new suits informed the UFCW that they would recognize the union but not the existing contract, and that workers would have to agree not to strike for nine months (Pins, 1982d). Out of desperation and economic necessity union leaders ceded to management demands. Soon the new FDL opened the cut and kill operations by paying its workers $6.00 an hour, "a far cry from the $14.00 an hour made by workers with the incentive program in the 1970s" (O'Hara, 1999:14). By mid-1983 the union lost much of its membership, down from 2,500 in 1979 to about 1,000 in 1982; and with its existing contract not being renewed by management, it was left without much bargaining power or political muscle (Jost and Erb, 1983).

Up until the late 1970s when Dubuque's long period of economic recession began, manufacturing activities dominated the city's economy. But affected by economic recession at the national level in the 1980s, thousands of industrial jobs were lost and the city's economic planners were forced to make a drastic change of direction for its future economic development.

In general, the city's workforce was affected by four major structural shifts in terms of newly created jobs and wage and salary scales. First, between 1980 and 1988 more than 4,500 workers were laid off in the manufacturing sector alone. Most of the jobs lost were in the high paying manufacturing firms employing 100 or more workers, many of them being union strongholds. In contrast, newly created jobs were mostly in small scale and private corporate chain stores, or in service and retail establishments that hired non-union workers and paid them minimum wages.

During the same period ancillary services and related companies such as colleges, city government, and health care institutions hiring 100 or more employees were able to create only 103 new jobs. In other economic sectors, employment for the wholesale trade, financial institutions, insurance and real estate agencies remained unchanged, while the retail trade and service sectors were able to create only 2,700 new jobs (Chaichian, 1991).

Second, at the same time that major manufacturing firms were reducing their mostly male work force, female workers were entering the job market in significant numbers. Thus during the 1980s the labor force composition by gender in Dubuque County took a rapid turn, as more women were hired to fill low paying, non-unionized and mostly part-time jobs. The most dramatic shift in gender-based employment took place in the ancillary services sector. While in 1980 female employees comprised 34.5 percent of all workers employed in the service sector, by 1988 they accounted for 66.5 percent of its work force. Considering the fact that jobs created in the service sector were mostly low wage, non-union, part-time, and seasonal with little or no benefits, this change is an indication of reduced earnings for female workers and their families. This contributed to what is known as the "feminization of poverty."[6] Warehousing and distribution activities also increased their share of female employees from 25.7 percent in 1980 to 37.5 percent in 1988. Even in the declining manufacturing sector there were slight gains for female workers at a time that thousands of male workers were losing their secure jobs. The loss of jobs and income for male workers in turn reduced their political power and negatively affected their self-esteem and mental health.

Third, in communities like Dubuque where a few major employers control a disproportionately high percentage of jobs, fluctuations in national and regional economic conditions could be disastrous for workers and their families. As an industrial town on the periphery of the American economy, periodic economic booms and busts in Dubuque are quickly translated into in- and out-migration of workers. For example, economic prosperity in the 1960-80 period led to an increase in Dubuque's population while the 1980s recession drained the city of its working class residents. Based on one estimate, in the latter period Dubuque lost more than 10 percent of its population (Elliott, 1995:8, Table 1).

Finally, Dubuque workers not only lost thousands of high-paying jobs to an economy in recession, but those who were lucky to maintain their jobs, and still others who were able to find jobs in service-related businesses had to compromise and settle for reduced wages and benefits. For example, after adjusting for inflation, in 1988 workers employed in production and related occupations had to take home $5,448 less than what they earned back in 1981. The income losses for clerical and service workers for the same period were $4,018 and $2,385, respectively.[7]

URBAN DEVELOPMENT PLANS AND RISE OF RACISM

Another development that had significant social and economic impact on Dubuque was the construction of a new highway that cut right through the old and mostly working class and low income neighborhoods in the "Flats" area. The highway corridor eliminated many lower priced yet solid housing units, forced the tenants out of their houses and neighborhoods; and negatively affected the remaining housing stock along the highway. A study by the Dubuque Housing Commission titled "*A Housing Impact Study of the Freeway Corridor Plan*" (1989:7) made a comprehensive evaluation and assessment of the new highway construction and its impact on low income housing stock and concluded that highway construction will eliminate 75 to 85 percent of residential units in five target areas of the freeway corridor.[8]

Thus in terms of actual numbers, up to 590 units were either converted to non-residential purposes due to rezoning, or demolished for new commercial and industrial development projects. By Dubuque standards, the assessed value of an affordable house in 1989 was below $30,000, and 95 percent of the residential units in affected neighborhoods were affordable houses for low income families. Another way to look at the impact of the highway corridor on people is to estimate the number of residents affected by it. Based on the 1980 census there were 1,493 people residing in five residential areas in the proposed highway corridor. The Housing Commission's report estimated that between 1,083 and 1,300 residents would be displaced if the proposed land use plan were adopted and implemented (op. cit.: 8-11).[9]

One of the working class neighborhoods devastated by the highway construction was the old enclave of the Irish, the Dublin, where the residents' anger and frustration in the 1980s was reflected in the pages of their newsletter, the *Little Dublin News*. At the same time that the editors poked fun at other ethnic and racial groups in town, they were mourning for their not so glorious but nostalgic past which was being destroyed by the city's economic development plans. During the planning stages of Highway 151 in the early 1980s the newsletter's editor commented,

> Getting back further down in Dublin, a lot of changes have been made over the years. The state still doesn't know what to do with our end of town or where to put their freeway. Seems like their motto is either tear it down or preserve it. But one thing they never will take away are the memories of the good old families that lived down there. (*Little Dublin News*, January 1981:7)

When in the late 1980s the city began to clear the highway path that ran through the Flats area and Dublin, the newsletter published the following eulogy for Dublin, reflecting the sentiments of a proud but defeated ethnic group:

> Isn't it a shame the way they're tearing down Little Dublin, just to build a concrete jungle and a short cut to Wisconsin? *Damn, when I see some of these buildings being torn down, I'd like to take a hack saw and remove some of the plumbing of these master*

> *minds who always "progress" — horse crap.* Last week Bill Seller's barber shop was razed. Sad thing about it, Peter Heinen was waiting for a haircut. Cannonball Weber's saloon also got the ax and it took two cops to remove Bob Beadle before he finished his brew. As yet, they're still undecided about the Huss House. To tear it down would be a shame and a blow to our economy, *putting some good bellhops like Popeye Gavin, Wad Powers out of work plus where all these cockroaches go?"* (*Little Dublin News*, October 1988:7)(italics mine).

ANATOMY OF A MISPLACED ANGER

Dubuque has long been a city divided along the lines of social class and economic opportunity, and the city's urban geography speaks of an uneven urban growth. The spatial segregation of the poor and working class from the middle- and upper-classes is further accentuated by Dubuque's peculiar topography: The former are concentrated in the "Flats" and the latter reside up on the bluffs (the "Hill") and beyond. Jonathan Raban, a British traveler and novelist who in his long journey on the Mississippi River visited Dubuque in 1980 best described the spatial manifestation of this highly stratified city:

> A sociologist might have created Dubuque as an elementary model of a stratified society. A woman cabdriver took about three minutes to explain to me how the whole structure worked. "I'm nobody around here," she'd said. "I come from the Flats." The 'Flats,' down by the river, was where all the nobodies lived. North Side was German, and Germans were nobodies hoping to be somebodies; South Side was Irish, and the Irish were the nobody nobodies. The cabdriver came from the Flats, South Side. Between the nobodies and somebodies lay the four-block-thick cavity insulation of the business district. Then, as bluffs began to rise steeply above the town, so the

> people and their houses grew more and more important. Right at the top of Dubuque life was Alpine, a rocky stratosphere of mansions and ranch houses. (Raban, 1981:144)

Similar to other communities but perhaps with conspicuous visibility, not only more money seems to have been spent on improving the quality of the urban environment in the middle- and upper-class neighborhoods but also on economic development projects that suit the interests of the elite in Dubuque. Examples abound, from lavish beautification projects, such as planting flowers along "Grand View," a main boulevard that ran through an affluent residential area, to a much superior quality of education and school facilities in the middle- to upper-class neighborhoods in the Hill area and newly developed southern and western parts of town. In addition, despite much talk about the positive effects of the newly opened highway on the community's economic development, its completion adversely affected the poor and working-class neighborhoods in the Flats area.

If one were to describe the overall mood in this blue-collar city in the 1980s and early 1990s, it would be a defeated, frustrated and frightened community that had lost many past gains achieved by hard work and the collective efforts of a proud and highly organized work force. It was a community with no apparent solutions or future hopes at hand. A combination of several factors, including the loss of good-paying and secure jobs, persisting poverty and unemployment and destruction of working class and low-income neighborhoods contributed to the formation of attitudes and sentiments of a citizenry which became increasingly sensitive to and intolerant of any new plans for social change.

Economic restructuring and uneven urban development in Dubuque greatly contributed to deterioration of community's economic welfare, workers' mental help, and an increase in the level and extent of prejudicial attitudes and racial discrimination. Those who stayed in Dubuque faced a highly depressed job market and an array of new problems, ranging from psychological pressures and depression, drug and alcohol addiction to difficulties in coping with an array of family-related problems caused by unemployment, underemployment and poverty (Ricchiardi, 1982a). According to *Protective Services* in Dubuque, there was a steady rise in the number of child and spouse abuse cases reported from October 1981 to May 1982. While before January 1982 the reported cases were about 30 a month, there were 55 cases of abuse reported in April alone (Ricchiardi, 1992b). During the same period, calls to mental health agencies for help, mostly by unemployed workers, increased drastically. There were four recorded suicides during the first five months of 1982 compared to an average of four cases for the entire year in 1981 (Pins, 1982c). Finally, the children of the unemployed were also affected by industrial and economic restructuring in Dubuque. Commenting on changes in his unemployed father's personality and moods, a teenager stated in an interview that "sometimes he seems bitter and full of hate. He gets grouchy and takes it out at us." One teacher talked about school children who did not want to go home after school "because of what is going on there" (Ricchiardi, 1982a). Youth were also deprived of a previously stable job market that offered them part-time and summer jobs, as these temporary and low-paying jobs were "being soaked up" by the unemployed and desperate adults scraping for survival (Ibid.).

A closer scrutiny of the social and biographical background of hate crime offenders indicates that all were in the 18 to 24 age range; and all came from working class and poor families in the Flats area (Arnold and Jaspen, 1991). Probably as a reflection of poverty, unemployment and economic injustice, police records on criminal activities also indicate that the majority of offenders came from the Flats area. For example, a survey of reported crimes to the Dubuque Police Department indicates that in 1992 about 50 percent of all crimes took place either in downtown, or at the North End, comprising most of the Flats area. The former was a dilapidated section of town in transition and housing the urban poor beyond the central business district; and the latter a residential area long known as a working class stronghold (Bagsarian, 1993d). It may have been soothing and comforting for many residents to blame those who burnt the crosses and then feel satisfied with their arrest, conviction and imprisonment. But these young offenders were the children of those who were brutalized by the economic restructuring of the early 1980s and also frightened by an uncertain future where prospects for secure jobs and stable families were not so great.

The racist attitudes of these members of the working class and especially those of the working poor in Dubuque have to be considered as misplaced anger. Unable to comprehend the dynamics of the national economic and political forces that have negatively affected their community, in the 1980s and 1990s some Dubuque residents used racism as an outlet to vent their frustration and aim their anger at prospective African American workers as handy scapegoats.[10] Although opposition to the proposed Constructive Integration Plan became a conduit for Dubuque citizens to vent their anger, racial tensions of the early 1990s did not boil overnight. The roots of conflict have to be traced back at least to the early 1980s when Dubuque plunged into one of its worst economic recessions. The city's unemployment rate in 1982 was among the highest in the nation, and Dubuque residents were beginning to cope with the consequences of massive layoffs. Many of the laid-off workers and their families moved out of town in search of jobs elsewhere. As a sign of the prevalent feeling of hopelessness and defeatism, Dubuquers often joked that "the last one to leave the city should turn the lights out" (Lamphier-Hoffert, 1993:6).

Labor-management conflicts of the 1980s seriously threatened the collective strength and legitimacy of organized labor and weakened its political muscle at the bargaining table. The outcome was a victorious business community that tried to salvage restructured enterprises in the face of a stubbornly persistent economic recession; and a defeated organized labor that was willing to sit down and negotiate with the management to save the remaining jobs and to make major concessions.[11] The escalation of racial tensions in Dubuque in the 1980s and 1990s is a sad commentary on an economy and a city, whereby the ruling class and those in charge of economic decisions failed two generations of Dubuque residents in their efforts to keep the businesses afloat.

CONCLUSION

This book is not a condemnation of Dubuque citizens for holding attitudes towards blacks, as many of them have been at the forefront of a relentless war against racism, sexism and social injustice. But this book is about "*any town U.S.A.,*" when its residents experience more or less similar historical processes of social and economic development. Sincere but futile efforts of a group of concerned citizens in Dubuque to achieve racial integration and harmony suggest that racial prejudice and discrimination cannot be single-handedly eradicated. First, the laws of motion of a capitalist economy contribute to the widening gap between the rich and the poor, pitting one sector of the working class against another so that business interests are secured and an acceptable rate of profit is maintained. Second, communities cannot in isolation and single-handedly eradicate racism as long as its ideological roots and contributing socio-economic conditions are not seriously questioned and tackled at the national level. Third, historical evidence indicates that racial and ethnic targets and scapegoats are products of specific historical circumstances.

Although as a result of the American experience with institutionalized slavery blacks appear to have been utilized as a "reference point" for all "nonwhite" groups, the nature and level of prejudice and racism against them is not a historical constant. Rather, as a reflection of a national trend racial and ethnic prejudice in Dubuque has evolved along two parallel historical tracks. The first track includes continued discrimination of blacks, but with varying degrees of intensity, who are culturally perceived as "reference points" for all nonwhite races. The second track is comprised of other ethnic and racial groups, both white and nonwhite, who are selectively singled out and then discriminated against as ethnic scapegoats. Both blacks and other occasional scapegoats are then held responsible for all social ills and economic problems. For instance, the overt public support for the Klan in the 1920s had a class base different from that in the 1980s and early 1990s, and targeted different groups. Back then, the Klan presence served the interests of the city's ruling elite by fragmenting a previously united working class and pitting one against another. Thus, by portraying workers with German background as "unpatriotic" and "un-American," the ruling elite were able to use them as a handy scapegoat to keep workers divided. While in the former period Klan sympathizers and members came from upper- as well as middle- and working class backgrounds, Klan support in the latter period was clearly provided by the working class and the poor. The racism of the 1980s was an intra-class conflict between a weakened and fragmented working class, organized and unorganized alike, and a perceived outside threat personified in the prospective minority workers, as suggested by the Constructive Integration Plan (CIP). There were also pro-Klan sympathizers among the business community and the ruling elite in the latter period, but "out of fear of disgrace" they could no longer mobilize their forces behind the Klan mask (Feagin and Vera, 1995:13).

This change in class based support for the hooded organization is also an outcome of the changes in the American economy after WWI. In one study, the socio-economic backgrounds of 150 Klan members are examined in the 1950s (Vander Zanden, 1960). The findings of Vander Zanden's investigation indicate that many of the individuals on his list belonged to marginal occupational groups which placed them somewhere between the middle-class and the working poor. This marginality is a precarious social class position, which in times of extreme social and economic pressure will lead to feelings of anxiety, insecurity and frustration. By providing a group identity and an illusory cause to fight, groups like the Ku Klux Klan appear to make sense to individuals at the margins of society (see also Johnson, 1976:1-11).

The liberal faction's failure to grasp the workings of the American political economy and Dubuque's social context inevitably led to the demise of the Constructive Integration Plan. Although sincere in their efforts, they should be blamed for their shortsightedness. Instead of advancing the cause of racial equality they contributed to the deterioration of race relations in town by ignoring the working class and the poor and excluding them from the decision making process. Our study of race and ethnicity in Dubuque indicates that "racists" come from all social classes, but they do not remain one in perpetuity. Unfortunately, most critical studies of racists and racist groups begin when these individuals or groups for various economic and political reasons become marginalized. As a result, strategies to deal with racism usually consider people with racist beliefs and inclinations as part of the problem, thus effectively excluding them when inflicted communities search for viable solutions.

Notes

1. The lynching of Nathaniel Morgan, an African American resident of Dubuque, by the mob in 1840 can also be linked to a sudden decline in lead mining business in the late 1830s. But it can also be viewed as an isolated act of violence, since it was not followed by more lynching or other extreme racist behaviors (see chapter 3).
2. For a discussion of race relations during this period see chapter 3.
3. Noting the difference in price structure in monopolistic and competitive industries, in *The Structure of the American Economy* Gardiner Means (1939: 139) observes that the term "monopoly" refers to "situations in which sufficient control would be exercised over price by an individual producer or by a colluding group of producers to make possible monopoly profits, i.e., profits above the rate necessary to induce new investment in other industries not subject to monopoly control." In contrast, during the competitive stage "a situation was in general classified as competitive if there

was insufficient control over price to make monopoly profits possible." See also *Monopoly Capital* by Paul Baran and Paul Sweezy (1966), in which they provide a framework to view the historical evolution of American capitalist economy and its transition from competitive to monopoly capitalist stage. Both monopolistic and competitive sectors of the economy have continued to exist side by side, but "the giant corporation, able to control to a considerable extent its level of price, output, and investment, is the typical firm in a dynamic sense in the monopoly capitalist economy." (Foster, 2000)

4. Later in this chapter I discuss the organized labor's position on immigration in the 1920s.
5. The Dubuque Packing Co. was later reorganized and renamed as FDL Foods, Incorporated.
6. The term was first used by sociologist Diana Pierce, who in 1978 studied female-headed households and brought their plight and increasing poverty to the nation's attention. See Pierce (1978).
7. Adjusted income for 1988 is calculated based on inflation rates for the 1981-1988 period, and it is the income workers should have earned to keep up with inflation. See Chaichian (1991, Table 10).
8. According to the report, at the time "there were a total of 324 buildings containing 664 residential units."(Ibid)
9. Highway 61/151 became fully operational in August 1993. The full impact of the corridor rezoning is yet to be seen.
10. Intra-class conflict based on ethnic antagonism has been studied and explained by several scholars. Bonacich (1972) develops an interesting theory known as the "split labor market." According to this theory, when there is a large differential in wage or "price of labor" within the same occupation, it produces a "three-way conflict between business and the two labor groups," with business attempting to replace higher paid workers with cheaper labor. Although the theory is not directly applicable to our case, the outcomes of a split labor market in terms of ethnic antagonism and conflict are very similar. See Howell (1982) and Boswell (1986) for an explanation of discrimination toward other ethnic groups, and Bonacich (1976) on black/white race relations.

11. Like many other industrial-based communities and regions hard hit by the economic restructuring process during the 1980s, the management-initiated "Labor-Management Council" was formed in Dubuque in 1988 (see Blocker, 1989; Scharnau, 1993).

EPILOGUE
DUBUQUE AND IOWA IN THE NEW MILLENNIUM

More than a decade has past since efforts by a group of concerned citizens to bring about racial and ethnic diversity to Dubuque were met by some residents' stiff resistance, and were eventually derailed by Dubuque's movers and shakers. When in 1992 the original citizen group that sponsored the Constructive Integration Plan (CIP) was replaced by a business-supported Council for Diversity (CFD), some observers predicted the latter group's ineffectiveness and short lived existence. Their vision was prophetic, as in fact the CFD was disbanded in June 1995 (see Pulliman-Hill, 1995: A5). A former member of the CFD summed up the main reason for its abrupt demise as "In the end, in 1995, they said we don't have any money. They [corporate sponsors] said pretty much, we accomplished what we wanted to do." (Ralph Scharnau, cf. Coyle, 2002b:2A)

As a credit to CIP supporters and CFD efforts, there were some accomplishments, at least in terms of organizing citizen discussion groups, educating the public and preparing Dubuque citizens for a more ethnically diverse population in future. For instance, in 1999 the city of Dubuque was recognized and awarded at the 6th annual Iowa Diversity Conference for its efforts to promote diversity.[1] The award recognized the Dubuque HRC and city administrators for the following initiatives:

1. Creation of the Dubuque Advisory Panel, a conduit for citizens to work with the police department to ensure equal treatment of people based on their race and ethnicity;

2. creation of the Dubuque Dispute Resolution Center to mediate neighborhood and racially-based disputes;[2]
3. establishment of Talk Circles, first in Dubuque and then in more than ten other cities in Iowa, that consisted of citizens from various ethnic and religious backgrounds who participate in group discussions on racial and ethnic diversity; and
4. supporting educational programs for children and students on human rights concerns, from sexual harassment to fair housing practices (Pieters, 1999:A3).[3]

Most efforts at the community level focused on education and plans to change people's attitudes toward other races and ethnic groups. For instance, in 1996 the Dubuque Community School District published a 40-page document to further promote the existing plan for a multicultural and non-sexist education. Some of the stated goals in the document were recognition of, and respect for diversity, sharpening students' skills in inter-ethnic and inter-racial communication and learning a second language (Krapfl, 1996:A3). An investigation of prejudicial attitudes among school teachers also led to the development of a teacher sensitivity training program (Brigham and Wright, 2001:334).

Despite the Dubuque HRC's more proactive approach in educating the citizenry about race relations, prejudicial attitudes continued to plague work places and schools in town. But probably as a sign of the HRC's increased power and active role in mediating in race-related complaints, several cases related to racial discrimination and hate crimes were taken seriously by the courts. For example, two former employees of FDL Foods, the city's second largest employer in the early 1990s, filed law suits against the company citing racial discrimination. In the first case filed in 1996, the plaintiff claimed that "he was subjected to racially hostile environment" and was attacked and severely beaten by white coworkers who allegedly did not like "having a 'nigger' working beside them." Yet he claimed FDL authorities "didn't acknowledge the problem and refused to take steps to resolve the situation" (Sweeney, 1996:A3). In the second lawsuit in 2001, another plaintiff reported "experiences with racial discrimination" in his workplace between 1990 and 1997. However, his complaints about the problem were dismissed by his employers and attributed to "personality conflicts." An administrative law judge reportedly sided with the employer, but his decision was later overruled by the HRC. In its ruling, the HRC indicated that the plaintiff's supervisor "was yelling in his face, monitoring his rest room breaks, and not allowing [him] to go home early while white coworkers with less seniority were treated differently." The HRC granted the black worker $72,292, its "largest award to date," for "lost wages and emotional distress" (Coyle, 2001:A3).[4] Finally, in early 2002 a teen-age student of Asian origin and her father were awarded $4,000 in the first hate crime case being tried in civil court in city's history. According to reports, the teen-ager was assaulted on her way home from school by a 17-year-old classmate who allegedly "called her derogatory names associated with her Chinese heritage." (Des Moines Register News Service, 2002a)

Dubuque's economy during the 1990s struggled to survive as some of its major industries closed their doors or reduced their work force. The major blow to Dubuque's already shattered economy came with the announcement by the FDL management in September 1995 that it would close its doors unless it could sell its hog-slaughtering plant. Thus began rounds of negotiation between Dubuque's civil leaders and FDL, the city's second largest employer, to find a qualified buyer. At the same time, management urged the United Food and Commercial Workers Union (UFCW) that represented FDL workers to ratify a contract with the company, since without a contract no purchase would take place. While the union settled for an already reduced hourly wage of $9.00, city leaders desperately sought after potential buyers. First, the Kansas City based Farmland Foods showed interest, but it later backed out. At this point FDL laid off more than half of its 1800 workers. Later on, IBP, a major meatpacking company became interested. But there were suspicions that it intended to purchase the plant and then close it down to eliminate competition. Dubuque civic leaders prevented the plant's sale to IBP through court injunctions, and once again Farmland Foods was lured by offers of economic development funds. Eventually, the company accepted the deal and the plant officially started to operate in mid-1996 (O'Hara, 1999:58-60).

With organized labor's diminished power in the work place, labor-intensive industries such as meatpacking reduced their work force and used coercive measures to increase their productivity, such as speeding up the production pace at their assembly lines. For instance, Farmland Foods was characterized by a union representative as a "pro at coercion," where workers were told "if they do not work to a specified level, their jobs will be moved elsewhere" (60). When Farmland took over the plant its management faxed a contract to the union office indicating that they were not interested in negotiating. Workers either had to pass the company-proposed contract, or else "they would be out of jobs"(61).

Similar to many other industries, economic restructuring in the 1980s also accelerated the deskilling process within the meatpacking industries. For instance, to increase worker productivity the new management also simplified their tasks. While in the past workers "would make all of the cuts on the piece of meat to remove the bone," under new management they made "one cut each on the piece of meat in removing the bone"(67).

In addition, plant managers used another strategy to undermine local workers' collective power and unity. At the same time that white workers opposed the Constructive Integration Plan, believing it intended to "recruit" blacks and migrant workers to come to Dubuque and undermining their job security, some businesses were quietly attracting and employing migrant workers. Of note is the Farmland Foods plant, where considerable numbers of Mexican and Bosnian workers were reportedly employed. There were also signs of rising levels of prejudicial attitudes among white workers at the plant. This was the case even before Farmland bought the plant from FDL. For instance, when O'Hara (1999:56, 58) interviewed FDL workers on the reasons for employees' alienation and diminishing morale, one worker spoke of how "he overheard a young person speaking about his reluctance to go to work" because "only Mexicans and Bosnians work there." Some told him "how there are now various languages spoken within the plant, further disabling workers from socializing with each other.

By 1999 the Farmland management had difficulty in attracting skilled meat cutters due to its low wages (O'Hara, 1999:15-19). The company was eventually sold to Smithfield Foods, which announced plans to fix up and reopen the facility, but it too closed the plant in 2000. With Farmland closing its doors, the city's civic leaders and planners began to search for alternative strategies to boost Dubuque's economy. In a report on Dubuque's economic "comeback" in the 21st century, a *Dubuque Telegraph Herald* reporter assured the readers of local leaders' awareness of the problem, and claimed that they tried to "wean Dubuque away from its traditional reliance on two huge local employers, the meatpacking plant and John Deere & Co." He then outlined the city's recent successes in attracting new businesses and creating jobs. Of note were a new 112,000 square-foot call center for the Retirement and Investment Services, a CIGNA subsidiary; a $17 million complex for manufacturing windows and doors; and construction of the first phase of the $200 million America's River Project, that reportedly would "revive the city's Mississippi River frontage with a new River museum and aquarium, convention center, and a hotel with an indoor water park" (De Witte, 2001).

But Dubuque's new emphasis on service-based industries, tourism, and small high-tech firms is a far cry from the city's tradition of relying on manufacturing activities in the past that created better paying blue-collar jobs with strong union presence. In light of big job losses during the 1980s and 1990s in meatpacking and farm equipment industries, new jobs are created but in much smaller numbers. This new so-called "post-industrial" economic strategy to attract high-tech industries and sell the city as a tourist attraction to outsiders has made the already defeated work force even more vulnerable to the uncertainties of a volatile economy and its job market. For instance, in its 2000-2001 annual report the Greater Dubuque Development Corporation boasted about a study by the Milken Institute, a California-based think tank, that ranked Dubuque 18th among the top 50 metropolitan areas for their high-tech output growth during the 1996-2001 period. Dubuque's achievements were reportedly in the areas of "computer programming and data processing, telephone communication services, and laboratory related products" (The Greater Dubuque Development Corporation, 2002). Yet this apparently remarkable achievement neither produced a sustained economic growth nor guaranteed stable and adequate job opportunities in town. For example, in the aftermath of the September 11 tragedy in 2001, in another study the Milken Institute ranked Dubuque 15th among 315 metropolitan areas that in 2002 would "experience the greatest job losses, based on the size of the working population"(Des Moines Register, 2002b).[5]

Despite some efforts by the city's movers and shakers, race relations did not drastically improve in Dubuque. Recalling racial tensions that shook Dubuque and briefly attracted the attention of the national media, in early 2002 the city's only newspaper, *The Telegraph Herald,* published a series of reports titled "Behind the Numbers." In the series several reporters looked at the city's black community and their concerns about living in a predominantly white city. "While the number of blacks more than doubled during the decade 1990-2000, blacks still represent 1.2 percent of Dubuque's population," said the first report. Chronicling turbulent moments in Dubuque' race relations since the Constructive Integration Plan's defeat, the reporter reminisced that in 1995 "a truck and two car loads of white youth drove through the downtown neighborhood shouting 'white power,'" and unknown perpetrators twice threw mud on a black resident's car (Sisco, 2002b:8A). But he then emphasized that some positive changes have also taken place in the area of human rights, mostly improvements in public accommodation for African Americans. A black resident noted that when he got off the bus in Dubuque "he had only $100 in his pocket and a bag of clothes," yet he had "no trouble finding a place to stay" (Crowin James, cf. Sisco, Ibid.). Another black resident recalled that a white landlord not only rented an apartment to her, but he also "helped her get a loan for her 1st month's rent" (Patricia Brown, cf. Sisco, Ibid.). Others also told of white Dubuquers who "overextended" themselves to help: "our [white] realtor... even offered to take me somewhere to fill out a job application"(Peggy Jackson, cf. Sisco, Ibid.). Ruby Sutton, President of the Dubuque HRC and a longtime local activist summed up the efforts of the Constructive Integration Debate on the city and stated she "never would have thought Dubuque would have come this far in this short time."(cf. Kittle, 2002:12A)

Yet despite improvements, what has persisted in Dubuque is a subtle racism. A former member of both the CIP and CFD stated that "not a whole lot has really changed since [the early 1990s]. Things really went covert" (Claudet Carter-Thomas, cf. Coyle, 2002b: A2). When asked about their experiences with race relations in town, several black residents declined to comment, and some indicated "the community would not want to know what they have to say about race relations in the city" (Coyle, Ibid.). Some residents also believe city leaders' efforts in the area of race relations are superficial and have produced little. When in January 2002 several neighborhood groups gathered to discuss diversity in Dubuque, some members questioned the utility of adopting racially inclusive slogans for the city: "just because the Martin Luther King Committee adopted the slogan, "Dubuque, Iowa: Dr. King's Neighborhood," does not mean that Dubuque has made progress in accepting and embracing diversity" (cf. Sisco, 2002a:A3). In fact, the CIP debate and ensuing racial tensions have further pushed prejudicial attitudes beneath a cover of social civility (Coyle, 2002b:A1).

Furthermore, discrimination in housing continued to be a prevalent problem in town. According to a December 2001 study done by the John Marshall Law School of Chicago, most people interviewed for their study of fair housing practices in town thought that "housing discrimination occurs regularly in Dubuque, and given the makeup of the community, it would be surprising if it did not." A survey of discrimination cases based on race and national origin filed with the Dubuque HRC during the 1990s also indicates the city's efforts to improve race relations has had little or no effect (cf. Coyle, 2002b"A2).

Yet despite opposition to the CIP in the early 1990s and continued prejudice toward blacks and nonwhites, by 2000 there was a significant increase in the number of both African Americans and residents of Hispanic origin. According to census data the number of black residents in the Dubuque MSA increased from 351 in 1990 to 964 in 2000 (Frey, 2001: Appendix E). During the same decade the number of Hispanics in Dubuque County also increased from 437 to 1065. The considerable number and presence of the latter group prompted the Dubuque HRC to offer Spanish lessons to its citizens "as an incentive for all people to feel welcome in Dubuque."(Coyle, 2002a: 2A)

Dubuque's continued struggle and preoccupation with prejudice and discrimination should be viewed as symptoms of a problem that has its roots in the state and national political economies. When Jonathan Narcisse, an African American activist and Iowa native was invited to speak at the 2002 Annual Martin Luther King event in Dubuque, he characterized Iowa as "one of the best places for white children to grow up in," yet "one of the harshest for African American children," where parents "lose at least half of them from school before graduation." He also alluded to the prevalence of racial profiling in Iowa whereby "it is impossible to drive from one side of Iowa to the other as an African American male without being stopped, detained and searched without cause"(Narcisse, cf. Nevans-Pederson, 2000:A3).[6] Narcisse's comments about the status of blacks in Iowa and prevalence of discrimination are supported by state data on black incarceration and unemployment rates. For instance, blacks in Iowa are incarcerated nearly ten times more than whites: while in 1999 blacks accounted for 2 percent of state's population, they comprised one-fourth of Iowa's prison population (The Associated Press, 1999). Likewise, in 2000 unemployment rates for white and black Iowans were 2.5 and 8.2 percent, respectively (Labor Market Information Bureau, Iowa Work Force Development).

While white-on-black prejudice and discrimination continues to affect blacks, Iowa's economic transformation and changes in its labor force composition in the past two decades have created a new problematic "race": the Hispanic migrant laborers. Lured and often directly recruited by Iowa employers in the meat packing plants and other industries in the 1990s, Hispanic migrant workers have come to Iowa in significant numbers. According to the census data Iowa's "Hispanic or Latino" population has more than doubled in a decade from 32,647 in 1990 to 82,473 in 2000.[7]

This is at a time when Iowa is loosing thousands of its younger and better educated residents to other states. As a sign of the state's "brain drain," a 1997 study conducted by the Iowa College Student Aid Commission found that 37 percent of college graduates with a bachelor's degree leave Iowa, and the percentage increases for holders of masters' and doctorate degrees to 54 and 56 percent, respectively (Heim, 2001:6). As young educated Iowans leave for better jobs and higher wages, existing and newly created jobs are mostly in the service sector and industries that require little or no skills.

Faced with a virtual brain drain and labor shortage, and in search of viable solutions, the state's governor and his policy makers are trying to encourage immigrants to come to Iowa. Thus followed by a recommendation by the 2010 Strategic Planning Commission, in 2000 Governor Vilsack pursued the idea of creating "Immigration Enterprise Zones" to attract immigrants while by-passing federal immigration regulations. Finding the idea impractical and faced with opposition, the governor abandoned the plan and instead announced that three Iowa cities of Marshalltown, Fort Dodge and Mason City would serve as "model communities." The governor hoped that with the state's financial backing the three communities would develop "strategies for both attracting immigrants and setting up the services necessary to handle an influx of new people" (Pins, 2000).[8]

The Iowa governor's immigrant recruitment campaign has met with stiff resistance, with the strongest opposition coming from the organized labor quarters. A 2001 *Des Moines Register* poll showed 66 percent of Iowans from "union households" opposed Governor Vilsack's efforts to recruit immigrant workers (Roos, 2001). Some union officials indicated that the plan is not necessarily a bad idea, but that it had the potential to be one: "we have real concerns about bringing in very low wage people, unskilled people that are going to end up flooding the low end of the wage market, becoming a basic burden on society."[9] In addition to the organized labor, there has also been a growing grass roots opposition to immigrant recruitment plans, specifically in communities that are either affected or will be in future by incoming migrant workers. In 2001, when the city council in Mason City by a vote of 4-1 approved the $50,000 state contract award for its participation in the Model City Project, many residents signed a petition to voice their concerns about the governor's plan. When asked for the rationale in signing the petition, one resident stated that she signed it because "we were not asked to be a model city. The mayor and the city council just snuck this through on us" (Mae Green, quoted in Kompas, 2001). A retired cement worker who also opposed Vilsack's plan believed that it was the "Mexican element" that has irritated residents:

> They'll run over the town if you let them — they're homing pigeons, sending all the money they make back home instead of spending it around here. Or

> they get on welfare the minute they can. People call it racism, but we call it stopping immigration (Leo Warner, quoted in von Sternberg, 2001).

A similar petition was also circulated in Fort Dodge, the other model city. A city council member who signed the petition echoed similar concerns: "we have got people in my area of town that are out of work. The economy is sinking. So why are we bringing immigrants in?"(Greg Nolting, quoted in Kompas, 2001). Amidst mounting opposition the governor called disagreement with his plan part of "a difficult but healthy debate," and warned Iowans that "given current population trends," without new comers by 2010 "the state will face a worker shortage of 450,000" (Vilsack, quoted in von Sternberg, 2001).

There are striking similarities between Dubuque's CIP that intended to attract blacks into town and Governor Vilsack's plans to recruit immigrants in order to promote racial and ethnic diversity. Likewise, one finds similarities in reaction to both plans. In particular, similar to Dubuque's case the governor's initiative has put labor unions between a rock and the hard place: supporting immigration recruitment plan would be detrimental to the welfare of their rank and file; while by opposing the plan they will be immediately branded by liberals as racist. Even worse, they will find themselves side by side the racist groups on this issue. Mark Smith, president of the Iowa Federation of Labor, best explained the union's concerns and frustrations and stated every time "he raises the mildest opposition to Vilsack's plan" he hears "from the right-wing hate groups who say it's the brown people invading us." He also blamed Iowa businesses and employers for their role in escalating the conflict and concluded "it's employers who want to work people for nothing who are the problem" (quoted in von Sternberg, 2001).

In general, state planners lack economic resources and political power to provide an alternative to a complex global economy that increasingly benefits from a highly mobile and cheap labor force. Similar to Dubuque's case, statewide efforts to find alternative strategies in response to economic restructuring, labor shortages and deskilling process tend to alienate longtime residents and victimize incoming immigrants. The end result is that the former resort to nativist and racist beliefs and ideologies in self-defense, while the latter are unjustly subjected to prejudice and discrimination.

If opponents of racial and ethnic diversity in Dubuque resorted to cross burnings and welcomed white supremacist groups to support their cause, Iowans opposed to the state's open-door migrant labor policy are using "English only" legislation as their political weapon. Similar to the 1920s when the "English only" policy was reinforced to deal with the "un-American" Germans in Iowa, it has been revived today in order to contain the threat by an influx of seemingly "un-American" Hispanic immigrants. Despite considerable opposition, the first victory for the new nativist movement was achieved in 2000 with the passage of a resolution by the Marshall County Board of Supervisors that made English the county's official language. In defending the resolution, one county supervisor stated that "it honored the 2,200-signature petition gathered by members of the local Veterans of Foreign Wars (VFW)." He then concluded that they responded to the veterans' request and "didn't see this as racism or Nazism" (John Soorholtz, quoted in the *Dubuque Telegraph Herald,* 2000). The passage of Marshall County's "English Only" resolution intensified the state's ongoing debate on making English Iowa's official language. After several setbacks, the introduced "English Only" bill to the Iowa house was eventually passed in 2001, followed by the Senate support in early 2002. Faced with public pressure and despite his initial hesitation in March 2002 the governor finally signed it into law. Of note is the governor's indecisive and confusing approach to the issue. While he still supported the promotion of diversity and welcomed immigrants, he was forced to endorse a policy that undermined new immigrants' rights in preserving and promoting their cultural heritage. At best, the "English only" bill will yield no tangible results, and at worst it will reinforce and fuel prejudicial attitudes toward newcomers who speak a language other than English (see Gribbin, 2002). In retrospect, organized labor in Iowa has to be recognized for its foresight and strong opposition to the "English only" legislation. As early as 1997 the IFL-CIO passed a resolution that strongly condemned "English-Only" legislation as a "myopic and bigoted effort by some that would only result in discrimination and hinder the competitiveness of the United States in a global economy (IFL/AFL-CIO, Resolution #12, 1997:47-48). Thus being dependent on political and economic forces beyond state boundaries, Dubuque and Iowa have entered the new millennium marred with uncertainties. In the area of race relations, after a long historical journey African Americans are still being discriminated against as Iowa's "reference point" for all other "nonwhite" races. But they may get a break in the new millennium, as new immigrants, in particular Hispanics, are being recognized as Iowa's new "problematic race."

My overall approach to race relations in this book is best explained by Pierre van den Berghe in the introduction to his pioneering book *Race and Racism, a Comparative Perspective:*

> At a more theoretical level race relations in the United States have, following Myrdal's lead, been interpreted more often as a moral dilemma in the hearts and minds of men rather than a complex dynamic of group conflict resulting from the differential distribution of power, wealth, prestige, and other social rewards.(1967:5)

Van den Berghe's reference is to the Swedish sociologist and economist Gunnar Myrdal. In his classic book, *An American Dilemma: The Negro Problem and Modern Democracy (1944)* he examined racial problems in the United States. Myrdal concluded that the "Negro problem" is a "moral dilemma" that violates the widely accepted precepts of the "American creed" and ideals of

American democracy, regarding the "essential dignity of the individual human being, of the fundamental equality of all persons, and of certain individuals' right to freedom, justice, and a fair opportunity"(3-4). For him, the main obstacle for racial equality was blacks' inability to assimilate into white European society, mainly because of resistance to such assimilation by whites. In a review of Myrdal's book, McKee (1993: 227) reiterates that "the dilemma between the highest ideal and self-serving prejudices was a dilemma for white people, not for black people; it was, in effect, a way of defining the white man's problem."[10]

I must conclude this chapter with the same words that I concluded my introduction to this book. Contrary to Myrdal's conviction, the "American dilemma," that is, "Iowa's dilemma," can neither be resolved by assimilation of blacks and other "nonwhite" ethnic groups into the "white" society, nor by simply changing whites' prejudicial attitudes toward nonwhites. Racism — in particular white-on-black racism — should be examined and understood as a socially created ideology that is intertwined with periodic turns and twists of the American political economy, has evolved historically, and is constantly modified and revised in response to political and economic developments, group and ethnic interaction dynamics and class conflicts.

Notes

1. The Iowa Diversity Conference was initiated by the state governor in 1994 as a response to racial tensions in Dubuque and other cities across Iowa.
2. By 1999 the Center had mediated more than 40 cases in town.
3. Promoted by the Iowa Civil Rights Commission in 1996, the "study circles" were community-based groups that were established in various urban centers to discuss racism and ways to improve race relations (see Patterson, 1998:18).
4. The ruling was appealed by the company.

5. For comparative job loss projections see the Milken Institute. Accessed 4-10-03: http://www.milken-inst.org/pressrel/rep3.htm.
6. He stated that he has been stopped "at least a dozen times in the last 18 months"(Ibid.)
7. Charvat, Sandra, and Willis Goudy. 2001. *Hispanic/Latino Residents by Specific Origin in Iowa's Counties, 1990 and 2000.* Iowa State University, placed on the census web site on May 18, 2001: http://www.soc.iastate.edu/census.
8. At the time, Marshalltown was already employing significant number of immigrants in its meatpacking industry.
9. Mark Smith, President of the Iowa Federation of Labor, interviewed by Roos, Ibid).
10. See chapter 6 in McKee (1993) for his appraisal of Myrdal's book.

BIBLIOGRAPHY

BIBLIOGRAPHY

Abu-Lughod, Janet L. 1991. *Changing Cities.* New York: HarperCollins Publishers.

Allen, William. 1865. *Letter to C. Childs.* State Historical Society of Iowa, Manuscript Collection. Iowa City, Iowa.

Anderson, Peter. 1969a. "The Invisible Man, Part I," *Dubuque Telegraph Herald*, (March 24):4.

-----. 1969b. "The Treasonable Path, The Invisible Man Part II," *Dubuque Telegraph Herald*,(March 25):4.

-----. 1969c. "We Are Gaining," *Dubuque Telegraph Herald*, (March 26):4.

-----. 1969d. "Dubuque Churches and the Black Man," *Dubuque Telegraph Herald*, (March 27):4.

-----. 1970. "Says Chalmers' Bridges May be Burned," *Dubuque Telegraph Herald*, January 11.

Annals of Iowa. 1903. "Slaves in Iowa," 3rd Ser., 6:66-67.

Arnold, William. 1991a. "Officials: Ad Against Minority Recruitment in Error," *Dubuque Telegraph Herald*, (September 18):1A.

-----. 1991b. "Hartig: Ad Focus Not Racist," *Dubuque Telegraph Herald*, (September 20):3A.

-----. 1991c. "Memories of Dubuque: Justice is Being Done," *Dubuque Telegraph Herald*,(November 8):3A.

-----. 1991d. "Chamber Offers Reward," *Dubuque Telegraph Herald*, (November 13):1A.

-----. 1991e. "Brady: Problem Imported," *Dubuque Telegraph Herald*, (November 14):1A.

-----. 1992a. "Diversity? Not About Plan," *Dubuque Telegraph Herald*, (March 29):1A.

-----. 1992b. "Commission OK's Diversity Plan," *Dubuque Telegraph Herald*, (April 14):1A.

Arnold, William, and Bruce Jaspen. 1991. "Racial Group No Stranger to Violence,' *Dubuque Telegraph Herald*, (November 11):1A.

Associated Press. 1999. "Iowa Blacks Imprisoned at High Rate," July 12, AP state and local wire.

-----. 2000. "State Commission; Number of Blacks in Prison a Concern," *BC Cycle*, August 20 (Sunday).

Auge, Thomas. 1976. "The Life and Times of Julien Dubuque," *Palimpsest*, 57(1):2-13.

-----. 1980. "Destruction of a Culture," *Gateway Heritage*, Fall, 1(2):32-45.

Bagsarian, Thomas. 1991. "NAACP Combats Race War with Ribbon-Bearing Drive," *Dubuque Telegraph Herald*, (November 11):1A.

-----. 1991b. "KKK Leader Attacks NAACP, Mayor, Plan," *Dubuque Telegraph Herald*, (December 1): 11B.

-----. 1992a. "Stop-Klan Group Plan to Counter KKK Rally," *Dubuque Telegraph Herald*, (May 7):1A.

-----. 1992b. "KKK Faces Wall of Protest," *Dubuque Telegraph Herald*, (May 15):1A.

-----. 1993a. "Cheers Likes Attention, But not Situation Context," *Dubuque Telegraph Herald*, (January 24):5A.

-----. 1993b. "Police Brutality vs. Statistics," *Dubuque Telegraph Herald*, (February 7):1A.

-----. 1993c. "NAACP Official: Drop Police Action," *Dubuque Telegraph Herald*, (March 6):1A.

-----. 1993d. "Breakdown of Dubuque's Crime," *Dubuque Telegraph Herald*, (May 9):1E.

Baran, Paul, and Paul Sweezy. 1966. *Monopoly Capital.* New York: Monthly Review Press.

Barnes, Charline j. 2001. *Life Narratives of African Americans in Iowa.* Chicago: Arcadia Publishing.

Barth, Gunther. 1975. *Instant Cities: Urbanization and the Rise of San Francisco and Denver.* New York: Oxford University Press.

Batio, Christopher. 1992. "Outtakes," *Argot*, (August):2.

Bell, Michael J. 1994. "True Israelites of America: The Story of the Jews of Iowa," *The Annals of Iowa,* 53: 85-127 (Spring).

Belluck, Pam. 2000. "Short of People, Iowa Seeks to be Ellis Island of the Midwest," *The New York Times,* (August 28): A1.

Belskey, Ruth. N.D. *101 Years With Dubuque Jewry*. Unpublished manuscript, the Dubuque Telegraph Herald Library, Dubuque, Iowa.

Bergmann, Leola N. 1948. "The Negro in Iowa," *Journal of History and Politics*, 46(1):3-90.

-----. 1969. *The Negro in Iowa*. Iowa City: State Historical Society of Iowa.

Berrier, G. Galin. 2001. "The Underground Railroad in Iowa," in Bill Silag (ed.), *Outside In: African-American History in Iowa 1838-2000.* Des Moines: State Historical Society of Iowa, Pp. 44-59.

Berry, Brewton. 1940. "The Concept of race in Sociology Textbooks," *Social Forces,* 18, 411-17(March).

Blocker, Sue. 1988. "Depression Hits Dubuque Harder," *Dubuque Telegraph Herald*, (February 23):25.

-----. 1989. "Panel on Labor, Management Exceeds Hopes," *Dubuque Telegraph Herald*, (March 13):1A.

Bloom, Stephen. 2000. *Postville: A Clash of Cultures in Heartland America.* New York; Harcourt, Inc.

Bluestone, Barry, and Bennett Harrison. 1982. *The Deindustrialization of America: Plant Closing, Community Abandonment, and the Dismantling of Basic Industry*. New York: Basic Books, Inc.

Bonacich, Edna. 1972. "A Theory of Ethnic Antagonism: The Split Labor Market," *American Sociological Review*, 37, October): 547-559.

-----. 1976. "Advanced Capitalism and Black/White Race Relations in the United States: A Split Labor Market Interpretation," *American Sociological Review*, 41, (February):34-51.

Boswell, Terry E. 1986. "A Split Labor Market Analysis of Discrimination against Chinese Immigrants, 1850-1882, *American Sociological Review*, 51, (June):352-371.

Bower man, J. Bialys. 1991. *A Guide to the Microfilmed Records at Carnegie-Stout Public Library, IA*. Dubuque County: Key City Genealogical Society.

Brewer, E. Cobham. 1898. *Dictionary of Phrase and Fable.* Philadelphia: Henry Altemus; cf. Bartleby.com, 2000. www.bartleby.com/81/. [accessed, 2-26-02].

Brig, Karla. 1991. "Dubuque Can Never Be Just Like It Always Was," *Dubuque Telegraph Herald*, (November 17):4A.

Brigham, Jeremy, and Wright Sr., Robert. 2001. "Civil Rights Organizations in Iowa," in Bill Silag (ed.), *Outside In: African-American History in Iowa 1838-2000.* Des Moines: State Historical Society of Iowa, Pp. 303-339.

Burchard, Esteban G. et. al. 2003. "The Importance of Race and Ethnic Background in Biomedical Research and Clinical Practice," *New England Journal of Medicine,* 348: 1170-75.

Burns Schuster, Judy. 1965. "Dubuque Negroes Say Poverty, Rights Linked," *Dubuque Telegraph Herald*, (November 18).

Calking, Homer L. 1962. "The Coming of the Foreigners," *Palimpsest* (special issue), XLIII (4):153-160.

-----. 1964. "The Irish in Iowa," *The Palimpsest*, XLV(2).

Calender, Charles. 1978. "Fox," in Bruce G. Trigger (editor), *Handbook of North American Indians, Volume 15*, pp.636-647. Washington, D.C.: Smithsonian Institute.

Chaichian, Mohammad A. 1989. "Urban Political Economy and Experiential Learning: Designing the Course Sociology of Dubuque," *Teaching Sociology*, 17:56-63.

-----. 1991. *Economic Restructuring and Changes in the Occupational Structure of Dubuque, Iowa: 1980-1989*. Unpublished paper presented at the annual meeting of the Midwest Sociological Society, Des Moines, Iowa.

-----. 1992. *Racial Tensions in Dubuque, Iowa: Report of Proceedings (testimony)*. Fact Finding Meeting before the Iowa Advisory Committee to the U.S. Commission on Civil Rights,(April 30-May 1):27-40, Dubuque, Iowa.

-----. 2005. "They Had a Dream: Failure of the Plan for Racial Diversity in Dubuque, Iowa," *Proteus,* 22(1): 28-36.

Chalmers, David M. 1987. *Hooded Americanism: The History of the Ku Klux Klan (3rd Edition)*. Durham, NC: Duke University Press.

Charvat, Burke, and Willis Goody. 1990. *1990 Census of Population and Housing, Summary File IA, Iowa: Dubuque City*. Ames: Iowa State University.

Cohen, Stanford. 1970. *Labor in the United States*. Columbus, Ohio: Charles E. Merrill Publishing Co.

Connor, Steve. 2001. "How Accusations of Racism Ended the Plan to Map the Genetic Diversity of Mankind," *The Independent,* (September 10): 3.

Conzett, Josiah. 1905. *Recollections of People and Events, Dubuque, Iowa 1846-1890*. Unpublished manuscript, Dubuque County Historical Society.

Cooper,Richard, Kaufman, J. and Ryk Ward. 2003. "Race and Genomics," *New England Journal of Medicine,* 348(12): 1166-70.

Couzin, Jennifer. 2002. "New Mapping Project Splits the Community," *Science,* 296: 1391 & 1393.

Coyle, Erin. 2001. "Commission: Farmland Guilty of Discrimination: $72,292 — Human Rights Commission Decides in Favor of Dubuque Man," *Dubuque Telegraph Herald,* (May 11):A3.

-----. 2002a. Dubuquers Go Back to Class to Learn Second Language," *Dubuque Telegraph Herald,* (February 15): A1.

-----. 2002b. "Many Find Prejudice in Subtleties," *Dubuque Telegraph Herald,* (March 18): A1.

CURE. 1992. *May 1992 Dubuque Summary of Statements*. Document courtesy of Citizens United for Respect and Equality, Dubuque, Iowa.

CURE Prescription. 1992. "Groups Join to Help Dubuque 'Can the Klan,'" 1(3), (May 22):1.

Des Moines Register. 1926. "Scores Fall in Sizzling Heat at Conclave," (August 29):6G.

-----. 1938. "Court of 1838 is Re-enacted," September 13.

-----. 1982. "Pack Sale Completed Before Judge OK's It," (October 16):3A.

-----. 1992. "Anti-Klan Rally Leaders Blast Police Department," (May 21):2A.

-----. 2002a. "Teen Awarded $4,000 in Hate-Crime Suit," April 16.

-----. 2002b. "Dubuque Listed 15th in Job Loss Due to September 11," January 11. Accessed 2-28-02: http:// www.cohenesrey.com/ instantnews/viewz.asp?newsid=891.

De Witte, David. 2001. "Dubuque's Comeback a Long Time in the Making," *Cedar Rapids Gazette,* July 29.

Dixon, Thomas. 1902. *The Leopard's Spots: A Romance of the White Man's Burden, 1865-1900.* New York: Doubleday.

-----. 1905. *The Clansman: An Historical Romance of the Ku Klux Klan.* New York: Doubleday, Page & Co.

Dockstader, Frederick J. 1977. *Great North American Indians: People in Life and Leadership.* New York: Van Nostrand Reinhold Company.

Dubuque City Directory. 1856-1857. Dubuque, Iowa: W.A. Adams Publishers.

Dubuque Daily Herald. 1875. "Colored Children in the Public Schools," (September 14):1.

-----. 1877. "De Gentleman of Color," (February 11):4.

-----. 1895. "Dubuque Hebrews Celebrate Feast of Yom Kippur," (September 18).

Dubuque Daily Times. 1863. "Dubuque Statistics," (June 4):1.

The Dubuque Housing Commission. 1989. *A Housing Impact Study of the Freeway Corridor Plan.* October 30, Dubuque, Iowa.

Dubuque Telegraph Herald. 1903. "To Organize Lodge," (September 16):8.

-----. 1905. "Color Question Enters School," (December 14):2.

-----. 1906. "Dixon's Story in Local Life," (May 9):3.

-----. 1907. "Race Equality Not Found Here," (May 6):1.

-----. 1913. "Dubuque's Rich Citizens, Who They Are and Their Wealth," (July 13).

-----. 1923a. "Local Legion Opens War on Ku Klux Klan," (February 13):1.

-----. 1923b. "Fiery Cross of Klansmen Seen,' (December 5):5.

-----. 1924a. "Third Fiery Cross of KKK Seen Here," (April 6):24.

-----. 1924b. "No More Arrests in Klan Affair," (June 15):2.

-----. 1925a. "Klan Permit to Parade Refused," (July 3):2.

-----. 1925b. "Klan's' Petition for Parade Denied," (August 25):5.

-----. 1925c. "56,000 Estimate at Klan Meeting," (August 31):10.

-----. 1926a. "Action Delayed on Klan Petition," (July 13):2.

-----. 1926b. "Klonklave Here Next Saturday," (August 26):1.

-----. 1926c. "Knights of Klan Coming Saturday," (August 27):2.

-----. 1926d. "Thousands Attend Klan KlonKlave," (August 29):18.

-----. 1938. "First Jewish Rites Held in Halls, Homes," (August 31):21P.

-----. 1964. "Irish Still Large Unit in Dubuque," (March 17):1.

-----. 1969. "City Rights Commission Hears of Bias Problems Faced Here," July 31.

-----. 1970. "FBI Gets Black Center Threat," March 8.

-----. 1990. "Synagogues Lament Decline in Friday Services," (July 14):10A.

-----. 1991. "8 Cross Burnings Unsolved Since '89," (December 9):1A.

-----. 1992 "Klan Fans Passions," (May 30):1A.

-----. 1993. "Pregnant Woman Who Accused Police Arrested Again in ED," (January 20):1A.

-----. 2000. "Racism Concerns Voiced at Public Hearing; Resolution Opposition: Marshall County Makes English Official Language," (October 23):A11.

The Dubuque Leader. 1923. "Immigration Millin,"" (June 1):1.

-----. 1925. "Warns Against Negro Congress," (August 14):1.

The Dubuque Times Journal. 1925a. "Klan Konklave Will be Held Next Saturday," (August 25):1.

-----. 1925b. "Klonklave Will be Held on Peru Road," (August 28):1.

-----. 1925c. "Monster Crowd Attended Dubuque Klan Klonklave," (August 30):1.

----. 1925d. "Klan to Hold Klonklave in City Next Year," (August 31):2.

-----. 1926a. "Klansmen Are Pelted with Rocks," (July 25):1.

-----. 1926b. "Klan Parade Regulations Are Discussed," (August 1):2.

-----. 1926c. "Klan Is Ready to Take Care of Crowd of 30,000," (August 27):2.

-----. 1926d. "Thousands in City to Attend 1926 Klonklave," (August 29): 2.

Dunn, L.C., and Theodosius Dobzhansky. 1964. *Heredity, Race and Society*. New York: The New American Library.

Duster, Troy. 2001. "Buried Alive: The Concept of Race in Science," *Chronicle of Higher Education,"* (September 14): B11-12.

Dykstra, Robert. 1982. "Dr. Emerson's Sam: Black Iowans Before the Civil War," *Palimpsest*, 63(3), (May/June):66-82.

-----. 1993. *Bright Radical Star: Black Freedom and White Supremacy on the Hawkeye Frontier*. Cambridge, Massachusetts: Harvard University Press.

Elliott, James R. 1995. *Cycles Within the System: Metropolitanization and Internal Migration in the U.S.,* Working Paper #95-21, Center for Demography and Ecology, University of Wisconsin—Madison.

Evans, Hiram H. 1927. "The Catholic Question as Viewed by the Ku Klux Klan," *Current History*, 26, (July):563-569.

Feagin, Joe, and Harlan Hahn. 1973. *Ghetto Violence: The Politics of Violence in American Cities.* New York: McMillan.

Feagin, Joe, and Hernan Vera. 1995. *White Racism: The Basics.* New York: Routeledge.

Finch, John. 1844. *Travels in the United States of America and Canada.* London: Longman, Reese, Brown, Green, and Longman.

Fleishaker, Oscar. 1957. *The Illinois-Iowa Jewish Community on the Banks of the Mississippi River.* Doctoral dissertation, Yeshiva University.

Flynn, Thomas, and Craig Takes. 1991. "Dubuque's Political Party Chiefs Speak Out: Enough!," *Dubuque Telegraph Herald*, (November 23):4A.

Fogarty, Thomas A. 1991. "Most Iowans Not Bigoted - Governor," *Des Moines Register*,(November 13): 1A.

Ford, Ramona L. 1988. *Work, Organization and Power*. Boston: Allyn and Bacon.

Foster, John Bellamy. 2000. "Monopoly Capital at the turn of the Millennium," *Monthly Review,* 51(11). Accessed 11-03-05: http://www.monthlyreview.org/400jbf.htm.

Frey, William H. 2001. *Census 2000 Shows Large Black Return to* the South, Reinforcing the Region's "White-Black" *Demographic Profile.* University of Michigan: Research Report, Population Studies Center.

Gabe, Catherine. 1983. "Cross Burnt in Church Lawn Possibly Racist," *Dubuque Telegraph Herald*, March 6.

Galena Daily Gazette. 1906. "Draws Color Line in Dubuque," (October 23):3.

Gallagher, Ruth A. 1916. "The Indian Agent in the United States Before 1850," *Iowa Journal of History and Politics*, 14(3):3-55.

Gannett, Lisa. 2001. "Racism and Human Genome Diversity Research: The Ethical Limits of 'Population Thinking,'" *Philosophy of Science*, 68:3, 479-92.

Giunta, Francis. 1992. *Racial Tensions in Dubuque, Iowa: Report on Proceedings (testimony).* Fact Finding Mission before the Iowa Advisory Committee to the U.S. Commission on Civil Rights, April 30-May 1): pp. 194-204. Dubuque, Iowa.

Gjerde, Jon. 1997. *The Minds of the West: Ethnocultural Evolution in the Rural Middle West, 1830-1917.* Chapel Hill: The University of North Carolina Press.

Glazer, Nathan. 1975. *Affirmative Discrimination: Ethnic Identity and Public Policy.* New York: Basic Books.

Glazer, Simon. 1904. *Jews in Iowa.* Des Moines, Iowa: Coch Brothers.

Gordon, Milton M. 1981. "Models of Pluralism: The New American Dilemma." *Annals of the American Academy of Political and Social Science,* 454: 171-188.

Gossett, Thomas F. 1997. *Race: The History of an Idea.* New York: Oxford University Press.

Goudy, Willis. 2001. "Selected Demographics: Iowa's African-American Residents, 1840-2000," in Bill Silag (ed.), *Outside In: African-American History in Iowa 1838-2000.* Des Moines: State Historical Society of Iowa, Pp. 23-41.

Gourley, Cathryn E. 1990. *Locations of Sauk, Mesquakie, and Associated Euro-American Sites 1832 to 1845: An Ethno- Historical Approach.* M.A. thesis, Iowa State University, Ames, Iowa.

Gradwohl, David M., and Johnsen, Nancy O. 2001. "A Kind of Heaven to Me," in Bill Silag (Ed.), *Outside In: African-American History in*

Iowa 1838-2000. Des Moines: State Historical Society of Iowa, Pp. 45-59.

Grant, Robert B. (Ed.) 1972. *The Black Man Comes to the City: A Documentary Account from the Great Migration to the Great Depression, 1915-1930.* Chicago: Nelson-Hall.

Graves, Joseph L. 2001. *The Emperor's New Clothes: Biological Theories of Race at the Millennium.* New Brunswick, NJ: Rutgers University Press.

Greater Dubuque Development Corporation. 2002. *Dubuque Ranked Nationally in High-Tech Growth.* Accessed 4-22-02: http://www.greaterdubuque.org/index.htm

Gribbin, August. 2002. "Iowa Makes English Official," *The Washington Times,* March 2. Accessed 3-4-02: http://www.washtimes.com/national/20020302-77938941.htm.

Haefner, Mary. 1938. "The Census of 1838," *Palimpsest,* 19(5), (May):185-192.

Hamer, David. 1990. *New Towns in the New World: Images and Perceptions of the Nineteenth Century Urban Frontier.* New York: Columbia University press.

Hanson, Gwen. 1991. "No Longer Proud of City," *Dubuque Telegraph Herald,* (November 17):4A.

Hanson, Jack. 1991. "Mourning Over the Racism in Dubuque," *Des Moines Register,* (November 14):9A.

-----. 1992. *Racial Tensions in Dubuque, Iowa: Report of Proceedings (testimony).* Fact Finding Meeting before the Iowa Advisory Committee to the U.S. Commission on Civil Rights, April 30-May 1): pp. 41-64. Dubuque, Iowa.

Hanson, Lyn. 1991. "Listening Post," *Dubuque Telegraph Herald,* (December 13):1A.

-----. 1993. "Churchill, NAACP Criticize Police," *Dubuque Telegraph Herald,* (February 1):1A.

Harper, Suzanne. 1993. *The Brotherhood: Race and Gender Ideologies in the White Supremacist Movement.* Unpublished PH.D. dissertation, University of Texas.

Hawthorne, Frances E. 1992. *African-Americans in Iowa, A Chronicle of Contributions: 1830-1992.* Des Moines, Iowa.

Heim, Ashley. 2001. *Iowa's Brain Drain: A Historical Comparative Analysis.* Unpublished paper, Mount Mercy College, Cedar Rapids, Iowa.

Hendricks, Michael. 1983. "Blacks Don't Move to the Area Because Few Are Here," *Dubuque Telegraph Herald*, (August 26):3A.

-----. 1984. "Duffy Resigns," *Dubuque Telegraph Herald*, April 29.

Hermann, Richard. 1922. *Julien Dubuque, His Life and Adventures.* Dubuque, Iowa: Times Journal Company.

Herndons, Lucia. 1981. "Black Family Called 'weird' for Moving to Dubuque," "*Des Moines Register*, (October 22):4.

Hernstein, Richard J., and Charles Murray. 1994. *The Bell Curve: Intelligence and Class Structure in American Life.* New York: Free Press.

Hill, James L. 1981-82. "Migration of Blacks to Iowa, 1820-1960," *Journal of Negro History*, 66(4):289-303.

The History of Dubuque County, Iowa. 1880. Chicago: Western Historical Company.

Hoffmann, H.J. 1924. *Letters to Paul Kamler, Clinton*. State Historical Society of Iowa, Manuscript Collection. Iowa City, Iowa.

Hoffman, M.M. 1930 *Antique Dubuque, 1673-1833*. Dubuque: Telegraph Herald Press.

Hoffman, Peter B. 1936. *Concise History of the City and County of Dubuque: 1833-1934*. Dubuque, Iowa: Center For Dubuque History, Loras College.

Hogstrom, Erik. 1999. "Speakers Say Education Can Fight Racism," *Dubuque Telegraph Herald,* (October 15):A3.

Howell, Frances B. 1982. "A Split Labor Market: Mexican Farm Workers in the Southwest," *Sociological Inquiry*, 52:132-140.

Hull, Jon D. 1991. "A White Person's Town?," *Time*, (December 23):39-40.

Hundred Percent American Songs as Sung by Dubuque Kounty Klan Kuartette (pamphlet). N.D. Courtesy of the Dubuque Historical Society, Dubuque, Iowa.

Hunt, Henry Thomas. 1971. *The Case of Thomas J. Mooney and Warren K. Billings.* New York: Da Capo Press.

Ignatiev, Noel. 1995. *How the Irish Became White.* New York: Routledge.

Iowa Advisory Committee to the U.S. Commission on Civil Rights. 1993. *A Time to Heal: Race Relations in Dubuque, Iowa.*

Iowa Federation of Labor, AFL-CIO. 1957. *Proceedings of the 2nd Convention.* Iowa City: State Historical Society of Iowa Archives.

-----. 1960. *Proceedings of the 5th Convention.* Iowa City: State Historical Society of Iowa Archives.

-----. 1977. *Proceedings of the 22nd Convention.* Iowa City: State Historical Society of Iowa Archives.

-----. 1995. *Proceedings of the 39th Convention.* Iowa City: State Historical Society of Iowa Archives.

-----. 1997. *Proceedings of the 41st Convention.* Iowa City: State Historical Society of Iowa Archives.

Iowa State Federation of Labor (ISFL). 1930. *Proceedings of the 35th Convention.* Iowa City: State Historical Society of Iowa Archives.

-----. 1950. *Proceedings of the 55th Convention.* Iowa City: State Historical Society of Iowa Archives.

-----. 1954. *Proceedings of the 59th Convention.* Iowa City: State Historical Society of Iowa Archives.

-----. 1955. *Proceedings of the 60th convention.* Iowa City: State Historical Society of Iowa Archives.

Iowa State Industrial Union Council, CIO. 1952. *Proceedings of the 14th Convention.* Iowa City: State Historical Society of Iowa.

-----. 1953. *Proceedings of the 15th Convention.* Iowa City: State Historical Society of Iowa Archives.

-----. 1954. *Proceedings of the 16th Convention.* Iowa City: State Historical Society of Iowa Archives.

-----. 1955. *Proceedings of the 17th convention.* Iowa City: State Historical Society of Iowa Archives.

Jaspen, Bruce. 1991. "Archbishop Calls for Catholics to Shun Racism," *Dubuque Telegraph Herald*, (November 19):3A.

-----. 1992 "New Plan: Cultural Diversity Without Quota, Tax Dollars," *Dubuque Telegraph Herald*, (March 24):1A.

Jaspen, Bruce, and Steven Weber. 1991. "Racial Crimes strain Police," *Dubuque Telegraph Herald*, (November 14):3A.

Jerde, Lynn. 1995. "The Irish of Dubuque, Iowa," *Irish America,* March-April.

Johnson, Kay. 1967. *The Ku Klux Klan in Iowa: A Study of Intolerance.* Masters Thesis, University of Iowa, Iowa City, Iowa.

Johnson, Russell L. 1996. *An Army for Industrialization: The Civil War and the Formation of Urban-Industrial Society in a Northern City.* Unpublished doctoral dissertation, University of Iowa, Iowa City.

Jost, Richard, and Gene Erb. 1983. "Union Gets Trashed; FDL Born in Dubuque," *Des Moines Register,*(April 19):1A.

Judd, Dennis R. 1988. *The Politics of American Cities: Private Power and Public Policy (3rd Edition).* Boston: Scott, Forseman & Company.

Juengst, Eric T. 1998. "Groups As Gate-Keepers to Genetic Research: Conceptually Confusing, Morally Hazardous, and Practically Useless," *Kennedy Institute of Ethics Journal,* 8(2): 183-200.

Kappler, Charles J. 1904. *Indian Affairs: Laws and Treaties, Volume 2.* Washington, D.C.: Government Printing Office.

Kelly, Suzanne P. 1992. "Klan Watchers Say New Image Doesn't Hide the Old Message," *Star Tribune* (Minneapolis), (May 30): 1A.

Kennedy, Randall. 1994. "Persuasion and Distrust: The Affirmative Action Debate." Pp. 48-67 in Nicolaus Mills (ed.), *Debating Affirmative Action: Race, Gender, Ethnicity, and the Politics of Inclusion.* New York: Delta.

King, M.C., and Motulsky, A.G. 2002. "Mapping Human History," *Science,* 296: 2342-43.

Kirchen, Richard. 1985. "Camaraderie 'Hallowed' to Society," *Dubuque Telegraph Herald,* (December 16):9.

Kittle, M.D. 2002. "Bakery Owner Just Taking Care of Business," *Dubuque Telegraph Herald,* (March 19):A1.

Kleniewski, Nancy. 2002. *Cities, Change, and Conflict: A Political Economy of Urban Life.* Belmont, CA: Wadsworth Thompson Learning.

Kompas, Kate. 2001. "Iowans Fight Immigration: Critics in the Three Cities Targeted for Aggressive Recruitment Petition the Plan to Attract Workers," *Des Moines Register,* July 5.

Kovel, Joel. 1984. *White Racism: A Psychohistory.* New York: Columbia University Press.

Krapfl, Michael. 1996. Diversity Plan Revamp," *Dubuque Telegraph Herald,* (November 2):A3.

Kraske, Steven. 1982a. "2 City Families Live in Fear After Racial Incidents," *Dubuque Telegraph Herald,* (November 2):3A.

-----. 1982b. "Right Chief Lorenz: Assess Attitudes of Officials," *Dubuque Telegraph Herald,*(November 10):1A.

-----. 1983a. "Local Group Wants to Question New Human Rights Appointee," *Dubuque Telegraph Herald,* (March 31): 3A.

-----. 1983b. "Good Times, Bad Times for Dubuque Black Residents," *Dubuque Telegraph Herald,* (April 24):3A.

-----. 1983c. "Duffy's Opponents Propose He Attend Cultural Seminars," *Dubuque Telegraph Herald,* (April 15):1A.

-----. 1983d. "Rights Task Force to Meet; Coalition Drop Demands for Duffy Resignation," *Dubuque Telegraph Herald,* (April 19).

-----. 1983e. "Being Black and a Dubuque," *Dubuque Telegraph Herald,* (April 23):3.

Kushnick, Louis. 1996. "The Political Economy of White Racism in the United States," in Bowser, Benjamin P. & Raymond G. Hunt (Eds.), *Impact of Racism on White Americans.* Thousand Oaks, CA: Sage Publications, Pp. 48-67.

Lamphier-Hoffert, Denise. 1993. "Iowa's 'Key City Unlocks Its Growth Potential, *Iowa Commerce,* 10(15):6-9, Summer.

Little Dublin News. Various issues of a monthly news letter published in Dubuque, Iowa. Center for Dubuque History, Loras College.

Loewen, James W. 2005. *Sundown Towns: A Hidden Dimension of American Racism.* New York: The New Press.

Lucy Nicholas. 1982. "Dubuque's labor History," in Russell Nash, *Dubuque Beginnings: Proceedings from a Sesquicentennial Community Workshop on Dubuque's Past, Present and Future,* pp.34-37, Dubuque, Iowa.

Lyon, Randolph W. 1991. *Dubuque: The Encyclopedia.* Dubuque, Iowa: Hoermann Press.

Madhubuti, Haki R. 1993. *Why L.A. Happened: Implications of the '92 Los Angeles Rebellion.* Chicago: Third World Press.

Mahoney, Timothy R. 1990. *River Towns in the Great West: The Structure of Provincial Urbanization in the American Midwest, 1820-1870.* New York: Cambridge University Press.

Maiers, Roger. 1992. *Racial Tensions in Dubuque, Iowa: Report on Proceedings (testimony).* Fact Finding Meeting before the Iowa Advisory Committee to the U.S. Commission on Civil Rights, April 30-May 1): pp. 431-451. Dubuque, Iowa.

Marger, Martin. 1991. *Race and Ethnic Relations: American and Global Perspectives.* Belmont, CA: Wadsworth.

-----. 2000. *Race and Ethnic Relations: American and Global Perspectives.* Belmont, CA: Wadsworth-Thompson Learning.

Marriott, Michael. 1987. "In Jersey City, Indians Face Rise in Violence and Hatred," *New York Times,* (October 12):II, 1.

Mass, Melvin, and Michael Stohlmeyer. 1991. "Labor, Management Deplore Racism," *Dubuque Telegraph Herald,* (December 5)4A.

McAllister, William. 1991. "Fiery Crosses Ignite Town's Worst Fears: Bid to Attract Minorities Resurrects Reputation that Dubuque Hoped to Shed," *Washington Post,* (November 17):3A.

McCormick, John. 1975. "KKK Had Tri-State Factions," *Dubuque Telegraph Herald,* (January 5):44.

McGarvey, Carol. 2000. "Famine Drove Them, Land's Looks Held Them," *Des Moines Register, March 20.*

McKee, James B. 1993. *Sociology and the Race Problem: The Failure of a Perspective.* Urbana, IL: University of Illinois Press.

McLemore, S. Dale. 1991. *Racial and Ethnic Relations in America.* Boston: Allyn & Bacon.

Means, Gardiner(ed.) 1939. *The Structure of the American Economy, Part I.* Washington, D.C.: U.S. Government Printing Office.

Mecklin, J.M. 1924. *The Ku Klux Klan: A Study of the American Mind.* New York: Russell and Russell.

Mercer, Helen. 1982. "The Cultural Environment of Dubuque," in Russell Nash, *Dubuque Beginnings: Proceedings from a Sesquicentennial Community Workshop on Dubuque's Past, Present and Future,* pp. 55-61, Dubuque, Iowa.

Meriwether, J. Bruce. 1992. *Racial Tensions in Dubuque, Iowa: Report on Proceedings (testimony).* Fact Finding Mission before the Iowa

Advisory Committee to the U.S. Commission on Civil Rights, (April 30-May 1): pp. 227-243. Dubuque, Iowa.

-----. 1993. "Diversity Council Dedicated to life in Tri-States," *Dubuque Telegraph Herald*, (June 10):4A.

Mihalakis, Elizabeth. 1993. "'Diversity' Will Divide, Conquer Us," *Dubuque Telegraph Herald*,(February 5):4A.

Miller, Kerby. 1985. *Emigrants and Exiles: Ireland and the Irish Exodus to North America.* New York: Oxford University Press.

Miller, Otis L. 1972. *Indian-White Relations in the Illinois Territory, 1789 to 1818.* Ph.D. Dissertation, St. Louis University.

Muellr, C.J. 1991. "put the Plan To a Vote," *Dubuque Telegraph Herald*, (November 17):4A.

Murphy, Lucy E. 2000. *A Gathering of Rivers: Indians, Métis, and Mining in the Western Great Lakes 1737-1832.* Lincoln: University of Nebraska Press.

Murray, Paul (ed.). 1951. *States' Laws on Race and Color*. Cincinnati: Women's Division of Christian Service.

Myrdal, Gunnar. 1994. *An American Dilemma: The Negro Problem and Modern Democracy.* New York: Harper & Brothers.

Nash, Russell. 1982. *Dubuque Beginnings: Proceedings from a Sesquicentennial Community Workshop on Dubuque's Past, Present and Future*. Dubuque, Iowa.

The Nationalist Movement. N.D. Civil Disobedience. Web site accessed April 3, 2002: http://www.nationalist.org/docs/ instruct/defiance.html.

Neal, Kathryn M. 2001. "Unsung Heroines: African-American Women in Iowa," in Bill Silag (ed.), *Outside In: African-American History in Iowa 1838-2000.* Des Moines: State Historical Society of Iowa, Pp. 365-383.

Nevans-Pederson. Mary. 2002. "Speaker at MLK Event Warns 'White Iowa' Not Immune to Crisis," *Dubuque Telegraph Herald,* (January 22):A3.

New Republic. 1923. "Why They Join the Klan," 36, (November):321.

New Sharon. 1926. "Miss May Francis Proven a Grafter," (May 26), in Agnes Samuelson's scrapbook collection, Box 10, Courtesy of the Iowa Historical Society, Iowa City, Iowa.

Neymeyer, Robert. 1995. "In the Full Light of Day: The Ku Klux Klan in 1920s Iowa," *The Palimpsest,* 1(76): 56-75.

Norman, Jane. 1991. "Iowa Lawmakers Face Issue of Anti-Semitism," *Des Moines Register*, (November 16):3A.

Official Year Book. 1938. Iowa State Federation of Labor.

O'Hara, James J. 1999. *A Study in the Oral Tradition of Long-Term Meatpacking Plants.* Masters Thesis, University of Northern Iowa.

Oldt, Franklin T. 1910. *History of Dubuque County, Iowa.* Chicago: Goodspeed Historical Association.

Palen, J. John. 1992. *The Urban World.* New York: McGraw-Hill.

Parish, John C. 1908. "An Early Fugitive Slave Case West of the Mississippi River," *Iowa Journal of History," 6:88.*

Paterson, Michael. 1998. "More Towns Discussing Racism, Race Relations, *Omaha Herald World,* (February 25):18.

Peterson, Henry K. 1957-1959. "The First Decision Rendered by the Supreme Court of Iowa," *Annals of Iowa*, 34:304.

Peterson, Jean E. 1996. "Jews Settled Here as Early as 1862," *Dubuque Telegraph Herald,* (December 6): 4A

Petersen, William J. 1966. "Julien Dubuque," *Palimpsest*, 47(3):105-119.

Pfohl, Eldon A. 1993. "Elite Gang Wants Social Engineering," *Dubuque Telegraph Herald,*(January 19): 4A.

Pierce, Diana. 1978. "The Feminization of Poverty: Women, Work and Welfare," *Urban and Social Change Review*, (February).

Pieters, Jeff. 1999. "Dubuque Wins State Honor for Diversity Work," *Dubuque Telegraph Herald,* (October 9):A3.

Pins, Kenneth. 1982a. "Dubuque's 23% Jobless Rate Tops Survey of U.S. Areas," *Des Moines Register*, (March 18):14A.

-----.1982b. "Dubuque Packing Closing Hits Like a Bombshell," *Des Moines Register*, (April 13):6A.

-----. 1982c. "Suicide Focus Attention on Jobless Rate," *Des Moines Register*, (June 2):3A.

-----. 1982d. "Rocky Start for Pack-FDL Marriage," *Des Moines Register*, (October 24):6B.

-----. 1983a. "Dubuque Rights Official Under Fire for Ethnic Jokes," *Des Moines Register*, (March 31):5M.

-----. 1983b. "Dubuque Protesters of Duffy Can Leave Town, Says Councilman," *Des Moines Register*, (April 7):1M.

-----. 1983c. "Racism Uproar Turns to Dubuque Dialogue," *Des Moines Register*, (April 17):3B.

-----. 1983d. "Dubuque: It's a Lot More Than a Place to Live," *Des Moines Register*, (December 18):1C.

-----. 2000. "Immigration Zone Plan Shelved," *Des Moines Register,* February 11.

Proceedings of the Annual Convention. 1927. The Iowa State Federation of Labor.

-----. 1929. The Iowa State Federation of Labor.

The Public School of Dubuque. 1878. *Twentieth Annual Report of the Board of Education of Dubuque, IA*. Dubuque, Iowa: The Herald Printing Co. Courtesy of the Dubuque Historical Society, Dubuque, Iowa.

Pulliman-Hill, Della. 1995. "Rights Commission: Hands Tied During Racial Crisis," *Dubuque Telegraph Herald,* (September 28):A5.

Raban, Jonathan. 1981. *Old Glory: An American Voyage*. New York: Simon and Schuster.

Redfield, Robert. 1958. "Race as a Social phenomenon," in Thompson, Edgar T. and Everett C. Hughes (Eds.), *Race, Individual and Collective Behavior.* Glencoe, IL: Free Press, pp. 66-71.

Report of the Advisory Commission on Civil Disorders. 1968. New York: Bantam Books.

Reynolds, David R. 1999. *There Goes the Neighborhood: Rural School Consolidation at the Grass Roots in Early Twentieth-Century Iowa.* Iowa City: University of Iowa Press.

Ricchiardi, Sherry. 1982a. "Children of the Unemployed," *Des Moines Register*, (May 5):1A.

-----. 1982b. "Share Crisis with Kids, Jobless Parents Advise," *Des Moines Register*, (May 9):5A.

Rittman, George. 1982. "Introductory Remarks." In Russell Nash, *Dubuque Beginnings: Proceedings from a Sesquicentennial Community Workshop on Dubuque's Past, Present and Future,* pp. 62-70, Dubuque, Iowa.

Roberts, David S. Jr. 1974. *The Politics of Iowa*. Unpublished manuscript, Dubuque, Iowa: University of Dubuque.

Rodgers, Randy. 1989. "Police Say They Know Who Wrote Letters," *Dubuque Telegraph Herald*, (March 1):3A.

-----. 1990. "Sentence - 10 Years for Youth in Cross Burning Case," *Dubuque Telegraph Herald*, (March 29):2A.

Roos, Jonathan. 2001. Immigrant Plan Hits Resistance; Many in Unions Resist Hiring of Immigrants," *Des Moines Register*, February 11.

Ryder, Thomas. 1970. "U of Dubuque Head Resigns," *Dubuque Telegraph Herald*, January 9.

Scharnau, Ralph. 1993. "Workers, Unions, and Work Places in Dubuque, 1830-1990," *Annals of Iowa*, 52, (Winter):50-78.

-----. 2001. "African-American Wage Earners in Iowa: 1850-1950," in Bill Silag (ed.), *Outside In: African-American History in Iowa 1838-2000*. Des Moines: State Historical Society of Iowa, pp. 217-241.

Schmidt, Eugene F. 1991. "Problem Begins in Ourselves," *Dubuque Telegraph Herald*, (November 11):4A.

Schaefer, Richard. 2001. *Race and Ethnicity in the United States (2nd Edition)*. Upper Saddle River, NJ: Prentice Hall.

Shaffer, Mary P. 1991. "Do Not Remain Silent," *Dubuque Telegraph Herald*, (November 17):4A.

Schwieder, Dorothy, Hraba, Joseph, and Elmer Schwieder. 1987. *Buxton: Work and Racial Equality in a Coal Mining Community*. Ames: Iowa State University Press.

Setliffe, William. 1922. "Where American Legion Stands," *The Dubuque Leader*, (March 31):1.

Sibley, Joel H. 1957. "Proslavery Sentiments in Iowa, 1838-1861," *Palimpsest*, 50(4):289-318.

Silag, Bill (ed.). 2001. *Outside In; African-American History in Iowa 1838-2000*. Des Moines: State Historical Society of Iowa.

Sims, Patsy. 1996. *The Klan (2nd Edition)*. Lexington: University Press of Kentucky.

Sisco, Becky. 2002a. "Discussion Centers on How to Become Dr. King's Neighborhood," *Dubuque Telegraph Herald*, (January 22): A3.

-----. 2002b. "Blacks Find City Inviting," *Dubuque Telegraph Herald*, (March 17): A1.

Somner, Lawrence J. 1975. *The Heritage of Dubuque*. E. Dubuque, Illinois: Telegraphics.

Sowell, Thomas. 1975. *Race and Economics.* New York: David McKay Company.

Stanley, Mary. 1985. "Population Relives 1860 Ethnic Break," *Dubuque Telegraph Herald*,(February 23):4.

Starobin, Robert S. 1970. *Industrial Slavery in the Old South.* New York: Oxford University Press.

-----. 1989. "Meeting Targets Racism," *Dubuque Telegraph Herald*, (December 8):3A.

Stevens, David. 1960. "Germans Dominate Tri-State Scene," *Dubuque Telegraph Herald*,(November 6):1 (Tri-State News).

Stromquist, Shelton. 1993. *Solidarity and Survival: An Oral History of Iowa Labor in the Twentieth Century.* Iowa City: University of Iowa Press.

Stuart, Paul. 1987. *Nations Within a Nation*. New York; Greenwood Press.

Sweeney, Kathleen. 1996. "Ex-FDL Worker Files Discrimination," *Dubuque Telegraph Herald*,(December 6): A3.

Swinton, Val. 1991. "Race in Dubuque: Bigotry Dies Hard," *Cedar Rapids Gazette*, (November 16):1A.

Swisher, Jacob A. 1926. "The Case of Ralph," *Palimpsest*, 7:33.

Talisman, Elsie, et. al. N.D. *Dubuque: Its History and Background*. The Dubuque County Historical Society, Dubuque, Iowa.

Taylor, William L. 1995. "Affirmative Action: The Question to be Asked." *Poverty and Race* (May/June): 2-3.

Telegraph Herald Special. 1977. *Our Early Years, Our SpiritedYears, Our Future Years.* A Three volume special edition prepared in observance of American Bicentennial. Dubuque, Iowa: Telegraph Herald.

Thomas, W.I., and Florian Znaniecki. 1918. *The Polish Peasant in Europe and America (Vol.1).* New York: Knopf.

Tobin, Neil. 1992. *Racial Tensions in Dubuque, Iowa: Report of Proceedings (testimony)*. Fact Finding Meeting before the Iowa Advisory committee to the U.S. Commission on Civil Rights, (April 30-May 1): pp. 217-226. Dubuque, Iowa.

Tolerance. 1924a. "On the Roll of the Ku Klux Klan," (August 10):4.

-----. 1924b. "Dubuque Kluxers Squawk!," (August 17):1.

Treneman, Ann. 1992. "Racism Still Simmers Below Dubuque's Surface," *Capital Times*, (May 22): 1E.

Tussman, Joseph (Ed.). 1963. *The Supreme Court on Racial Discrimination*. New York: Oxford University Press.

UAW Local 94. ca 1978. *The Spirit and Times of Local 94-UAW: Our Local Union's History* (a commemorative booklet published by the Dubuque UAW on the occasion of its 30th anniversary). Dubuque: Local 94 Education Committee.

Ukupseni Declaration. 1997. *Declaration of Indigenous Peoples of the Western Hemisphere Regarding the Human Genome Diversity Project*. Accessed January 9, 2002: http://www.ankn.uaf.edu/declaration.html.

U.S. Bureau of the Census. 1933. *Abstract of the Fifteenth Census of the United States*. Washington, D.C.: U.S. Government Printing Office.

-----. 1952. *A Report of the 17th Decennial Census of the United States, Census of Population: 1950, Vol. II. Part 15, Iowa*. Washington, D.C.: U.S. Government Printing Office.

-----. 1973. *The 1970 Census of Population and Housing, Census Tracts for Dubuque SMSA, IA*. Washington, D.C.: U.S. Government Publishing Office.

-----. 1983. *The 1980 Census of Population and Housing, Census Tracts for Dubuque SMSA, IA*. Washington, D.C.: U.S. Government Printing Office.

-----. 1990. *Summary Tape File STF3A- Sample Data*. Data prepared by the city of Dubuque Community and Economic Development, Dubuque, Iowa.

-----. 2000. *The Black Population in the United States, March 1999*. Accessed January 4, 2002: http://www.census.gov/prod/2000pubs/p20-530.pdf.

U.S. Commission on Civil Rights. 1992. *Racial Tensions in Dubuque, IA: A Report of the Proceedings*. Fact Finding Meeting before the

Iowa Advisory Committee to the U.S. Commission on Civil Rights, April 30-May 1. Dubuque, Iowa.

Van den Berghe, Pierre. 1967. *Race and Racism: A Comparative Perspective.* New York: John Wiley & Sons.

Vander Zanden, James W. 1960. "The Klan Revival," *American Journal of Sociology*, 65,(March):457-462.

Van Speybroeck, Christopher J. ca.1986. *The Jewish Community of Dubuque, 1833-1930s*. Dubuque, Iowa: Center for Dubuque History, Loras College.

Villarosa, Linda. 2002. "A Conversation with Joseph Graves: Beyond Black and White in Biology and Medicine," *New York Times,* (January 1): F5.

Von Sternberg, Robert. 2001. "Trouble Over Immigration Brews in Mason City," *The Minneapolis Star Tribune,* July 23.

Wade, Richard C. 1964. *Slavery in Cities: The South 1820-1860.* New York: Oxford University Press.

Waldman, Carl. 1988. *Encyclopedia of Native American Tribes*. New York: Facts on Files Publication.

Wall, Joseph F. 1978. *Iowa: Bicentennial History.* New York: Norton.

We Want To Change. 1991. Statement of Case, the Constructive Integration Task Force, April 8, Dubuque, Iowa.

Webster, James. 1991. "Racism a Product of Fears," *Dubuque Telegraph Herald*,(November 17):5A.

Whitcomb, William. 1992. *Racial Tensions in Dubuque, IA: A Report on the Proceedings(testimony).* Fact Finding Meeting before the Iowa Advisory Committee to the U.S. Commission on Civil Rights, (April 31-May 1): pp. 65-84. Dubuque, Iowa.

Wiley, Deborah. 1992. "New Group Formed to Promote Cultural Diversity in Dubuque," *Des Moines Register*, (March 25):2.

Wiley, Deborah, and Jack Hovelson. 1992. "Klan Rally in Dubuque Ends in Scuffles, Broken Window," *Des Moines Register*, (May 30):1A.

Wilkerson, Isabel. 1991. "Seeking a Racial Mix, Dubuque finds Tension," *New York Times*,(November 3):1.

Williams, Colleen. 1991. "Integration Plan Not the Answer," *Dubuque Telegraph Herald,*(November 19):4A.

Williams, Joe. N.D.a. *History of Knights of Columbus- Council #510, Dubuque, IA, Volume 1:1900-1939*. Loras College: Center for Dubuque History. Dubuque, Iowa.

-----. N.D.b. *History of Fourth Degree Knights of Columbus, 1906-1980*. Loras College: Center for Dubuque History. Dubuque, Iowa.

Wilkie, William E. 1987. *Dubuque on the Mississippi: 1788-1988*. Dubuque, Iowa: Loras College Press.

Wise, Joseph. 1925. "Warns of Race Hatred Promoter," *The Dubuque Leader,* (August 7):1.

Wolf, Jack. 1941. *A Century with Iowa Jewry*. Des Moines, Iowa: Iowa Printing and Supply Co.

Yates, Steven. 1994. *Civil Wrongs: What Went Wrong with Affirmative Action.* San Francisco: ICS Press.

INDEX

NAME INDEX

SUBJECT INDEX